PLAYFUL
PARENTING

Rose N. Grasselli

Priscilla A. Hegner

illustrations by Barbara Goodson

PLAYFUL PARENTING

*Games to Help
Your Infants and Toddlers
Grow Physically,
Mentally & Emotionally*

A PERIGEE BOOK

Perigee Books
are published by
The Putnam Publishing Group
200 Madison Avenue
New York, New York 10016

Published simultaneously in Canada by General Publishing
Co. Limited, Toronto.
Published by arrangement with Richard Marek Publishers

Library of Congress Cataloging in Publication Data

Grasselli, Rose N. (Rose Nava)
  Playful parenting.

  "A GD/Perigee book."
  Reprint. Originally published: New York : R. Marek
Publishers. 1981.
  Bibliography: p.
  Includes index.
  1. Play. 2. Infants—Care and hygiene—United
States. 3. Child rearing—United States. 4. Exercise for
children—United States. I. Hegner, Priscilla A. II. Title.
HQ782.G7 1983   649'.57   82-20547
ISBN 0-399-50725-6

Designed by Elizabeth Woll
First Perigee printing, 1983
Printed in the United States of America

        5   6   7

To my daughters, TANIA, ANGIE and TINA,
    without whom this book would not have been possible.
    I love you!
And to my husband, LES,
    for his encouragement, understanding and support.

RNG

With love to my family . . . RICK, JENNY and TY.

PAH

Every effort has been made to trace the ownership of nursery rhymes and finger plays and to fully acknowledge their use. Many of the selections are traditional, with the author(s) unknown. If any errors remain, they will be corrected in subsequent editions on notification of the publisher.

WE WISH TO THANK:

The parents in our classes for their laughter, support and friendships, and for allowing us to share in their children's beautiful beginnings.

Our illustrator, Barbara Goodson, for her endless patience and lovely sketches; her husband, Bob, for taking many of the photographs that Barbara worked from; our photographer, Susan Faludi, for her exceptional ability to photograph children in action; our friend and fellow author, Karen Green, for being in the right place at the right time and for sharing her expertise; Jane Jordan Browne, our agent, for her guidance and knowledge; our editor, Marie Powers, for her talent and enthusiasm; our publisher, Richard Marek, for believing in our work; our families and friends for caring and believing in us; the numerous professional individuals who gave generously of their time and ideas over the years, particularly Diane Rosentreeter, for her creativity, Dr. Greg Gilman, optometrist, who read the manuscript and gave suggestions, and Lenora Kerr and Carol Richmond of The Kid's Place in Irvine, for their information on the latest educational toys.

Finally, we wish to thank the following individuals for giving us permission to use material from their books. Bonnie Prudden, *How to Keep Your Child Fit From Birth to Six*; Dr. Janine Levy, *The Baby Exercise Book*; Elizabeth Matterson, *Games for the Very Young*, originally published by Penguin Books Limited as *This Little Puffin*; and Louise Bender Scott and J. J. Thompson, *Finger Plays and Flannelboards*, copyright 1960, with permission of Webster/McGraw-Hill to reprint the following: "I Am a Top"; "I'm a Little Puppet Clown"; "A Birthday Cake"; "This Little Clown"; "Counting at the Circus"; "Monkey See, Monkey Do"; "I Am a Snowman"; "The Wind"; "Readiness"; and "Riding the Merry-go-round."

CONTENTS

Part I

PLAYFUL PARENTING IS BORN

Chapter 1

WHY PLAY
WITH
OUR BABIES?

Becoming a parent is a joyful experience and a frightening one. We are faced with the thrilling yet demanding role of satisfying the needs of a completely helpless little person.

When our daughters were born, we each thought that parenting must involve more than simply feeding, changing diapers and bathing a baby, because our little ones were kicking, wiggling, cooing—responding to life. Our pediatricians stressed the need to stimulate our girls from an early age, but we wondered how we should interest them—with what, how long, when, where and why?

With the desire to see our children grow healthy and strong, and encouraged by their wriggling enthusiasm, we began to look for answers. From our physical-education backgrounds we knew the importance of proper sensorimotor training and, with extra study, we soon discovered the tremendous impact of starting a loving and playful program of developmental movement for infants and young children.

The experts' opinions about sensorimotor stimulation for children are uniform and emphatic. Child developmentalist Dr. John Bower writes that a child's basic motor skills, perceptual development (learning through senses) and cognitive (thinking) skills become established during infancy. In *Total Baby Development*, Dr. Jaroslav Koch observes that babies whose muscles and senses are stimulated become more receptive to their surroundings, leading to a fuller life intellectually, emotionally and physically. And Dr. Burton L. White concludes in *The First Three Years of Life* that, "The informal education that families provide for their children makes more of an impact on a child's total educational development than the formal educational system."

Nowhere were such findings more emphatically substantiated than in the nationwide Project Head Start. Educators had hoped to give disadvantaged preschoolers a head start to prepare them for kindergarten, but they discovered that the program was already too late. Trained adults could not, even with the richest of resources, make up for what the children had lacked developmentally during their first three years of life.

Drs. Daniel D. Arnheim and William A. Sinclair suggest in their book, *The Clumsy Child*, that many classroom problems—awkwardness, perceptual-motor or neurological dysfunctions, social and emotional inadequacies—may be prevented or lessened to a great extent by a planned program of movement and multisensory experiences begun in infancy.

Once we knew *why* it was important to play with very young children, we asked, "Why aren't parents *doing* it? Why didn't we know *how* to play with our babies?"

Lack of awareness, we discovered, is the primary reason. The general public does not realize the importance of developing an infant's learning foundations through play.

Most hospitals now have prenatal classes for expectant parents, but they do not offer new parents *post*natal classes in infant growth and development. Many pediatricians do not adequately counsel parents about how to provide early sensory and physical stimulation for their babies.

Because of the increased mobility in America, the family unit is breaking down. Unlike the past, grandparents, aunts, uncles and cousins are not always around to play with infants and to suggest imaginative recreational activities for them.

Urban sprawls and mass transportation have also greatly limited access to the hills, trees and grass which help young children develop motor skills and senses. Automated conveniences have eliminated the need for children to use their senses and muscles to hang clothes, wash dishes, and so on.

The increase in the number of working mothers, the busy schedules of young parents and the disinterest of baby-sitters have often forced babies and young children to spend too many waking hours in infant seats, playpens, walkers, strollers and car seats. There they are not even required to make the beneficial posture adjustments they would make if they were being held or carried. Today's toddlers often lack children-oriented indoor and outdoor spaces and attention from people who can respond to them as individuals.

We decided to go to work on our own babies, setting up a program that used everyday activities to stimulate their muscles and senses. After several weeks our babies were having fun—and so were we!

Friends and neighbors with children grew curious about our activities, so in 1972 we began to meet regularly in a play group. From that modest beginning we spent the next nine years developing and teaching a simple, progressive, daily program of developmental movements and sensorimotor experiences that offers children the opportunity to reach their maximum potential. We call the program *Playful Parenting*.

Playful Parenting has received support from doctors, nurses, physical therapists, college professors, child-development specialists and, most important, parents. The program has been tested by more than six thousand participants through recreation centers, YMCAs, preschools, day-care centers, gymnastic schools and a special university grant program, and it has been licensed by the California State Regional Center for the Handicapped.

Its success can best be measured by the enthusiasm of the thousands of parents who have taken part in it. These comments express typical feelings:

"Diaper Play makes me feel important as a parent. It gives my job credibility."

"My husband and I spend lots more time watching and playing with our son now. We feel more relaxed, and he is more expressive."

"Having twins is double work, but Mini Play gives me different things to do with each twin by himself."

"Angie takes my hand every day, pulls me over to the record player and says, 'Time for Mommy to play with Angie.' "

"Toddler Play gives me ammunition for all occasions: what to do while waiting in the doctor's office, on rainy days, for fussy times . . ."

"Tyler and I like to get together with other moms and children to do the activities. Afterward the moms can visit while the children explore."

Playful Parenting is specifically designed for children six weeks to three years of age. We are delighted to bring it into your home.

Chapter 2

ALL ABOUT
PLAYFUL
PARENTING

COMMON PHASES OF DEVELOPMENT

Frank and Theresa Caplan, authors of *The First Twelve Months of Life* and *The Second Twelve Months of Life,* point out that although personalities differ greatly, most children pursue certain activities at about the same age. Having a knowledge of common phases of development allows parents to follow their child's growth pattern from birth, enabling them to observe and to identify problems should they occur.

The same phases of development allow *Playful Parenting* to provide activities that meet the needs of your child as he or she matures and requires new challenges.

PLAY GROUPS

The program is divided into three play groups: Diaper Play, for children six weeks to twelve months of age; Toddler Play, thirteen to twenty-four months; and Mini Play, twenty-five to thirty-six months. We choose to begin the program at six weeks because by this time you are well acquainted with your newborn, and he or she stays awake for longer periods.

The program is further broken down into behavioral guidelines, lists of supplies, suggestions for setting the atmosphere and warm-up games, followed by developmental movements, exploring activities and other sensorimotor experiences.

Each month or combination of months includes:

1. HOW DO YOU DO? briefly discusses some background information on kinds of behavior to expect at each age level.

2. SUPPLIES lists innovative equipment and materials that make *Playful Parenting* a more resourceful and challenging program.

3. GETTING READY offers a variety of activities designed to arouse your child's interest in movement. In the first year these include massaging, rocking, tipping, spinning and rolling. In the second and third years come tension and relaxation, rhythms, body awareness, finger play, locomotion and pretending.

4. MOVING OUT includes an assortment of developmental movements. In the first and second years:

> *Reflex Movements* stimulate your child to act reflexively to responses that are normally present at a particular age.
> *Prompted Movements* encourage your child, with your guidance, to stretch and contract his muscles, arousing excitement and creating additional free movement.
> *Partner Movements* allow you and your child to move together.
> *Assistive Movements* allow you to support your child in individual movements.
> *Active Movements* require your child to move alone.

And, in the third year:

> *Balancing Movements* involve floor play and refined use of the supplies, stressing the use of both your child's left and right sides.
> *Up and Away Movements* include fun airborne activities to challenge large-muscle coordination.
> *Playing with Objects in Space* introduces the use of four "grown-up" activities: throwing, catching, striking and hitting.

5. EXPLORING suggests delightful, unusual media to stimulate your child's creativity and imagination. Through Silly Pool and Super Stuff, he or she can explore such touchables as bubbles, feathers, scarves, pudding and gelatin.

6. ALL AROUND shows your child curious and fascinating ways to use his five physical senses and how to develop a sixth "social" sense. He'll experience smelling, tasting, touching, seeing, hearing, body positioning, manipulating, imitating, imagining, communicating, problem solving and socializing.

These guidelines may sound formal, but the program is easy to follow. Each movement, as well as its educational value, is thoroughly described. Necessary steps are detailed, and illustrations accompany many of the movements. Nursery rhymes, both familiar and new, provide rhythm and verbal support. A recommended number of daily repetitions for each movement is included. If your baby spends time in a day-care center and/or needs the extra stimulation that premature, high-risk or developmentally disabled infants often do, you may want to repeat some movements more than the recommended number. Your doctor can best advise you in these cases, but you will not overstimulate your child as long as you use common sense. If your baby is colicky, wait until he is calm before beginning.

CREATING THE RIGHT ENVIRONMENT

There is nothing more wonderful than feeling secure in your environment. Therefore, it's important that your child's first learning experiences be positive and happy. Keep the following tips in mind when you design the play environment.

Space for the program may be a garage, family room, basement, bedroom or, on a sunny day, a backyard or park. There should be ample room to move freely and safely. The greater the area, the more your child will move. Lively, spontaneous movements enhance circulation, breathing, digestion and many other bodily functions.

Temperature of the space should be warm—between 72 and 76 degrees Fahrenheit when your child is very small, and somewhat cooler when he or she is older and more active.

Clothing tends to restrict movement and lessens touching experiences. To get the full benefit of the activities, your child should wear little or no clothing except for diapers. Shorts are fine when he is older. For safety—and for touching—shoes should *not* be worn on the equipment.

Music, singing, whistling and nursery rhymes add a special dimension to the atmosphere. The pleasant association between music and activities helps develop rhythm, language and listening skills. You may vary the selection, depending on your mood and goals for the day.

Time for *Playful Parenting* is whenever you feel it is right. Choose a time when your child is rested and you are not rushed. Some parents prefer after bath, while others like to do the activities in two to five ten-minute segments. We recommend fifteen to thirty minutes a day for Diaper Play—longer if you and your child are feeling particularly relaxed and silly. During Toddler Play and Mini Play, increase the variety of activities and the time to thirty to sixty minutes a day. Many of the movements may be repeated, and one session a day should include Dad.

If you are consistent in doing structured activities at about the same time and in a familiar place, even as a tiny baby, your child will learn to anticipate that "special playtime." Consistency in quality and quantity of attention also reinforces him or her to move up to more challenging tasks.

Use *common sense* to keep your child safe. Never leave her unattended on the equipment if it is too advanced for independent play. In fact, your presence and encouragement give the nod to try new things. Only when your child feels secure will she become totally involved in the activities.

You can also set up your home to stimulate your child indirectly. Integrate some play activities into your household routine. When you cook, allow your child to smell and taste. While you are changing a diaper, keep the feely bag handy and let him sample the textures. During bath time talk about body parts. While you are grocery shopping give him different items in the cart to manipulate. As you watch your bundle of energy grow, you will learn the best ways to handle his needs.

SETTING THE MOOD

You are your child's first teacher, and research shows that your child's total development depends on the diversity of stimulation that you provide.

The activities offered in this book will guide you in teaching your child something new and useful every day. Encourage him to reach toward these experiences, but never force. Let him play at his own pace.

Allow your little one time to explore his environment freely. If you let him amuse himself, he will develop independence and the ability to solve problems. Remember, the object of this program is not to *accelerate* development, but to fully *cultivate* your child's potential from an early age.

The accent in *Playful Parenting* is always on having fun and enjoying the activities. At no time should there be a sense of fear or drudgery for you or your child. Be patient, have reasonable expectations and reflect positive feelings about any accomplishment, large or small.

GOALS

You may wish to keep the following goals in mind when playing:

> to express affection through physical closeness: touching, hugging, rocking
>
> to form a foundation of communication for problem solving and joyful, daily living
>
> to playfully work together to achieve goals.
>
> to establish a firm basis of support and trust
>
> to develop basic physical skills: agility, body control, coordination, endurance, strength and flexibility
>
> to develop desire and confidence to do physical activities
>
> to make sensorimotor experiences pleasurable daily occurrences
>
> to foster language development and self-expression
>
> to make the parenting responsibility an imaginative and rewarding experience.

ENJOYING YOUR BABY

Since adults cannot remember what it was like to be a toddler, we have difficulty understanding what our baby's early experiences mean to him. Self-esteem is very important; a child needs to have his feelings and ideas respected.

Be as tactful and calm as possible when your child is concentrating on an activity. Remember that his rate of development is uniquely his. Do not expect him to complete an exercise on the first try. Many skills take months of practice. As time passes, you will see tremendous growth and improvement in your child's abilities.

When you realize that you, too, are learning from the program and that you are not expected to be an expert, you will do a splendid job of caring for, loving, tracking the progress of, being sensitive to the problems of and meeting the needs of your child. Your little one's self-esteem will flourish, and you will become better attuned to your *own* feelings. Naturally, you will make some magic memories as you share the activities of the next few years. But, best of all, you will enjoy the satisfaction and pleasure of interacting with your child as he or she grows.

Happiness is being a playful parent—or being the child of a playful parent!

Part II

DIAPER PLAY

Six Weeks to Twelve Months

INTRODUCTION

Diaper Play is the start of an exciting adventure for you and your baby. Each month your little one will reach new milestones, and you will be proud of your role in fostering the achievements.

You may experience fears and mixed feelings about being a parent. These are normal emotions, because your baby can't tell you why she is crying or why she is unhappy. You will learn to communicate in your own special way, though, as she grows from a tiny baby into an independent little person.

Diaper Play provides you with activities to nourish your baby's intellectual, physical and emotional growth. You will massage, rock, roll and spin him and stimulate his muscles to grow properly. He will see, touch, hold, hear, smell and taste many interesting things. Surround him with happy talk as you play to encourage good language development and self-expression. Be yourself, have fun with your baby and let him know that you love him by telling him that he is very special and important. Meet with other mothers and fathers, too, to share ideas, talk about your problems and seek and offer solutions. Most of all, smile, and enjoy watching your baby grow into a well-rounded, caring and self-confident individual.

Chapter 3

THE EMERGING PERSONALITY
Six Weeks through Two Months

HOW DO YOU DO?

By the time your baby reaches six to eight weeks of age, she has grown from an oblivious little being whose total concern is comfort into a person who has specific likes and dislikes and a genuine interest in her surroundings. Her eyes are alert. She communicates by various cries and shows excitement and delight through wiggles, kicks and sounds. Your baby's schedule may even be fairly predictable: eating times are followed by naptimes, then short crying spells and wakeful times—perhaps for a period of ten hours a day.

A child's new wakefulness allows her to observe many things of interest. Sounds attract her attention. She can see an object held nearby, though moving objects hold her attention longer. She may be able to hold a small object for a time and bring it to her mouth to suck.

Your baby's skin is still highly sensitive to temperature changes and to the contrast between soft and hard materials. She is drawn to your smooth, warm skin and enjoys being held, rocked and lovingly talked to. She is quickly becoming your companion, and she is beginning to look at others as individuals and to enjoy their company as they do hers. She is ready for Diaper Play.

Imagine being your baby. You are bathed, dried with a fluffy towel, diapered and laid on a soft blanket in a warm room. Then imagine being massaged, stretched and firmly exercised while music plays, then being handed interesting objects to touch, see and hear, all while being gently talked to.

Sound terrific? That's exactly how your baby will feel. Let's begin!

SUPPLIES

soft blanket—to lay your baby on
beach ball—partially inflated, 36-inch ball
feely bag—pillowcase or drawstring bag to hold scraps of softly textured massage materials (softies)

GETTING READY

Cuddles. This wonderful massaging game, akin to an athlete's warm-up, arouses your baby and makes her more responsive to the developmental movements.

Tenderly massage your baby from head to toe, front and back, in a hand-over-hand motion while talking lovingly to her. Different soft fabrics such as terry cloth, satin, and crushed velvet may be used to massage.

Expand this touching communication by gently pressing different parts of your baby's body as you say, "Here's your knee, your ankle, your toes," and so on. Notice the contentment, the pleasure and the movement of the tiny body in response to your touch.

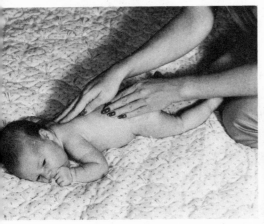

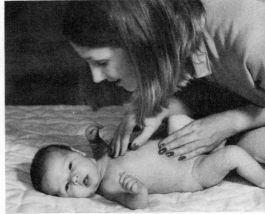

Massaging with intermittent cuddling and kissing may be done for two to three minutes. This helps set a precedent of receiving pleasure from relationships with other people.

Rock 'n' Roll. "Refreshing" and "engaging" best describe this game. "Refreshing" because the movements can relax or exhilarate your baby, and "engaging" because each time your baby loses his balance, he will work to right himself. The balancing mechanism, along with muscle development, eventually allows him to move efficiently while he is upright.

Place your baby on the beach ball while holding him securely around the middle. Hum or sing a favorite tune to set a slow and steady rhythm to rock him back and forth, side to side and round and round, first on his tummy and then on his back, for two or three minutes. As the weeks progress and he gets used to the motion, the rocking and rolling may become more vigorous.

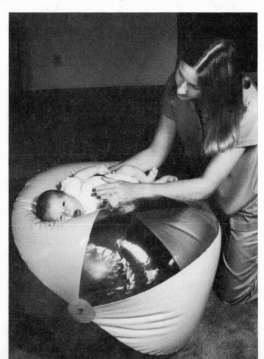

MOVING OUT

Reflex Movements

TAFFY PULL

Value: "My, what a strong grasp you have!" is a father's response to this movement, which encourages your baby to open and close his hands and stretch arm and shoulder muscles.

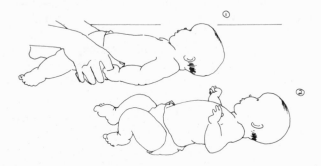

Here's How: Lay your baby on his back. Place your index fingers in the palms of his hands, stimulating his reflexes. When he has grasped your fingers, draw his hands gently toward you until his arms are stretched to their fullest. Slip your fingers out of your baby's grasp and his arms will spontaneously pull backward, returning to their original bent position. A good variation is to draw your baby's arms up over his head, then release them.

How Many: Two extensions; may be repeated daily. (For additional hand-grasp stimulation, give your baby a bright rattle to hold for a few moments.)

TIGERS

Value: This movement stimulates and develops the muscles which control your "tiger's" thighs—the muscles eventually used to creep, crawl and walk.

Here's How: Place your baby on his back. With one hand, grasp both ankles from underneath and gently pull until his legs straighten. Using the fingers of

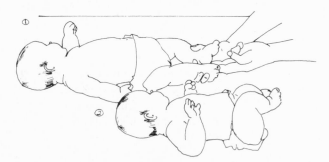

your free hand, stroke the soles of his feet. He will bend his toes downward and immediately draw his legs up into a bent-knee position.

How Many: Three pulls; may be repeated daily. (Do a second set when you are changing a diaper.)

HI-HO

Value: Most grandparents can hardly believe their eyes when they observe a grandbaby doing this walking reflex movement. Reassure them that in no way does the exercise speed up your baby's ability to walk before maturation allows. But it *is* fun, and it stimulates and strengthens many of the leg and lower-trunk muscles that will be involved in walking.

Here's How: Kneel behind your baby, holding beneath her arms, and draw her into a full standing position. Tilt her forward slightly to stimulate the walking action. In the correct position your baby will take rhythmical steps, touching

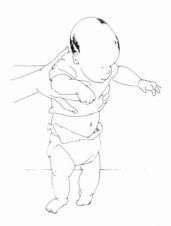

the entire soles of her feet to the surface of the floor. She will "walk" on a level plane, step over low obstacles and perhaps even walk up an incline. A firm surface is more desirable than a spongy one.

How Many: Both you and your baby will enjoy this movement, but caution should be taken that it is not overdone. Your baby should do the walking reflex for five to ten seconds *once* a day.

PUSH-AWAY

Value: Often a baby's movements remind us of a little animal's. The action in this movement seems like that of an inchworm. Push-Away stimulates muscle action in your baby's feet, legs and thighs, giving her the sensation of forward motion that will someday become creeping, crawling and walking.

Here's How: Place your baby on her tummy with her feet tucked close to her body. Apply firm hand pressure against the soles of her feet and a push-away

reaction will occur. Her legs will straighten and her body will inch forward. She may even let out an "Oof!" as if she had just moved a mountain. Pat her bottom in acknowledgment of the effort.

How Many: Three push-aways in succession, once a day.

Prompted Movements

WIPERS

Value: Singing, "Row Your Boat" or "London Bridge" creates a slow and steady rhythm for your baby to perform this movement, which stretches arm, shoulder, chest and upper back muscles.

Here's How: Place your baby on your lap so that you can see each other. Allow him to grasp your forefingers with each hand. Gently spread his arms out to his sides as far as possible, then bring them across his chest and return them to their starting position. (At first you may need to secure each grasp with thumb and forefinger.) Be happy as you sing:

> *London Bridge is falling down, falling down, falling down.*
> *London Bridge is falling down, my fair lady'o.*

How Many: Eight movements; may be repeated daily. (Dad can do the second round of this exercise. His special attention just before mealtime may help your baby be more content while the family dines.)

BOW 'N' ARROW

Value: This movement stimulates muscle activity and increases flexibility in your baby's arms and shoulders. He will need this to reach for objects, crawl and, eventually, play ball or shoot a bow and arrow.

Here's How: To ready your baby, place him on his back on your lap, looking into your face. Have him grasp your forefingers, and gently stretch his arms out as far as possible. Then move them in an alternate manner in as many directions as possible, while singing "Ten Little Indians." You will feel more strength and resistance in your baby's arms as the days go by.

How Many: Repeat for the duration of the song; may repeat entire exercise twice daily.

BOO!

Value: This is a great movement because it contains the element of surprise. Boo! mobilizes the major leg, hip and thigh muscles and joints, which will be used to creep, crawl, walk and jog.

Here's How: Place baby on her back on the floor and grasp her legs around the knees, straightening them. Move her legs upward toward her head, stretching the backs of thighs and legs, then return them to the fully extended position. When her legs are by her head, spread them and say "Boo!" You will love watching your baby's coos and chuckles.

How Many: Four stretches, once a day.

Time out for hugs and kisses. Sometimes, in the beginning, you get so wrapped up in the mechanics of the movements that you forget to smile, hold, smell, think and *tell* your little one what a wonderful person he or she is.

PUSS 'N' BOOTS

Value: Here is a movement designed to stretch and stimulate activity in your baby's back, thigh and leg muscles.

Here's How: Lay your baby on his back in your lap or on the floor. Grasp below his knees and hold the legs down straight. Then push your child's legs into a bent-knee position with his thighs touching his tummy. Return the legs to a straightened position. As you sing the first verse of "Farmer in the Dell," your baby will make the association between rhythm and movement:

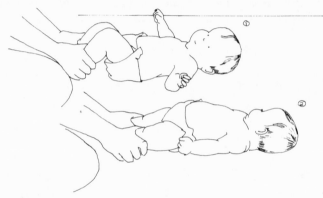

The farmer in the dell, the farmer in the dell,
High ho the dairy'o, the farmer in the dell.

How Many: Four knee bends, once a day.

ALL AROUND

Besides enjoying structured games and movements, your baby delights in being exposed to experiences that increase his awareness of himself and his surroundings. Integrate into your everyday routine activities to stimulate his touch, sight, hearing and movement and observe how he responds with a different action or sound for each new stimulus.

Touching

The sense of touch is quite acute; even at six weeks your baby may respond to a particular sensation as though mesmerized. The activity may be continued as long as it does not appear to irritate him. A good time for touching is after bath, when your baby wears little or no clothing. Choose one or two touching experiences each day.

With your baby on your lap, talk softly and gently rub his skin in *circles,* from head to toe and front to back, using your hands or soft materials from the feely bag. Your baby will enjoy the switch to a single hand *stroking* while snuggling on your shoulder. The strokes should be gentle and rhythmic, much like you would stroke a kitten. Varying the rhythm from fast to slow and using light to firm pressures will interest your baby, but never stroke harshly. You may also take your baby's hands and help him stroke his own body and your face and arms.

Lay your baby on his back and tummy on different types of *cushy materials,* such as blankets, towels, sheets, quilts, robes or pieces of thick clothing. Describe to your baby what the material feels like: "This is bumpy, silky," and the like. Another touching experience for your baby is to *pat* his body gently with your fingertips, varying the speed and pressure. Try saying this rhyme as you pat the soles of his feet:

> *Pat your little feet together,*
> *Pat them on my cheeks,*
> *Pat your little feet together,*
> *And lay them down to sleep.*

Seeing

Your baby should have a variety of visual experiences to enhance total development. Brightly colored, oddly shaped objects capture his attention and stimulate his ability to focus. Mobiles help him focus on and track a moving object.

Select multicolored *patterned sheets* for your baby to see. Attach *bright objects* to the crib, and place a toy where she can swipe at it. Safe and pretty *mobiles* can be made from ordinary household goods—plastic lids, felt, feathers and cardboard. We also recommend the Semper toy line, which features different toys to attach every few months. Change or rotate media, and remove your baby's *crib bumpers* when she is awake to allow her to view the surroundings.

Hold a bright object like a *flashlight* 8 to 12 inches in front of your little one and let him track the light from one side across the middle of his body. This will help him learn to move his eyes, which is important for future reading readiness.

Paint a simple *happy face* on cardboard and securely attach it to the side of the crib. The face should be about the size of an adult face, including all the features—dots for eyes, a line for a nose, an enlarged line for a smile and ovals for the ears. Your baby begins early to recognize facial features and will respond to a happy face with increased activity. Leave the happy face up for short periods each day.

Hearing and Language

When your baby's hearing is stimulated by a variety of sounds, he is encouraged to increase his attention span and to make his own sounds, which will later become words.

For short periods during the day, your baby should hear a variety of *background sounds,* such as a radio, stereo, television or tape.

Talk and sing directly to your baby. Encourage him to imitate your sounds. He can also produce sounds when a *bell or rattle* is tied to his bootie or wrist or placed in his hands.

Body Positioning

Placing your baby in a variety of positions assists him in gaining maximum body control, self-awareness and balance.

Rocking your baby can be very pleasurable. Rock him while he lies on his tummy, sits up and lies on his back or on either side. Move him back and forth, up and down and side to side. Your baby may also like to be rocked while being fed. This can relax you, and your baby will enjoy your warmth and the sound of your voice when you sing or hum softly.

Turning develops balance. Hold your child closely in your arms or against your shoulder, supporting her head, and sing or laugh as you spin with her. Your baby should also be *carried* in different positions: facedown as well as faceup in your arms, horizontally on both right and left shoulders and in front of you with her back to your chest. These experiences make an infant more conscious of her "space."

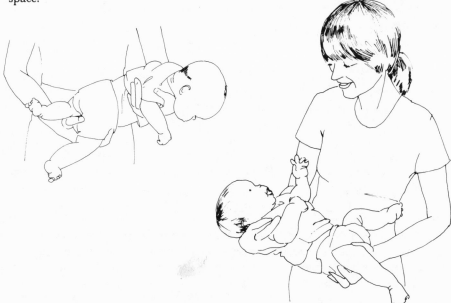

While he is in his crib, it is best for baby to alternate between lying on his tummy and on his back so he can *look around*. Place him in different locations within the crib, such as at each end and near each side. Also, place the crib at different angles in the nursery and position his portable crib in different nooks within the house so he can see new surroundings.

While carefully holding your baby's head and shoulders up, let him *flail his arms* freely in the bath water. Special bathtubs are available for your babies so that they can safely kick the water.

Swinging is another pleasant body-positioning experience for your baby. Place your infant on his back or tummy in the middle of a soft blanket. By grasping both ends of the blanket tightly, you can gently sway your baby side to side, back and forth and round and round. Two people can do this more easily than one and are really necessary as baby grows and gains weight.

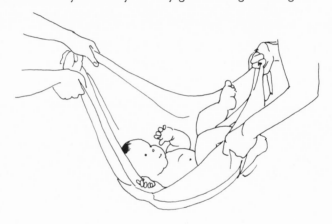

Socializing

Your baby's emotional growth begins at birth. He responds to others' feelings and behaviors. Reinforcing infant smiles with nods, talk and smiles and discouraging tears, frowns and fusses make babies very "smiley" indeed!

Place baby nearby when the *family gathers* for meals, TV-watching and other at-home activities. Infants love to be held and comforted by older brothers and sisters, grandparents, aunts and uncles. Your baby will like to be close while there is *activity* about the house, too. Tell him about your chores.

Feeding is one of our basic social experiences. Your baby should always be held by a family member or close friend during feedings. She will respond hungrily to the warmth and companionship of a helpmate. And a wonderful way to expand your baby's social circle and to relay your rhythmical motion is to carry her in a *front pack* while you are shopping and running errands.

Chapter 4

CREATURE
OF HABIT
Three Months

HOW DO YOU DO?

At three months your baby's developing abilities may surprise you. A baby this age can hold his head up without a lot of bobbing. He can associate certain activities with people: when he sees his bottle or sees you preparing to feed him, he may smack his lips, coo and wiggle all over. These actions demonstrate that memory is developing.

Your wiggler is also learning cause and effect. When he swipes at dangling objects, he makes them move. He is gaining bodily control and now holds onto objects voluntarily. His most exciting discovery is himself: he discovers that his hands and feet are parts of him and that they can explore his face and body.

You, too, are becoming more familiar and confident in caring for your little one. You may spend a lot of time just watching him, talking to him, listening to him and encouraging him to gurgle and coo. As your baby shows greater pleasure in his surroundings, exercise time becomes more playful.

SUPPLIES

beach ball—partially inflated

big dish—a saucer used for sledding

cushies—soft fabrics to wrap up and lay your baby on, such as a bathrobe or nightgown

feely bag—containing an ever-expanding collection of softies (chiffon, nylon and cotton velour)

record—slow waltz to provide a definite beat for rocking and other rhythmical activities.

33

GETTING READY

Cuddles 'n' Circles Wrap your baby snugly in a cushy material, such as a robe or towel. Cuddle, kiss and talk lovingly as you slowly unwrap him and massage his body with gentle, circular motions. Don't forget to lightly massage sensitive areas, especially the skin around his lips, eyes, ears and between his thighs and arms. Continue to massage with hands or softies for two or three minutes while you turn him from his back to his tummy and on each side. How adored he feels—ready to play!

Rock 'n' Roll. Your baby likes being king of the mountain on the beach ball. Support him in a sitting position atop the ball and repeat the rocking and rolling movements of back and forth, side to side and round and round. You can feel the righting reflex at work as he uses tummy and thigh muscles to stay upright.

Your child may like the familiar positions of lying on his back and tummy while the motions are repeated more vigorously. Introducing a cadence or using a waltz record for a steady rhythm will make the two or three minutes seem like seconds.

Big Dish. This tipping and spinning game relaxes and intrigues your baby. Tipping employs the balancing mechanism in his inner ear.

Place your baby on his back in the dish and gently tip him back and forth and side to side, then slowly spin him in clockwise and counterclockwise circles. Each time you spin, center your child so he can see your smiling face and hear a

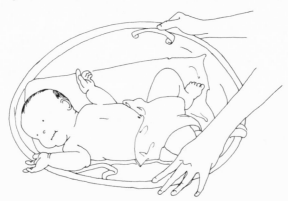

familiar "Hello!" Using cushies inside the dish will give your little one different tactile sensations. Play Big Dish with your baby on his back and tummy for a total of one to two minutes.

MOVING OUT

Reflex Movements

HOT CROSS BUNS

Value: Once your baby is happily aroused, Hot Cross Buns stimulates the muscles that turn hips and trunk, preparing her for the day she will roll from her back to tummy.

Here's How: Lay your little one on her back and kneel in front of her feet, looking into her face. Grasp one ankle and foot and cross them over her other leg until her foot touches the floor, and her hips and trunk will follow.

How Many: Two repetitions of Hot Cross Buns will have you rhythmically alternating your baby's left and right feet four times; may be repeated daily.

> *Hot cross buns, hot cross buns,*
> *One a penny, two a penny, hot cross buns.*

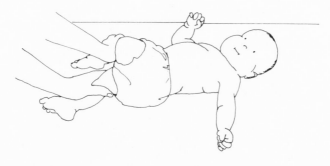

APPLE TURNOVER

Value: This movement helps prepare baby to roll from tummy to back.

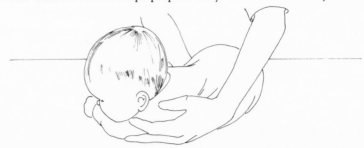

Here's How: While your baby lies on her tummy, kneel at her side near her head. Gently lift her shoulders slightly and fold one arm under her chest. The trunk and hips will automatically follow to turn her over. Repeat, first to one side, then the other.

How Many: Two turnovers on each side; may be repeated daily.

Prompted Movements

TWINKLE TOES

Value: We want your baby to feel beautiful from the top of his head to the tip of his toes. Twinkle Toes pays special attention to the feet, stimulating those ankle and foot muscles important for eventual walking, dancing, skiing.

Here's How: Lay your baby on his back, in front of you or on your lap. Grasp his ankles and heels and touch the heels of his feet together, following with the soles and toes of his feet. Hold this position for two or three seconds, then return his feet and legs to your lap or the floor.

Your baby will flare his toes when the soles of his feet touch, much like a little flower spreading its petals.

How Many: Four toe-touches; may be repeated daily. (A convenient time to do the second round is after a diaper change.)

JAM 'N' JELLY

Value: This movement stimulates your baby's shoulder, chest and upper-arm muscles as well as increasing the flexibility of the entire shoulder area for reaching, creeping and crawling endeavors. The actions may help your baby be a whiz on a tennis court someday!

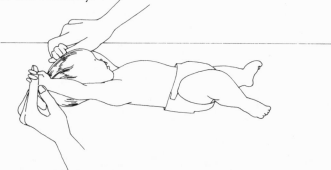

Here's How: Place your baby on his back. Kneel at his feet, tell him to get ready and have him grasp your thumbs. Gently raise his arms from a fully extended position at his sides to an overhead stretch about in line with his ears. Let him use his muscles to hold your fingers as long as possible during the movement. Tell him that you can feel him growing stronger and more capable every day!

How Many: Four stretches while whistling or singing a favorite nursery rhyme; may be repeated daily.

THE ARCH

Value: Three-month-old babies like this movement, perhaps because they see a curious upside-down world, or because this movement stretches the neck muscles that get so much use.

Here's How: Kneel at your baby's feet while she rests on her back. Encourage her to grasp the index fingers of your hands, then gently pull her upward until her neck and upper back are *slightly* arched. Hold this position, count to three slowly, then lower her. The movement must be done in a slow, steady manner without jerking your baby or overly arching her back.

How Many: Two arches; may be repeated daily.

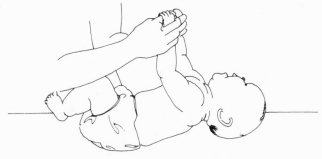

Before you begin the next movement, lie on your back and rest your baby on your tummy or hold him close while you do a few leg lifts.

ONE UP, ONE DOWN

Value: One Up, One Down encourages flexibility in your baby's lower back and hip region by stimulating the bottom and thigh muscles. This symmetrical movement will first be used when your baby crawls and, later, when he roars around the driveway on his tricycle!

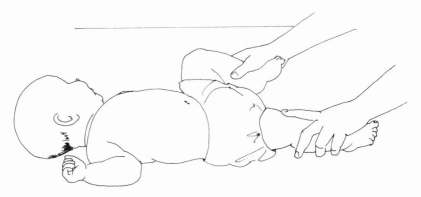

Here's How: Kneel at your baby's feet while he lies on his back. Grasp his lower legs and, from a fully extended position, alternately bend one knee up to touch or nearly touch his tummy, then return it to the full extension.

How Many: Alternate four times on each leg while singing "Twinkle, Twinkle, Little Star"; may be repeated daily.

> *Twinkle, twinkle little star,*
> *How I wonder what you are.*
> *Up above the world so high,*
> *Like a diamond in the sky.*

[Cradle your little one in your arms while you finish the song.]

> *When the blazing sun is gone,*
> *When he nothing shines upon,*
> *Then you show your little light,*
> *Twinkle, twinkle all the night.*

THE DOLPHIN

Value: You may often find your three-month-old lying on his tummy with his head up and his legs flexed, much like a dolphin arching its back. This movement strengthens your baby's bottom and lower-back muscles and stimulates the muscles located in his back and neck region, allowing him to assume his favorite dolphin position and, eventually, to sit and walk upright.

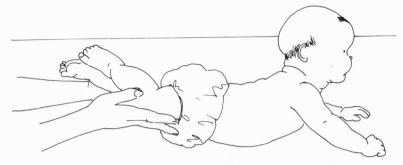

Here's How: Place your baby on his tummy and kneel at his feet, looking toward his head. Slide your hands under his thighs and lift them gently and slowly until your baby lifts his head and arches his lower back slightly. Hold for a slow count of five or until his head drops back to the blanket.

How Many: Two lifts; may be repeated twice daily.

ALL AROUND

Studies show that when a baby's organic needs (food, sleep, dryness) are satisfied, she will seek stimulation from and interact with the environment. Your infant is rapidly displaying these traits. Playtime after feedings may be as long as an hour and a half. And, although your baby's sense of taste is still fairly static, the senses of smell, touch, hearing and sight can be stimulated in many pleasant and interesting ways.

Smelling

Your baby cannot identify various smells, but smell associations are part of her everyday life. It is important that your child encounter different smells, which are closely associated with taste, since both are important to her survival. Make a game of smelling as baby gets older and can identify odors.

Mom should wear different *perfumes* and Dad should use *colognes* and after-shave lotions when feeding and playing with baby.

Pleasant *household smells*, such as bath oils and deodorants, should be presented to baby. To "present" a smell, put a dab on your hand or on a piece of facial tissue and pass it under your baby's nose several times. Remember that your baby is extremely sensitive to harsh and toxic smells, which should be avoided.

When you prepare meals, present different *food smells* to your baby and describe them to him. When you have fresh fruit in the house, help your baby fondle some and say, "This is an orange. It is round and bumpy. It smells sweet and fresh."

Touching

At this time in you baby's life, he is more aware of touch than any other sense. Give your curiosity seeker as rich a variety of tactile experiences as possible by choosing one or two of the following each day.

Your little one loves to be *stroked*. A good time for this is during feedings. Also stroke your baby with materials of moderate temperatures, such as a clean diaper right from the dryer or a cool cheek just in from a snowstorm. (Be sure that the temperatures are *not* hot or cold!)

Tapping is an interesting sensation for your learner. Using your first two fingers, gently tap parts of your baby's body, naming them as you go. Or tap in fast or slow sequences, like a chipmunk scurrying all over his body.

While your baby is nude, let her *wiggle freely* on different textures, such as carpet or upholstery samples. Give her *touchies* that are rough, smooth, lumpy, and so on. Help her fondle objects that have different shapes—a round ball, a square block, a hard metal spoon. Keep in mind, though, that she will bring everything to her mouth to feel and taste.

Seeing

Your three-month-old can now see across a room and is beginning to see more detail. He stares at his hands for long periods, and his ability to bring them together and focus on them is part of hand-to-mouth organization—a primary means of learning that integrates smell, taste, touch and sight.

Tie a brightly-colored *balloon* on a string over baby's crib, near enough to move if he swipes at it or kicks it. Placing interesting objects at different distances will also help develop depth perception.

Let your baby see his environment and respond to hanging objects from different *points of view*, such as sitting with support, reclining in an infant seat or being propped on one side.

Your baby is learning more about himself every day. Replace the happy face with a *mirror*. Put it near your baby for several minutes, two or three times a day.

Seat your little one in different *places* about the house, as well as outside, so that he may observe shapes and movements, such as the shadows tree branches make on a wall.

Hearing and Language

Your baby's vocalizing is becoming more expressive. She may whimper when tired, coo when delighted and wail when hungry. Respond to these sounds, as feedback tells your baby that she is important and loved. As she builds a basis of communication, stimulate the maturation of hearing and speech.

Talk to your baby as you move around the house so that she will follow your *sounds and movement*. Expose her to house noises: electric razor, hair dryer, ticking clock, whistling teakettle, vacuum, telephone.

Hold your baby close and show pleasure when he makes baby sounds. Let him feel your lips as you say, "mama," "daddy," "baby," "I love you."

Body Positioning

Frequent changes in body position keep your baby happily occupied during waking hours. Your baby will like the closeness while you play *Tick Tock*. Sit on the edge of a couch, legs together, and lay him on his back atop your legs. Move your legs together in a side-to-side motion while you repeat, "Tick tock, tick tock."

Gently *bounce* your baby at different speeds while holding him on a partially inflated beach ball, on a bed or on your lap. He will enjoy trying this on his back, side and tummy. A bouncinette is another lovely toy, constructed so that the slightest movement causes a bounce. The bouncinette's shape also lets your baby look around, and its mesh is airy and refreshing on a hot day. A mother of twins can really benefit from using this toy; as she feeds one baby, the other can bounce!

Encourage your baby to change positions by moving from one side of him to the other and *calling him to find you*. Offer him toys from the left side, right side and front.

Swinging in a *porch swing* or under the trees is a beautiful way to spend time with your infant. He enjoys your warmth, the motion, outdoor noises and views.

Socializing

While your baby's world expands, social stimulus becomes more important. Your baby is beginning to recognize family members and searches with her eyes and wiggles in anticipation at the sound of a familiar voice. Your family's sensitivity to baby's needs will help her believe in herself.

Take your baby to *visit friends*. Allow them to hold, touch, talk to and feed your baby. *Strolling* can be relaxing and interesting, too. Strangers will stop to admire your little one and to chat with you. Umbrella strollers are convenient, but as soon as your baby can sit up, a regular stroller allows him to maintain his own balance and look around better.

A *playpen* is useful for short periods and when you are picnicking or traveling. It keeps baby safe from unclean surfaces and animals, and lets her be close enough to enjoy activities without being endangered by the crashing and banging of older siblings and neighborhood children.

Chapter 5

EAGER BEAVER
Four Months

HOW DO YOU DO?

At four months your baby is like a sponge, absorbing every experience that comes her way. Your eager beaver takes great pleasure in examining objects—touching, tasting, smelling, looking and listening. Mealtimes are social happenings with solid foods that are a bit messy but mmmm . . . good! Baths are splashing adventures. And, much to your delight, baby is sleeping through most nights and the length of playtime has doubled.

Your baby is gaining more body control. She is able to keep her head erect while sitting and can hold it in mid-position while lying on her back. Improved muscle control also allows her to arch her back and, perhaps, roll from tummy to back. The small muscles of her hands explore her face, clutch at her clothes and meet in the middle of her body to play with the fingers.

With color and three-dimensional perception developing, your baby's eyesight is almost at adult level. She can now grasp objects lying nearby and bring them to her mouth. Brightly colored and moving objects hold special appeal, and she enjoys seeing herself in a mirror. She is going from cooing, chuckling and talking to herself to laughing aloud and showing excitement during play. Your eager beaver is truly ready for movement time!

SUPPLIES

> feely bag—different textured cloths (softies) plus media such as feathers, smooth wood and a soft artist's paintbrush to use in massage
> cushies—expanded variety of interesting fabrics: warm sheets from dryer, coat lining, rabbit pelt
> beach ball—fully inflated
> big dish
> small bolster—covered foam bolster 10 inches in diameter and 24 inches long

GETTING READY

Cuddles 'n' Stuff. Switch on your favorite music and slowly take three deep breaths while your playmate wiggles freely on an interesting cushy. While singing or whispering to your baby, use a new medium—maybe a feather, cotton ball

or smooth stone—to tenderly massage his entire body for one to three minutes. The massaging (hand over hand, circles or strokes) should range from very slow motions and gentle pressure to motions that are progressively faster and more vigorous.

Rock 'n' Roll. Affectionate squeezes and expressions encourage your baby as he feels the exhilaration of having less support while rocking on the ball. Grasp either arms or feet as you move him forward, backward, sideways and round and round while he is on tummy, back and side. His attempts to right himself using

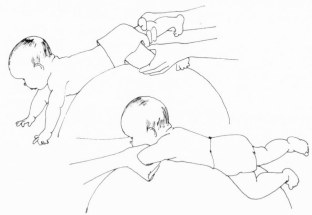

the inner-ear balancing mechanism are more dramatic than ever. (If, however, your baby finds the lack of support frightening, return to holding him securely around the middle and try again later to grasp just feet or arms.)

A variety of tempos, from waltzes to jazz, may be used to rock one to three minutes. Cushies placed between your four-month-old and the ball will further stimulate him.

Big Dish. Playing Hello, Good-bye! with the spinning and tipping big dish makes your baby laugh and smile. The activities may be continued as described at three months, but try spinning baby two or three revolutions.

Small Bolster. Babies take to this new game quickly. Your eager beaver may like to lie on his tummy on the bolster with support around his middle and initiate his own game by pushing with legs and feet. He also likes to rock for-

ward and backward on his tummy, back and side. Always start slowly and progress to faster motions. Isn't it exciting to watch him grow stronger, develop muscles and initiate games?

MOVING OUT

Reflex Movements

SOARING

Value: Dads and babies usually have a wonderful time with this movement, which teaches baby not to fear heights—and to trust you. The activity also strengthens the neck and back extensor muscles that will eventually help her creep, crawl and walk.

Here's How: Lie on your back and place your baby on you, tummies together. Holding firmly with both hands around the chest and tummy area, lift baby slowly to a position just over your face. Now, smile! Your baby will lift her arms and legs to form an arched back. Hold for a count of five and return her to starting position before she droops.

Once you feel confident lifting her, add fun-filled variations. Move her from side to side and back and forth, or gently twist and turn her. (Dad may want to

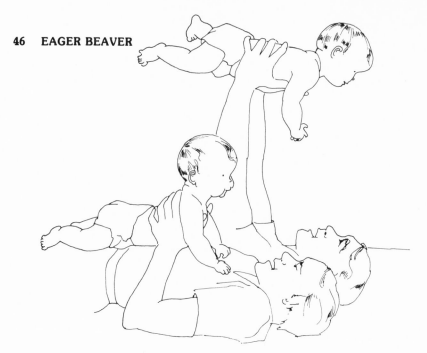

buzz baby around, making airplane sounds.) For added excitement, stand and play. Your baby will love it!

How Many: Two lifts, may be repeated daily.

CATERPILLAR

Value: After you and baby have been soaring, bring your flier back to earth to do the Caterpillar, which stimulates leg and back muscles.

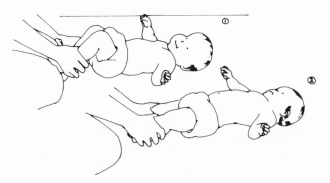

Here's How: Place your baby on his back. Kneel at his feet, looking into his face. Put his heels on your bent knees and lightly stroke the soles of his feet with your fingers. He will push hard against your knees, lift his bottom off the floor, arch his torso and inch backward.

Eventually your little caterpillar will push hard enough to arch his entire back and support his body weight on his shoulders—an accomplishment worth many kisses!

How Many: Three movements; may be repeated daily. (You may even discover your baby inching his way across his crib or blanket—practicing his Caterpillar!)

LOOK ABOUT

Value: Your baby is becoming quite a star. This movement shows off his strong back muscles while encouraging him to focus on objects placed in high places.

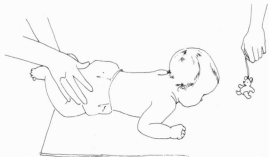

Here's How: While your baby lies on his tummy, kneel at his feet looking toward his head. Place a colorful toy on a higher plane in front of him. Hold both legs firmly against the floor, encouraging him to arch his back and look about, and count slowly to three. Ask baby about his discovery: "Look about, look around. What do you see so high off the ground?" After two repetitions allow him to explore the toy.

How Many: Two movements; may be repeated daily.

Prompted Movements

SCISSORS

Value: The purpose of this exercise is to stretch and stimulate the lower back and hip muscles. Most moms and dads relate to it easily from their own movements and sports experiences and may wish to do eight to ten themselves before exercising baby.

Here's How: While your baby lies on his back, kneel at his feet and smile into

his face. As you grasp his strong lower legs and ankles and move them up and down in a kicking motion, sing, "Row, row, row your boat,/Gently down the stream/Merrily, merrily, merrily, merrily,/Life is but a dream." Extend each scissor kick to each leg's full range of movement.

How Many: Eight kicks with each leg; may be repeated daily. Finish with a few fast flutter kicks and big hug!

BUTTERCUP

Value: Babies are often compared to flowers, needing tender loving care to blossom fully. Buttercup is the first of a series of movements in which your TLC helps prepare your baby to sit up by strengthening and stimulating her neck muscles.

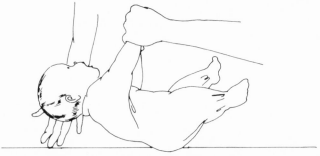

Here's How: Lay your baby on her back. Kneel at her feet and hold both of her hands with one of yours. Place your free hand behind her head for support. Gently pull her arms and bring her into a semi-sitting position. She will lift her head forward and stretch her legs upward. Hold for a slow count of three and lower her down by supporting her head.

How Many: Two movements, once daily.

LITTLE PUPPET

Value: With your help, your baby is going to stand! He may literally screech with delight at the accomplishment, which increases leg strength and helps him gain confidence and trust in the upright position.

Here's How: Seat your baby with feet outward, facing you, as you sit on bent knees. Grasp both hands and gently stretch his arms, pulling him to a standing position. As his weight comes down on his feet, he will automatically push down on the floor and attempt to stand. Let him enjoy his moment, then lower him. How proud you both are!

How Many: Three movements; may be repeated daily.

HIPPIE

Value: This movement may earn you a look of "You're kidding!" from bystanders, but never mind—go right ahead! It exercises baby's hip and lower-back muscles, improving flexibility and preparing him to turn from tummy to back.

Here's How: Place your baby on his tummy and kneel at his feet. Spread his legs slightly and, while holding one leg in place, lift the other up and over toward the floor. Alternate legs, then finish with a gentle leg and back massage.

How Many: Four lifts on each side, alternating.

ALL AROUND

You and your four-month-old are establishing a unique relationship. Your tone of voice and body language express your feelings, and she is learning to communicate likes and dislikes. Your baby must still rely on you, however, for all stimulation. She depends on your care and sensitivity, and tuning into her personality will make your days pleasant and rewarding.

Not every sensorimotor experience will appeal to your baby. Choose thoughtfully, and remind yourself to maintain a balance. One area should not be overdone to the exclusion of another. The following ideas were favorites among parents in our classes.

Smelling

During daily activities in the *kitchen* and *around the house*, continue to present smells to your baby as discussed in Chapter 4. Describe to your baby the *baby smell* of squeaky clean hair ("delicious"), freshly diapered bottom ("sweet"), and newly laundered clothes ("yummy"). Identify the *animal smells* when a pet comes in from the rain or when pet food is opened.

Touching

Your baby can use his hands now with more agility. He holds objects with a mitten grasp and may even transfer an object from one hand to the other. Toys keep him mentally stimulated and teach him about his world.

Try to provide your baby with many different, nonirritating *items to grasp*—lids, cups, flexible toys, curlers, and the like. *Dangle* a textured ball or crib gym where your baby can kick it.

Seeing

Child developmentalist Dr. Jerome Bruner writes, "The more a baby sees, the more he wants to see." Offer your baby ample opportunities to view his environment.

Buy a *crib gym* or make your own by securely tying brightly colored plastic objects to a wide strap and draping it across the playpen or crib. *The strap must be fastened tightly at both ends.*

Hold your baby in front of a *mirror* so he can see his whole body—and you. Watch his attentive reaction. He may smile, wiggle and vocalize at his reflection but will probably be puzzled by your image and prefer to touch and look at you directly.

Hearing and Language

Your baby's vocal abilities are becoming more varied. She practices new sounds over and over and babbles with pleasure to amuse herself. She is learning to imitate oral sounds, such as coughing or clearing her throat. She can also make noise at will now, which becomes a terrific game! The following suggestions will help refine her hearing and language abilities.

Encourage friends, relatives and siblings to play and *chat with baby* on a one-to-one basis. They will most likely be rewarded with grins, giggles and other antics.

Crumple different types of paper, such as tissue, newspaper and cellophane, while you have your baby's attention. Give him *toys that make sounds*, such as a block with a bell in it or discs on a chain. Make *sounds to accompany* playtime activities, such as buzzes, bonks and thunks.

Encourage your baby to make *humming and mumbling noises* by repeating his. Make silly sounds and let him feel your cheeks, chin and lips. See if he will try to make the noises, and praise his attempts.

Body Positioning

According to sensorimotor specialist Dr. Daniel Arnheim, "The most important sense organs to the acquisiton of skilled movement are vision, touch, and the sense of movement." The following body-positioning experiences allow your baby to practice using the three senses to gain body control, self-awareness and balance.

A *net hammock* allows your baby to watch goings-on while he sways back and forth. (What a wonderful way to put him to sleep for an afternoon nap!)

Your baby will find making waves on a *waterbed* a curious experience. Roll her by pressing down on the bed next to her, or gently bounce her and roll her from side to side. A waterbed is also a nice place to lie down and snuggle your baby and to share a few quiet moments or a nap. The tightness of a *trampoline* gives your baby very different sensations than the waterbed does. You may also gently roll her over and over on it and tamely bounce her on tummy and back. (A regular bed may also be used.)

A *Flying Saucer* is a heavy shallow, plastic disc on wheels. Using a blanket inside will add to the sensations your baby gets as you pull him on his tummy or back. Later, baby will enjoy a ride while seated and, eventually, he will pull the saucer by himself.

Socializing

Dr. Benjamin Spock writes about companionship with your baby:

> Be quietly friendly with your baby whenever you are with him. He's getting a sense of how much you mean to each other all the time you're feeding him, bubbling him, bathing him, dressing him, changing his diapers, holding him or just sitting in the room with him. When you hug him or make noises at him, when you show him that you think he's the most wonderful baby in the world, it makes his spirit grow, just the way milk makes his bones grow.

Your baby also enjoys *stepping out* to the market or shopping center, or going for a bicycle ride to the park in your backpack. In public environments moms and dads share feelings and observe how other parents care for their children.

Chapter 6

LITTLE PAL
Five Months

HOW DO YOU DO?

At five months of age your baby shows the first signs of becoming a real little pal. She thrives on being part of the family and likes to go where the family goes. Brothers and sisters are great entertainers, and Dad's presence usually means playtime—although Mom is still the greatest. Baby's reaching out to other family members is an important step toward self-sufficiency.

Language is all-important. Your baby loves to listen, is fascinated by the faces and lips of people who talk to her and literally glows when people respond to her verbalizations.

Your little pal likes to be propped up now and surrounded by objects to touch. Eyes, fingers and mouth work well together, and reaching and grabbing help her develop depth perception. She is learning the characteristics of objects, such as size, shape and weight. Baby will handle and look at an object that fascinates her and repeat the motions of her hands over and over.

Your five-month-old will also cling when held, and if you bounce her on your knee, she will try to imitate your movement to prompt you to repeat it. She can propel herself by rocking, rolling and twisting, and after naptime she's ready to go! Diaper Play is a highlight of the day.

SUPPLIES

cushies.
feely bag—odds and ends of soft material scraps (softies) and other massaging objects, such as a baby's hairbrush, fuzzy yarn pom-poms or seashells; we also suggest that you add a small jar of baby oil and/or baby powder.
beach ball—fully flated.

big dish.

small bolster.

mirror—wall mirror large enough for baby to see entire body reflection.

barrel of fun—Remove the ends of a large packing barrel, place a roll of foam inside and add color and/or texture to the outside with nontoxic paint, kitchen carpet and/or contact paper.

GETTING READY

The activities for your five-month-old are terrific. Let's get started!

Cuddles 'n' Stuff. A pleasant addition to this massaging game is to sprinkle baby powder or baby oil in your palms. Your hands glide over your baby's body and make the skin tingle.

Sing a lullaby during the one to three minutes of massaging. Your baby knows something good is going to follow!

Rock 'n' Roll. That something good is playing Poppety-Pop on the fully inflated beach ball. Lay your baby on his back on the ball, and press on his thighs to hold him. Tip the ball slowly forward, and the movement will help your little pal sit up! This prepares him to sit and allows him to practice balancing.

This game is even more stimulating when you rock your baby on his back, forward, backward, sideways and round and round before doing Poppety-Pop.

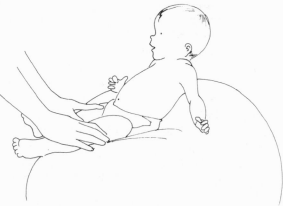

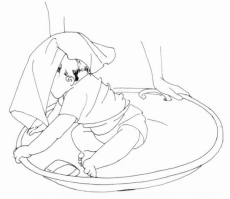

Big Dish. A lively variation is to place your baby in the big dish and cover him with a lightly woven cloth. Tip and spin him in the familiar directions, take off the cover and say, "Boo!" He will love the surprise. The action also reassures him that you can disappear and come back and alerts him to feeling without seeing the action. Play this two or three times.

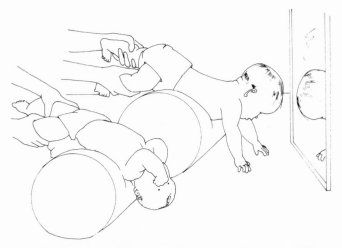

Small Bolster. A full-length mirror adds an exciting dimension to the bolster game as you rock your baby forward and backward on her tummy and back while *only* holding arms or legs. The invigorating motions make her smile while her eyes, inner ears and muscles work to balance.

Lean close to your baby and point to her facial features, exclaiming, "I see Tina's eyes. I see Tina's ears. Watch Tina smile." Touch the mirror "nose" and then your baby's nose. Help her do the same, and remark how beautiful she is. Rock on the bolster for one to three minutes, with short breaks for touching and pointing out facial features.

Barrel of fun. Playing Peek-a-boo with your pal in the barrel of fun makes him more than ready to "move out."

Place your baby head first into the barrel on his back or tummy and rock him gently from side to side. Bend down at first so baby can see your expressions of

approval and hear your encouraging voice before you begin to disappear and reappear, chanting, "Peek-a-boo, where are you? Peek-a-boo, I see you!"

MOVING OUT

Reflex Movements

UPSY DUBSY

Value: This movement shows off baby's talents while strengthening neck and back muscles and broadening space awareness.

Here's How: With baby lying on his back, grasp his upper legs with both hands and lift him slowly until his head is off the floor. Then set him down gently, touching his head first and rolling him down onto his back.

At five months your baby's back will be fairly straight. But at six and seven months, he will arch his back and lift his head to look around. One cheek will touch first when he is lowered; then gently roll him down onto his tummy. With lots of praise and applause, your baby will know he is doing something wonderful!

How Many: Two lifts; may be repeated daily.

PULLY WULLY

Value: If a poll were taken among the babies doing these exercises in our classes, Pully Wully would probably be rated number one. This movement employs that favorite upright feeling while strengthening neck, back and abdominal muscles.

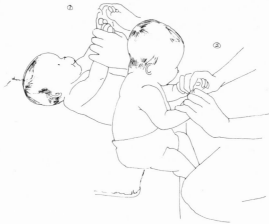

Here's How: Place baby on his back and kneel, facing him. As he grasps your thumbs, pull him slowly to a seated position. He will tuck his head forward and draw his legs toward his tummy as he sits up. Pause for a few seconds, then lay him down.

Remember that at this age your baby *should not sit for long periods of time*, because his back muscles and spine are not strong enough to support his weight. He may, however, push into a stand from the seated position. Allow him to do so, then offer support under his arms while he stands. He feels so accomplished that he may stamp his feet and bounce up and down!

How Many: Two sit-ups; may be repeated daily.

TUMMY BALANCE

Value: You may often enter the room to find your look-alike bobbing on her tummy with arms and legs outstretched. Tummy Balance encourages her to assume this posture, strengthening neck and back muscles while helping her adjust to being on her tummy.

Here's How: Place your baby on her tummy on the floor and shake a bright,

noisy toy in front of her, just out of reach. While she is reaching for the toy, she will lift her head and stretch out her arms and legs. Count to ten slowly, then give the toy to your pal to explore.

How Many: Two stretches, may be repeated daily.

Prompted Movements

TUMBLEWEED

Value: Tumbleweed prepares your partner to turn from back to tummy by stimulating muscle action in the trunk and hips.

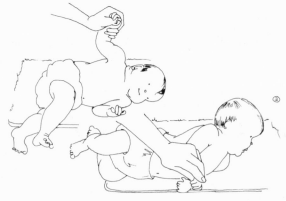

Here's How: Once you are kneeling on the floor, face to face with your baby, let him grasp one of your fingers and pull him gently over onto his opposite side. His trunk and hip will follow. Allow him enough time to roll back or all the way over onto his tummy by himself.

How Many: Two rolls on each side; may be repeated daily.

Time again for a seventh-inning stretch. Play soft music, lie on your tummy next to baby and discover how beautifully she is growing—and how your life is changing. Talk about anything that comes to mind. Feeling refreshed again, caress her, tell her how glad you are to have her and carry on.

THE BANANA

Value: We call this exercise The Banana, but parents in our classes often refer to it as the baby push-up. It strengthens neck and back muscles required for standing.

Here's How: Place your baby on her tummy and kneel at her feet. Allow her to extend her arms, then grasp her pelvis and lift her back and legs until they are shoulder level from the floor. Hold for a count of five and lower legs to the floor.

In the beginning, some babies balance on their elbows. Later in the fifth month they may extend their arms. (This is also a good time for you to do a few push-ups. See if you can increase *your* number this month!)

How Many: Two push-ups; may be repeated daily.

SWAN

Value: Most people think of the swan as a graceful bird with a wide wingspan. This movement stretches the chest and shoulder muscles and expands baby's lungs, much like the motion of a swan just before flight.

Here's How: Lie baby on his tummy and kneel at his feet. Take his hands, draw his arms out to his sides and lift the upper portion of his body back and off the floor. Your baby will lift his head. Hold this position for a count of three and lower him to the floor. Be cautious not to arch his back past his waist. Sing this rhyme to match the movements:

> *Little swan, little swan,*
> *Let me see you fly.*
> *Little swan, little swan,*
> *Lift your arms to the sky.*
> *Little swan, little swan,*
> *So high, so high.*

How Many: Two stretches, once a day.

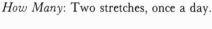

PUSH 'N' POINT

Value: Let's take time to stretch *all* the muscles in your baby's feet to prepare them to push, jump, tap and walk.

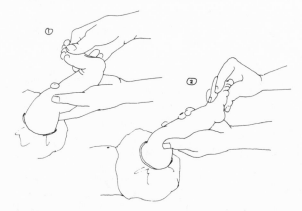

Here's How: Lay your baby on his back in your lap and place the left foot in your hand. With your other hand, gently press and push back against the sole of his foot with your thumb. Relax the foot, then wrap your fingers around the toes and arch and pull the foot to a point. Follow by turning the foot first to the outside, repeat Push 'n' Point actions, turn foot to the inside, repeat and set down. Ditto for the right foot.

If your baby flexes his foot, distract him with a tickle or a toy so he relaxes and you can complete the movement. A mother in one of our classes made up this jingle:

> *Push 'n' point, push 'n' point, turn it all around.*
> *Push 'n' point, push 'n' point, set it on the ground.*

How Many: One complete movement on each foot; may be repeated daily.

ALL AROUND

By now you are finding that your five-month-old enjoys exploring objects, and his developing abilities allow him to entertain himself. Try these new challenges in addition to sensorimotor experiences from previous months.

Smelling and Tasting

Smelling and tasting are brought together now because of your baby's more varied diet and her ability to bring everything within reach to her mouth.

Give your five-month-old *warm and cold foods* to taste and feel—cold yogurt, frosty whipped cream, icy juice cubes, warm applesauce, room temperature mashed bananas and lukewarm pudding. Let her experience foods from different taste groups—sweet, sour, bitter and salty—such as a drop of honey, a lick of dill pickle or lemon and a tiny dot of butter. Talk about the food—its color, smell, texture—and watch baby's expression change with each sample. We suggest *only* a taste; we do not recommend that your baby consume any food other than what your doctor recommends.

Talk to baby about *outdoor smells*, such as grass clippings, rain, flowers.

Touching and Manipulating

Touching is now a prelude to manipulating because of your baby's increased ability to handle objects. He has begun to initiate his own experiences, such as making a toy squeak. This is a milestone in your child's life, for the ability to initiate gives him things to think about.

Your explorer has a good time holding and putting a *spoon* into his mouth during feedings. Sets of different *textured objects*, such as four or five small, hard blocks or yarn balls, interest five-month-olds. Ask how they feel: soft? hard? fluffy?

Place your baby near the sides of his crib or playpen and let him push and *kick textured fabrics* that you have draped and anchored securely over the edge with large safety pins.

Sight and Language

Your baby can see clearly now, as demonstrated by direct hits when he reaches for toys. Muscle control has developed from his eyes to his head, arms and hands. Asking him about what he sees and does as he uses eyes and hands begins the language process of naming.

Place your baby on a patterned sheet and *point out and identify the animals*, clowns or fairy-tale characters. Point to objects on wallpaper and trace their shapes.

Baby will often play with feet and hands. Encourage him by playing rhymes on *fingers and toes*. "This Little Pig Went to Market" and "Ten Little Indians" are favorites.

Use sound words like "boom!" "bump!" and "pow!" when baby taps or pushes over a *tipping toy* that rights itself. Attach a *balloon* to your baby's wrist with a ribbon, then describe the balloon and its motion: "Look at Jenny shake the big, round, red balloon!"

Hearing and Language

Your five-month-old can grunt, squeal, purr and make "raspberries." Talk to him, offer a toy, pick him up and tell him how great it is to hear him talk to encourage him to make more sounds. Your feedback is as important to his speech progression as are the following activities.

Shake a rattle behind your baby and to his left and right to see if he turns to *locate the noise.* If he or she catches on, you might say, "Where's the rattle? Here it is!"

Sing and recite *nursery rhymes* to your playmate as you carry her and change diapers. Five months is a good time to refresh your memory of favorite childhood nursery rhymes by borrowing a library book or purchasing your own. The repetition of word patterns and sounds will interest and delight your baby and, if it is continued, will aid reading readiness. Also, while holding your baby, march and *chant the cadence* "hup, two, three, four!" Some friends and relatives may know other terrific marching and singing cadences to add to the fun.

Holding your five-month-old closely and swaying to different tempos while *humming the beat* will relax you both.

Imitating

Your baby's interest in faces and voices stimulates her to imitate your sounds, facial expressions and actions. Play games to encourage these attempts. *Shake your head* from side to side and see if your little pal will move *her* head from side to side. *Smile* and see if she will return your sunshine, or *place a mirror* in front of her while she plays. She will be fascinated by the "other" baby and may even reach out to touch it.

Body Positioning

Discovering movement in various positions will excite your baby enough so that he will attempt even more daring moves. This is a natural learning device to gain balance, body control and space awareness.

Jumping in a *Jolly Jumper* is a tantalizing activity for your baby. Beginning with one dainty push and progressing to both feet, he will soon be bouncing down and up, down and up. Three to five minutes—possibly longer—will be sufficient time for your five-month-old to enjoy the jumper. Increase play periods to ten or fifteen minutes at six and seven months of age and move to longer times as leg and back muscles strengthen. Secure the jumper outdoors, too, where your bouncer can watch his shadow and see others playing. A warning, though: once he is able to crawl and explore, the jumper will not be as interesting—too confining.

Wait till you tell your friends that your five-month-old *skateboards*! Place your baby on it on his tummy and guide him around the floor, allowing him to use hands and feet to push while you hold him around the middle. Skateboard wheels allow your baby to move quite easily, and older brothers and sisters like to help. Be sure, though, that the board is made of flexible plastic with no sharp edges or points.

Rolling is a fun way to stimulate your baby's awareness of her body in space. Gently roll her over and over on fabrics of different textures. Using a couch cushion as an incline will help your "roly poly" move with less assistance. Make up a rhyme to match your baby's speed.

Socializing

Bath time is fun time for a little water and many bobbing toys. He will splash! He'll like company, too, so go ahead and lay him safely on your lap, placing his head on your bent knees, and invite an older sibling to join in the fun. Once he learns to sit well, allow him more freedom in the tub but *never*, under *any* circumstance, leave him unattended in the water—even for a few seconds.

Swimming is good exercise, very pleasurable, a wonderful social happening and really mandatory for your baby if your home or apartment has a pool. Often babies begin to paddle before five months, but visit swim schools, read books and articles and discuss the subject with one or two doctors before beginning lessons.

Your baby loves *being near older children*. Their talk, laughter and activity amuse him for long periods.

Your baby is curious about the family *pets* and enjoys watching and touching them, under your supervision. If you present your animals to your baby in a gentle manner, you can help curb a pet's jealousy.

Rocking is worth mentioning again. Though not every baby takes to it, there is no nicer way for a child to feel your comforting warmth. This can be the perfect place to lean back and hum, close your eyes and daydream, sing your favorite songs or read to your child. Rocking can also comfort a sick or colicky baby, especially if you gently rub or pat his back. And it is a lovely way for relatives and friends to share their affection for your five-month-old.

Chapter 7

A PERSONAL STYLE
Six and Seven Months

HOW DO YOU DO?

Each baby chooses a personal style of locomotion in preparing to crawl. At six or seven months your baby may twist, flop, roll, creep, scoot on his back, crouch on his knees and lurch forward or bounce on his bottom—sometimes going forward, more often moving backward.

But go baby will—everywhere! Take notice of his wonderful new ability to move around and make sure that the surroundings are safe: plastic plugs should safeguard unused wall sockets, cords should be taped out of reach, toxic materials should be stored in high cupboards and valuables should be perched on mantels and high shelves. These precautions enable you to relax and enjoy your baby's progress.

Your baby is busy, busy, busy gaining new skills. He probably sits well at six months and at seven months can plop into a seated position easily. He can travel to objects, reach for them, transfer them from one hand to the other and enjoy exploring and manipulating them.

Your baby still loves to be held, rocked and talked to when he has his bottle, though he now likes to hold the bottle himself! Feeding time in the high chair, on the other hand, is crazy. Your monkey may blow bubbles, spray, smear and mangle his food while making noise and enjoying himself immensely. Teething biscuits, pieces of toast or bananas may keep him occupied while you spoon in the solids.

The clown comes out in baby at other times. He makes faces, plays with Dad's hair while riding on his shoulders, draws a diaper over his face and waits for you to find him and drops things over the side of his high chair or crib to lure brothers and sisters into play. You can almost see and hear his thinking wheels turn. Boy, is he ready for Diaper Play!

SUPPLIES

feely bag—rubber ball large enough for your baby to hold and too big to fit into his mouth

beach ball—fully inflated

mirror

small bolster

barrel of fun

big dipper—styrofoam swimming pool toy

dowel—18-inch piece of ⅜-inch or ½-inch diameter dowel

rings—two rubber swimming-pool-toy rings, 6 inches in diameter

GETTING READY

Cuddles 'n' Stuff. As soon as your baby gains mobility and can sit up, it is sometimes difficult to get him to lie down, even for the pleasurable experience of massaging. We suggest that you now play this game for one to three minutes while your baby sits up and listens to quiet background music.

Give softies to your baby and see if he will rub them on face, arms and legs. Use expressions such as, "aah," "ooh" or "mmm" as *you* feel the materials. Then listen to see if he does the same.

Sit behind your growing baby and massage his back, neck and ears while talking lovingly. You may also softly run your finger or the rubber ball around his back in different patterns. He will often sit very still following this sensation. Then make patterns on his chest with a thimble or cotton ball, naming body parts and facial features.

Rock 'n' Roll. While your rock 'n' roller lies on her back, grasp her feet. As she rolls backward toward the mirror, ask, "Who's that? That's Molly. Look at Molly upside down!" Think of other playful questions to ask your baby as she

watches herself roll forward, backward, sideways and round and round for one to three minutes, both on her tummy and seated.

In the seated position rock your child, very slowly at first, holding her thighs. You will notice her abdominal muscles working to keep her upright and you will be amazed at her strength, body control and balancing ability. Music to fit the occasion might be "Top of the World."

Small Bolster. By now your baby is a pro at lying on the bolster on his tummy and pushing off with his toes. With your help, he may now push over far enough to touch the floor with his hands, grab a toy, then rock back until his feet touch the ground again. To accompany his squeal of excitement or look of quiet contentment, sing this jingle:

> *Touch your hands, touch your toes,*
> *This is the way the game goes.*
> *Rocking, rocking, back and forth,*
> *See how nicely baby grows.*

What a nice relationship you and your baby are developing . . . cooperating, sharing, relaxing. How quickly one to three minutes go by!

Barrel of Fun. This body and spatial-awareness game may surprise and even baffle your baby at first. Roll him from left to right, right to left and then from left to right again for one to two minutes, being cautious not to startle him by moving the barrel too fast. Soon he will anticipate, and even help, roll over and over in the barrel while you slowly turn it. You may wish to kneel on the floor so that your baby can easily see and hear you as you sing, "Roly poly, roly poly, over and over goes my baby."

Big Dipper. "Pop! Goes The Weasel!" is a perfect song to sing while spinning and tipping your baby in the big dipper. Motions are much more exaggerated now than in the big dish, and more exhilarating to your baby. Cover baby's face

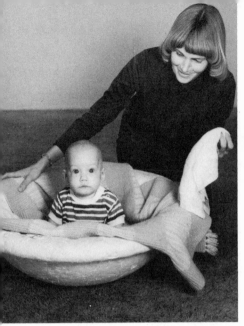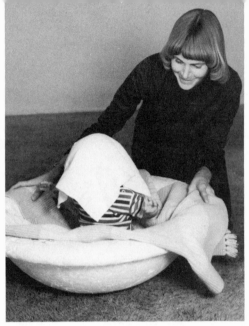

with a diaper and, while she is seated, spin her from left to right, right to left and left to right again. When you come to "pop" in the tune, uncover her. Sing the rest of the song, tipping her from side to side and back and forth and giving her a quick kiss when the song says to. After a fast, final spin your baby's face will sparkle with animation at her staying seated for so long.

All around the cobbler's bench,
The monkey chased the weasel.
The monkey though 'twas all in fun,
Pop! Goes the weasel!
I've no time to wait or sigh,
No patience to wait till by and by,
Kiss me quick, I'm off, good-bye,
Pop! Goes the weasel.

MOVING OUT

Reflex Movements

STAR THRUST

Value: Every infant has an inborn energy force that drives him to move forward, and this movement stimulates and develops the chest, arm, leg and back muscles that will propel him forward when he crawls.

Here's How: Stand next to baby while he lies on the bed on his tummy. Grasp him around his middle and lift him several inches off the bed. Baby will draw himself into a crawl position and kick and stretch as if crawling. A bright, wiggly toy just out of reach and some cheerful encouragement from you will stimulate even more movement. Count slowly to ten and set him down where he can explore the toy.

How Many: Two movements; may be repeated daily.

Prompted Movements

LADYBUG

Value: After touchdown your star chaser may enjoy being a little earth creature who walks on his hands. This is a wonderful movement for family participation. Someone can hold baby, one can rattle a toy and another can clap with excitement when baby finishes.

Here's How: Place baby on his tummy and kneel behind him. Place a rattle or toy just out of his reach. Lift his legs together, level with his extended arms. He may begin to walk on his hands right after the toy or he may need more assistance from you. If so, roll one side of his body forward till he moves his hand, then roll the other side.

This splendid accomplishment is just the beginning. With your assistance, your baby will soon be walking on his hands straight up and down. And most likely someday he will take first place with a friend in wheelbarrow races at the park!

How Many: As long as baby will walk on his hands; twice daily.

STICK STRETCH

Value: For the first time your baby is going to hold something other than your fingers to complete a movement, one that strengthens his grasp and stretches arm, shoulder and chest muscles, which are useful for reaching, holding and manipulating objects.

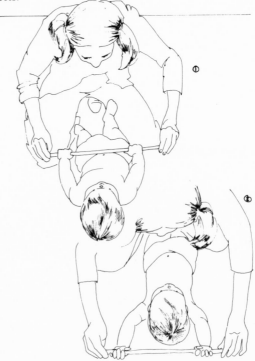

Here's How: Place baby on his back and kneel at his feet. With his hands shoulder-width apart, help him grasp a dowel. Bring the dowel to his hips, then stretch it over his head and from side to side. He may also like to sit up and stretch to the rhythmical beat of "Yankee Doodle."

> *Yankee Doodle came to town,*
> *A-riding on a pony,*
> *He stuck a feather in his cap,*
> *And called it macaroni.*
> *Yankee doodle, doodle doo,*
> *Oh Yankee doodle dandy,*
> *All the lads and lassies are*
> *As sweet as sugar candy.*

How Many: Eight stretches or for duration of song; may be repeated daily.

Assistive Movements

LEGS

Value: Exploring an attractive toy will keep your baby quietly amused while she strengthens the upper leg and abdominal muscles necessary for correct sitting, walking and future zooming on a water slide or bobsled.

Here's How: Sit on the edge of a chair. Place your baby faceup on your lap, extending her legs over the edge of your lap. Hold her legs up from underneath

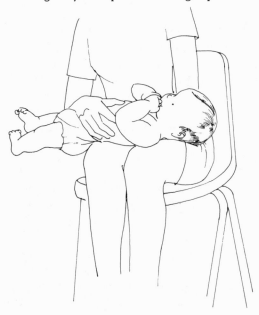

while pressing gently on her chest. Gradually release her legs; she will hold them out straight. Keep one of your legs slightly raised under baby's bottom so she is slightly tilted and there is no strain on her back. For the same reason do not let her legs droop over the edge of your lap.

How Many: Once daily until your baby is able to hold her legs out straight for ten seconds; then it may be repeated twice daily. Baby deserves many jubilant squeezes for this triumph.

RING-A-DING

Value: This movement is a close second to Pully Wully in popularity, for your baby is now very interested in standing. He may wiggle with joy and smile broadly if you rub the neck, abdominal, leg and hand muscles that are working so nicely together.

Here's How: Place your baby on his back and kneel at his feet. Offer him a rubber ring in each hand, then let him pull with his arms and push with his feet to stand for a count of five or less. Lower him to the floor. (Hold both rings in one hand so you may place your other hand behind your baby's back in case he lets go of the rings.)

How Many: Two stands; may be repeated daily.

ROCKING HORSE

Value: You may be one of many parents grunting "Oof!" during this movement while your baby grins from ear to ear. The closeness of rocking together rhythmically is delicious, especially while singing "Ride a Cock Horse."

Here's How: Sit on the floor and bend your knees. Place baby on your lap, looking into your face. Hold her underneath the arms, then rock back and forth with your knees bent, just as if you were doing a sit-up. After a while your baby will hold just your finger and vigorously help push and pull while maintaining her balance—which will be greatly appreciated by tired you!

Ride a cock horse to Banbury Cross,
To see a fine lady upon a white horse,
Rings on her fingers and bells on her toes,
She shall have music wherever she goes.

How Many: Rock for the length of the song, until baby seems to lose interest or *you* run out of steam! May be repeated daily.

SWISH

Value: No movement delights your baby or dazzles an onlooker more than this body and spatial awareness one. Your baby senses your confidence in handling her and will respond to the sensation of turning quickly upside down with more movement and, possibly, laughter.

Here's How: Stand beside your bed and place your baby on her back on the bed, her head near you. Grasp her around the waist and upper back with your

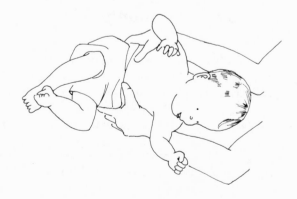

fingers spread. Lift her up, turn her onto her left side, make a circle in the air to the right, and finish in starting position. Reverse the movement and lay your swisher down on the bed again with lots of pats, smiles and tender words.

How Many: Two lifts; may be repeated daily.

ALL AROUND

In his book *The First Twelve Months of Life*, Frank Caplan writes, "The infant's relentless practice of his sensory, physical, and mental abilities, in fact, testifies that the need to learn is at least as important as pleasure-seeking in determining behavior during the first two years of life." The following sensori-motor experiences, when playfully shared, offer your little sponge the best of both worlds.

Smelling and Tasting

Mealtimes are seeing, hearing, touching, manipulating, socializing, smelling and tasting extravaganzas! Your child may play Mr. or Ms. Choosy, but wants to participate more and more in the feeding process. Keep calm and maintain a sense of humor about the antics. Try these suggestions to keep the atmosphere pleasant for sharing, learning and eating.

Your baby may have great interest in using a *cup with a handle*. Have an older sibling offer him a little juice in a plastic one, first turning the handle to one side, then offering it again with the handle turned the other way. See if he uses both hands to pick it up, if he turns it around or if he lifts it by the handle.

If you wish to relax and enjoy a long meal, place the *mirror* in front of your baby while he eats. He will watch that "other baby" eat every morsel of food.

Seeing, Touching, Manipulating

According to Dr. Greg Gilman, optometrist and visual-training specialist, activities that combine the use of hands and eyes are the best learning experiences for visual development. These seeing, touching and manipulating experiences link baby's senses and skills to develop information-processing abilities.

Offer your baby a two-foot piece of *flexible hose* to bend and examine. He will learn that he can change its shape. Challenge him in a playful game of tug-of-war.

Furnish your protégé with objects of many *different qualities* to scrutinize— wooden shapes, a paper drinking straw, sandpaper. Give your baby a toy and watch to see if he exchanges it from *one hand to the other*. Offer a wooden spoon or other *long object* for your investigator to reach for and grasp from different angles and distances. This gives him practice in perceiving and managing a curious item.

Floating toys and *moving objects* in the bathtub are fun challenges for baby. Encourage him to trap them. Move your little one past a *stationary object* and let him reach for it. After two or three passes let him grab it. Cuddle him and tell him that he has a terrific reach.

Baby will enjoy playing with his hands, feet and a big *fuzzy ball* suspended over his playpen or crib. He may grasp it with both hands, both feet or all four together, demonstrating how his muscle control has now extended from his head to all extremities. A multipurpose *activator* may be purchased to hang over his crib. These stimulate your baby's senses and help him learn cause and effect, such as pulling a cord to ring a bell.

Hearing, Seeing and Language

Your baby's sense of hearing can alert him to danger and is a valuable means of communication. Hearing is also closely linked with vision and listening ability in developing attention. Assist your baby in locating sounds and in increasing her attention span.

Give your baby a *bell* to shake and explore while you say to her, "ring, ding-a-ling, ding-dong."

Your little seeker will delight in playing *Hide and Seek with Noises*. From various places in a room, shake a rattle or squeaky toy. Call to him and watch him turn, locate the sound, crawl and find it. Give him a big hug-a-bug and tell him what good listening ears he has. You can share some quiet times, too, with simple *picture books*. Make appropriate sounds for each picture—"meow" for a kitty, "moo" for a cow.

Hold your baby close, put on a record and move to *match the music*: happily, peppily, smoothly, jerkily or slowly. Your talented singer-dancer may even make his own sounds and movements.

Bring *environmental sounds* to your baby's attention—running water, chirping birds, barking dogs. Turn a light switch on and off and say, "Where's the light?" See if baby will make the connection and look at the light. Likewise, show him a clock and say, "Tick, tock."

During *conversations* look into your baby's eyes, laugh and touch her as you repeat her consonant, vowel and babbling sounds. Talk to her when she calls or mumbles just as though a real conversation with words were taking place.

Allow your goer to explore objects that make noise when they are manipulated, such as waxed paper, a lidded plastic bowl with a spoon inside or a ball with a bell inside. Many interesting, safe *noise-making* toys are also available for different age levels.

Imitating

Show your baby how to *clap his hands* or how to bang a plastic toy on the floor.

Wave bye-bye to someone, and see if your baby will wave, too. He may only open and close his fingers a little, but the attempt will thrill the whole audience.

Cover your face with your hands and pull them away, saying, *"Peek-a-boo!"* Help your baby cover his eyes with his hands and see if he tries it by himself. A willingness to try demonstrates a growing sense of security.

Pucker your lips in a kiss on your baby's cheek and encourage him to try it by bringing his head close to your cheek. Most often he will open his mouth on your cheek, and you can hug and thank him for the nice, wet kiss.

Body Positioning

In a more advanced version of *Huddles*, your baby will find rolling together on soft textured surfaces truly terrific! Lie on your back and place him on your chest. Put one hand on his bottom and your other hand behind his head and roll over and over together. He will *not* be smothered; your elbows take the weight as you roll onto your tummy.

You may have a good time making a *Fuzzy Wuzzy texture board*. So that baby can creep and crawl, it needs to be twelve to eighteen inches wide and at least three to four feet long. Thick cardboard, pegboard or plywood are ideal backings to which you can glue many materials for your explorer to feel as he moves along it. Most flooring-supply stores are happy to give away old samples. Use rubber cement to attach them and change the samples every so often, making your board useful for months to come (see Appendix).

Jumping not only strengthens your baby's leg muscles but gives him a pleasurable, rhythmic sensation. While standing beside a bed or sitting in a chair, pick up your pal under his arms and let him down into a bent-knee position, with toes touching a surface or your lap, then lift him again. After a few tries, baby will begin to push himself up. Do this fast or slow to your favorite rhyme.

For happy togetherness, play *obstacle games*. Your baby will enjoy crawling over you, and you can relax and give a helpful nudge if she needs it. Lie on the floor and place your baby on one side of you. Jangle a toy on the other side. At first she will probably lie across your legs, push off with her feet and tumble onto her hands and arms. Soon, however, she will be crawling over you like a champ.

Expand your *leg ladder* by including Dad or an older sibling in the fun. Sit side by side on the floor and part legs to form spaces, like ladder rungs. Your hurdler will scramble over each obstacle to reach a toy, especially if encouraged by applause and cheers.

Once you play *Red Rover* with your little pal, she is apt to sit on your foot or leg and bounce up and down whenever you are seated! Sit on the edge of a couch or chair and cross your legs. Place baby on your foot or crossed leg. While supporting her by her hands or lower arms, bounce her up and down with your leg, then swing her over while uncrossing your leg. Sing, "Red Rover, Red Rover, Angie cross over!" (This is a special grandpa delight!)

Socializing

We are always tickled when we wish the parents and babies in our classes a half-year birthday. The six-month mark always seems to come as a happy shock. Some say that they did not know time could pass so quickly: others cannot even remember what life was like B. B. (Before Baby).

At this point we want to extend our congratulations to *you* and *your* baby, for you, too, are through one-half of the first all-important year . . . a year in which he grows and develops faster than at any other time. Admit it, aren't you proud?

When your family has a *barbeque* or picnic, your little companion delights in being part of the gathering by being nearby in a playpen or on a blanket or by happily being passed around, talked to and played with.

An *evening stroll* to view the lights and feel the cool air will interest your baby. If you live in a neighborhood with *front lawns and sidewalks*, visit with other adults and children. Your goer will have a marvelous time exploring grass, sidewalks and the like.

While you are *window-shopping*, your alert observer likes to be carried on his tummy across your bent arms and hands or tucked under one arm. Allow him to reach out and touch large objects—furniture, leaves, tree trunks, windowpanes and doors.

First-time parents are generally reluctant to leave their baby with anyone but a good friend or relative, but there are dependable *baby-sitters* for a six- or seven-month-old. Look for someone who enjoys talking to and playing with children, and offer proper instructions and backup support. Your little one will form a real attachment and grin happily whenever the sitter arrives.

Now is not too early for you and a few other parents with babies about the same age to form a *play group*. Meet once a week and let the babies explore while the parents share ideas, laughter and viewpoints about community and world events. If you are isolated or new in your area, an advertisement in the local paper usually brings a good response. Play groups offer adults opportunities to express feelings and exchange recipes, medical updates, books, toys, records and equipment. Your baby has wonderful exposure to other little ones, and you'll be amused at the variety of looks and touches. And if you are excited about the activities in this book, you can share and enjoy the program together!

Chapter 8

THE EXPLORER
Eight Months

HOW DO YOU DO?

What a dramatic and exciting month this is as your baby starts to crawl forward and pull up to stand. His curiosity is strong; you find your bright-eyed explorer peeking from under tables and chairs, behind doors and drapes and inside closets and cupboards.

As a parent, brace yourself: this month is a dramatic change for you, because your baby's intense quest for adventure is equaled by his ability to follow you. Before you know it, he is maneuvering himself with tremendous speed from one end of the house to the other. Allow your baby the freedom to investigate his surroundings. Clear the room where baby spends his wakeful time of all unsafe items, and replace them with things he *can* reach for and play with, such as books and colorful blocks. Preventative care will provide a more relaxing and less exhausting atmosphere, particularly if you have twins. An expandable fence which gives your baby plenty of space can also be effectively used, especially outdoors.

One noticeable characteristic of your busy eight-month-old may be a keen interest in tiny particles such as crumbs. He may stare intensely at them and, as he discovers his "pincer" grasp (thumb and forefinger working together), he may pick them up and bring them to his mouth. A small wad of paper may fascinate him and, if you're not observant, he may eat it—along with a little bug or two!

Your baby is also experimenting with the basics of quantity, for he can place one object after another into a container. He experiments with objects by turning them with his hands in all directions, banging them and bringing them to his mouth. He also likes to look at things from different angles. You may find him shaking his head, pivoting and laughing at his own silliness.

Your baby often babbles a variety of happy sounds and mimics your mouth and jaw movements. He may make vowel and consonant sounds—"ma," "mu," "da," "e" and "be." He turns his head and torso toward familiar sounds and is beginning to recognize some words. Continue eye-to-eye contact with your sunny one as you talk and respond to his sounds. As time goes by, he will show greater interest in words and phrases.

If you have occasion to watch other eight-month-olds, notice the differences now in the speed and manner in which they learn new skills. Each baby has a unique approach to learning. Some are quiet by nature and spend time observing and manipulating objects; others are gregarious, moving constantly and poking noses and fingers into every nook and cranny. Parents with quiet babies are often concerned that their little ones are not learning fast enough, and parents of very active babies think that their children are hyperactive. Both reactions are normal. We advise selecting a variety of activities to suit your baby's personality and interests, and gently encouraging either the active developmental movements or the quieter activities, depending on your baby's tempo. Either way, get ready to have a wonderful time playing with your alert, energetic and beautiful explorer.

SUPPLIES

beach ball—fully inflated.
parachute—large sheet, light blanket or parachute.
small bolster.
barrel of fun.
big dipper.
Teeter-Totter—may be purchased; made of durable, molded plastic.
dowel.
big ladder—6-foot orchard ladder, 12 inches wide, with rungs 12 inches apart.
ramp—ironing board in collapsed position, slanted against couch front, cushions removed.
silly pool—wading pool, large enough for several babies to sit in and play comfortably. Use tortilla flour, dry noodles of assorted shapes, dry oatmeal, water and bubbles.

GETTING READY

Even though baby is crawling, he needs you to be close and to reassure him that you still enjoy playing.

Cuddles and Chitchat. It is hard to catch your baby-on-the-go, let alone get her to hold still for some Cuddles. However, she will love chitchat games in which

you touch her while acting out a rhyme, such as "Creepy, Crawly Little Mouse."

Walk your fingers up baby's legs and arms and around her tummy, then tickle her under the chin, saying:

> *Creepy, crawly goes the little mouse,*
> *From the barn to the house,*
> *Into the pantry finds the shelf,*
> *Sees some cheese and helps himself.*

With this next rhyme vary the pressure of your fingers to create interesting sensations on different body parts. What better way to develop the sense of touch and to encourage listening skills?

> *Round and round the haystack,*
> *Goes the little mouse,*
> *One step, two steps.*
> *In his little house.*

Rock 'n' Roll. Your goer is now ready for a more challenging game on the big ball to develop balance and space awareness. Place him on his back and grasp his

right arm and right leg. Slowly rock him forward and backward almost to the floor, then spin him around quickly. Now smother him with kisses! Do four times on his back, then four times on his tummy, holding his left arm and left leg. Add your own favorite rhyme.

Bubbles. A large sheet, light blanket or parachute is a wonderful medium to capture your baby's attention. Your responsive one likes to crawl on it, be wrapped in it, be stroked with it and feel its fluffiness as you shake it and make it gently billow on the floor. Use one to three minutes a day while listening to pleasant, airy music.

Small Bolster. Continue to play background music while sitting your baby astride the small bolster while you hold his thighs from behind. Move him and the bolster to the right so that he touches the floor with his foot, then pushes off to the other side. Do four times on each side. Then place a wiggly toy to one side

and have him reach for it from astride the bolster. Repeat on the other side. Give him the toy and tell him what good reaching arms and fingers he has.

Barrel of Fun. Baby may now be trying to crawl through the barrel on his own power. Often he'll stop in the middle and giggle as if to say, "Okay, I'm ready, rock me!" Begin rocking from side to side, then roll him over and over slowly. A couple of trips through will be sufficient. When you stop, be ready to greet him with much praise if he crawls through the barrel. Also, update the textures inside the barrel from foam to interesting carpet remnants.

Big Dipper. Turn the big bowl over now and use it as a mountain for your youngster to climb. She may put a collection of objects inside and take them out with great pleasure. She may even like you to place it over her head and lift it off while she sits on the floor. While you sing "Little Boy Blue," let her play fast spinning and tipping games for a total of three to four minutes or until she loses interest.

Two to Tee. The Teeter-Totter is a very popular toy, offering social interaction between young babies. It is especially wonderful to own if you have twins, but can be used with one baby, too: simply put a doll on the other seat! Your

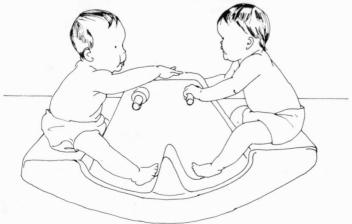

eight-month-old will love the up-and-down sensation as he develops spatial awareness and body control. Sing "Rock-a-bye Baby" and rock until the rhyme is over.

> *Rock-a-bye baby on the treetop,*
> *When the wind blows the cradle will rock,*
> *When the bough breaks the cradle will fall,*
> *Down will come baby, cradle and all.*

MOVING OUT

If your baby is to learn the basic rules of his physical world, his environment must be an active one. Some psychologists say that to miss any one stage of physical development may lead to later deficiencies in spatial perception, left-right relationships and even word and picture correlation. Pay special care to the crawling, standing and walking stages of maturation. These exercises provide playful opportunities to develop these three key areas.

Reflex Movements

MOUNTAIN CLIMBING

Value: Your little adventurer feels a thrill of achievement as she climbs up to your shoulders.

Here's How: Kneel on the floor, holding baby's hands and standing her in front of you. As you raise her arms, she will walk up the front of your body until she reaches your shoulders. Lower her with lots of pats and praise for being such a good mountain climber.

Another beginning position is to lay your baby on a bed while you stand on the floor in front of her. Her feet will press against your thighs. Grasp her hands, and as you lift her to a standing position, she will start to climb.

How Many: One movement; may be repeated daily.

Prompted Movements

TICKLES

Value: You bend over and smile directly into your baby's face during this delightful movement, which strengthens leg muscles and develops flexibility in back and hip joints.

Here's How: Place baby on his back while you kneel at his feet. Gently hold his left leg down while lifting his right leg up and across his body to tickle his left ear. Say, "Tickle, tickle!" and he will smile and laugh at the sensation. Return to starting position. One leg may be more flexible than the other, but eventually he will be able to reach his ears with both.

How Many: Two tickles with each leg, alternating; may be repeated daily.

STAND UP

Value: This movement, done to the old football cheer, "Lean to the left, Lean to the right, Stand up, sit down, Fight, Fight, Fight!" strengthens your baby's leg and arm muscles and helps him stand—and sit!

Here's How: Seat baby on your lap and grasp his lower arms with his fingers around your thumbs. Lean him slightly to the left, slightly to the right, and as you pull him toward you, he will push his legs against your stomach and stand up. Gently pull his arms forward and down, and he will sit down while you clap his hands together three times. He will love it!

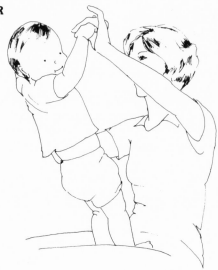

A variation of this movement is to use a box or stool about six inches high and seat your baby on it. Repeat the movements as above.

How Many: Two complete movements; may be repeated daily.

Partner Movements

TUMMY SURFING

Value: This terrific movement, practiced by parents for generations, strengthens lower-back muscles and develops baby's awareness of moving in space. (The movement is also good for *your* legs and thighs!)

Here's How: Sit on the floor with your knees bent and stand your baby, facing you, in front of your legs. Holding her hands, slowly lean back until your back is on the floor and baby is lying on your lower legs. Raise and lower your legs by bending your knees as you stretch your baby's arms to the sides.

How Many: Eight extensions up and down may be repeated daily.

Assistive Movements

PULLING UP

Value: This movement gives your baby the opportunity to pull himself to a standing position and to develop arm and leg strength and balance.

Here's How: Place your baby on the floor a few feet away from a chair. Hold an enticing toy atop the chair and watch him crawl to it and pull himself up. Allow him to play with his reward and praise him for his fine effort.

How Many: Two pull-ups; may be happily repeated many times a day if you place bright objects on chairs and couch cushions where he plays.

TABLE HANDWALK

Value: Your baby has already enjoyed walking on her hands on the floor. Now we would like her to walk on a higher surface. With your help, we want her to do a handwalk along a table top.

Here's How: This movement takes teamwork: one player jingles a colorful toy to encourage your star and one holds the handwalker. Both should cheer, too!

Clear the area around a dining or coffee table. Hold your baby in the air and lower her onto the table hands first. As her hands touch, lower her lower body

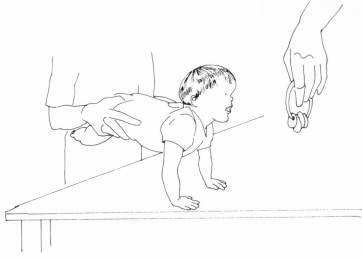

and legs parallel to the tabletop. Have the teammate call to baby and jangle the toy, and off you go around the outside of the table!

How Many: One circle around the edge of the table; may be repeated daily.

Active Movements

A PERSONAL STYLE

Value: This movement lets your baby show off her clever, adorable style of crawling while she explores the big ladder. Body control, balance, eye-hand coordination and spatial perception will make her more self-reliant.

Here's How: Place the big ladder flat on the floor. Kneel beside your baby at one end of the ladder. Place a squeaky toy one rung ahead of her and encourage her to crawl along the ladder, managing the rungs "in a personal style." For variety place different textures under the ladder—a foam pad, terry-cloth towel, silky material or a fuzzy-wuzzy board.

How Many: Move the length of the ladder; may be repeated daily.

CHOO-CHOO CLIMB

Value: Your growing baby's abilities are leading to new adventures. She is ready to try the challenge of crawling up and down a ramp. Watching her meet this challenge may remind you of the saying from *The Little Engine That Could*: "I think I can, I think I can!" Making train sounds may excite your little engineer, and a bright toy helps persuade her that the trip is worthwhile.

Here's How: Prop an ironing board against cushions from a couch to form an incline. Place your baby at the bottom of the ramp and kneel beside her. Encourage her to climb up, then turn her around to come down. Covering the ramp with different textures, such as throw rugs or fuzzy blankets, makes a trip more interesting and lends traction.

How Many: One round trip up and down; may be repeated daily.

EXPLORING

Silly Pool

This is about to become a highlight of your baby's exploratory moments. A wading pool is perfect for this activity because it is large enough to keep everything—including your baby—inside, and still allow room for movement.

Mediums for this age may include *tortilla flour*, *dry noodles* of assorted shapes,

dry oatmeal and *water and soap bubbles.* Tortilla flour is especially nice because it feels cool and compresses when squeezed. Just empty a package or two of the media into the pool and let baby start to play. An assortment of bowls, spoons, scoops, funnels and containers adds to the fun.

Relax, sit back and enjoy watching your baby pat, poke, smear, push, drop and, of course, taste. Other children may join to make the experience even sillier. Their responses to the media make the activity that much more educational for *your* baby. Encourage the merrymaking with your laughter and cheers.

ALL AROUND

Thus far you have surrounded your baby with a marvelous sensory environment. The more she explores with her eyes, ears, voice and body, the more sensations she will *want* to experience. Your baby is sensitive to all stimuli, and a rich sensory environment will benefit her total development.

The following experiences will challenge your constant learner to further develop her potential.

Smelling and Tasting

Offer your baby a variety of *food tastes*: small pieces of chicken, raisins, cubes of soft bread, broken crackers, peas, corn and cut-up green beans and fruits. Talk about how they taste, smell and feel. Give her *fruit juices*, such as apricot nectar, grape and peach. Offer her a contrast of sour and sweet and let her drink a small amount from a cup.

Under your supervision, allow your baby to hold and smell different flowers, like gardenias or roses. Let him smell citrus scents—lemons, limes and grapefruit; many aftershave lotions and colognes have citrus smells. Expose him to scented soaps, sachets and facial tissues. Bring him into the kitchen so he can smell the breakfast bacon, toast and coffee.

Seeing, Touching and Manipulating

During the eighth month offer your baby objects with different sizes, shapes and textures. He is learning to judge objects by their sizes; he is developing eye-hand coordination.

Give your baby a variety of *textured balls* that can be grasped only by using both hands—plastic, rubber, sponge, football, baseball, basketball and clear plastic. He can push and crawl after them. Place an upside-down cup in front of baby and see if he will *turn the cup over.* If not, demonstrate.

Develop his *pincer grasp* by offering him small pieces of food to pick up with his thumb and forefinger. This skill is important for good handwriting. Eight-month-olds work diligently to *take off socks* or booties. Praise his efforts, even if it means a little more work for you.

Let your curious one pull a *toy on a string*. If he does not use the string to pull the toy, show him how; this is an important lesson in cause and effect.

Old magazines or catalogs of her own will occupy your baby for long periods. She can have a wonderful time crumpling paper while developing finger dexterity and eye-hand coordination. Let her look at and tear pages, but be watchful that she does not eat the paper. A book made of stiff cardboard pages with different *noisemakers* interests your baby, too.

Take your baby outdoors and let him feel surfaces: bricks, sidewalks, rocks, grass, flowers, leaves, and so on. Allow him to crawl on different textured surfaces such as sand, dirt, grass, cement, linoleum and gravel. Tell him what they are and how they feel: "rough," "gritty," "smooth," "bumpy," "grainy."

Up till now we have been using the *feely bag* primarily as a softies holder for massaging purposes. Now we suggest that you use it to collect materials for your baby to feel—aluminum foil, sponge, wax paper, sandpaper, plastic scouring pad, felt scraps and the like. Talk about the feel of something scratchy or soft, rough or smooth.

Hearing, Seeing and Language

Research indicates that a child who misses early hearing and sound experiences will have later difficulties with language and abstract reading skills. These experiences encourage baby's hearing and language development.

Let your baby play with *blocks that have bells* in them. Your little one may be able to *label some objects by their sounds*, such as a train that "choo-choos." Play this game for a toaster ("pop-pop"), a timer ("bzzz-bzzz"). Identify familiar sounds such as a ringing doorbell or the neighbor's barking dog.

Use everyday situations such as feeding, bathing and dressing to enjoy *small talk* with your baby, increasing his passive vocabulary. During developmental movements increase his understanding of words and actions by repeating terminology, such as "Please sit up," "Please stand up," "Please lie down." After a while your baby will do the movements at your verbal request.

Encourage family members to play *seeing games*, like Peek-a-boo and Hide 'n' Seek, with your bundle of energy. These are his first games of visualization and develop his visual memory.

At this age your baby can probably only do one of the five activities on the *Surprise Box* toy: pushing the lever up or down. He will be enchanted with it, though, and will soon complete all five.

Imitating

Place a toy in front of your baby and let him see it. Then cover it with a diaper and see if he pulls the diaper aside to find the toy. If not, playfully show him, then repeat *covering the toy*. He will be so pleased with himself when he discovers the toy.

Whistle and see if your baby will pucker her lips to imitate you. Give her a *cup and spoon* and show her how to stir in the cup.

Body Positioning

Stand your baby in front of a couch while you hold a balloon on a string in front of her feet. Show her how to kick it (if she doesn't do it accidentally!). Eventually she will kick it deliberately.

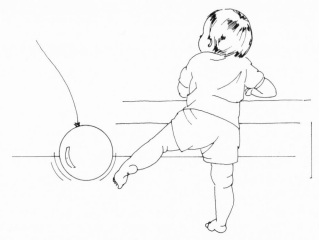

Turn on some lively music and hold your baby tightly while you *sway and bop* to a beat. You may also hold him away from you and sway him.

Your pal would now enjoy a car seat propped high enough so that she can watch the passing scenery. As you drive, talk to her about her world or recite nursery rhymes.

Socializing

A happy atmosphere strengthens your baby's emotional ties with you and other people close to him. With this in mind, your baby is bound to enjoy *traveling*. He best enjoys outings where he can actively explore while having contact with adults and other children—the beach, parks, zoos.

The *expandable play yard* is a great piece of baby furniture to have when you are camping or picnicking. This allows your baby freedom to move and, often, older children will join the play, providing great company for your eight-month-old. Family members can gain affection from the littlest member of the family by playing simple *social games* with him: Pattycake, Come Find Me, Who's Behind the Paper, Sing with Me and Let's Make Raspberries.

Chapter 9

THE MISCHIEVOUS ONE
Nine and Ten
Months

HOW DO YOU DO?

If the house or apartment is quiet and your nine- or ten-month-old isn't in sight, she is probably into exploratory mischief: pushing the telephone buttons, splashing in the toilet bowl, unrolling toilet tissue, dumping a planter, pulling on drapes, unshelving books or turning TV or stereo knobs. When you begin to look and call for her, she scoots away from the scene of the crime or sheepishly shakes her head and says, "No!"

Do these episodes sound familiar? Your baby is mischievous, alert—and adorable. She is also busy improving crawling, climbing and standing skills, and large motor development is advancing aggressively. She sits easily, may crawl up stairs or climb on chairs and may be working very hard at taking that first big step. This progression usually takes several months, and your baby moves at her own pace, but it may happen something like this:

First she may pull herself up by holding onto furniture and then sidestep along the furniture. Later she may anchor with only one hand, using her free hand to maneuver toys and maintain balance. Finally she may stand alone. The first daring step is usually from one piece of furniture to another or, happily, to you.

Recognizing dimensions becomes a new challenge for your nine- or ten-month-old. She reaches for small objects with her thumb and fingers and large objects with both hands. She can now reach behind her for a toy without looking, and she may point, poke and touch with an extended index finger. As she learns to walk, she may also carry a small object in each hand and bang both together at the center of her body.

Your capable baby may also drop one of two blocks to reach for a third or put one of two objects into her mouth to grab a third. She may even be able to stack one block on top of another. She can usually uncover a toy that has been hidden and enjoys finding the ball under the diaper—showing off her memory and displaying trial-and-error learning.

Your little rascal is learning words and appropriate gestures, such as saying, "bye-bye" while waving. Her passive vocabulary is growing rapidly; she reacts to words that identify familiar people, animals, objects and everyday activities. She listens with interest to familiar rhymes and songs and may understand simple commands, such as "Please get your bottle." She is beginning to use words meaningfully and may say "dada" and/or "mama" as specific names—much to your delight!

Intense concentration on her environment often makes your baby very sensitive. At playtime she may cry if another child cries. She may fear familiar activities such as baths, and may show hurt, discomfort, sadness and anger. Understanding and, perhaps, taking a new approach—such as bathing *with* her for a while—help the fear pass.

She loves to imitate you, rubbing herself with soap and playing the game of pointing to body parts. She also copies other babies' antics and movements and quickly learns from siblings to finger-feed herself. By the end of the tenth month, she will probably finger-feed herself an entire meal, drink from a cup and hold her bottle.

All these accomplishments show that your baby is becoming a dynamic person, an individual with developing muscles, feelings and skills. She deserves love, praise and all the special activities designed just for her pleasure in Diaper Play.

SUPPLIES

> parachute
> big bolster—covered foam bolster 14 inches in diameter and 24 inches long
> barrel of fun
> big dipper
> Teeter-Totter
> little ladder—4-foot long ladder; each 1-inch rung is 6 inches apart
> ramp
> big ladder
> silly pool—with whipped cream, angel-food cake, rice paper, peanut butter, cooked pasta, mashed potatoes

GETTING READY

Cuddles and Chitchat. Here are two tickle rhymes to develop physical closeness and encourage language development. With your hands mime the actions suggested by the words and watch him giggle and squirm in anticipation of the tickles.

> *Slowly, slowly, creeps the garden snail,*
> *Slowly, slowly, up the wooden rail.*
> *Quickly, quickly, runs the little mouse,*
> *Quickly, quickly, round about the house.*

Begin this game by running your index finger around baby's palm, then jump your finger up his arm and tickle him under the arm.

> *Round and round the garden, went the teddy bear,*
> *One step, two steps, tickle under there.*

Bubbles. Watch your baby's face glow when you bring out the parachute and switch on some peppy music for a frolicking round of Bubbles. Baby loves to lie on the parachute, be stroked with it and pulled on it. Make billowy bubbles around him and let him pat them, poke them and crawl under and over them with you. Talk about your games and suggest, "Let's play choo-choo! Pop the Bubbles or Hide 'n' Seek!" Bubbles helps your baby develop body and space awareness while thoroughly enjoying himself for three to five minutes daily.

Big Bolster. The advantage of this new game is that you can play more exaggerated and stimulating rocking games. Your baby still likes to rock forward and backward, sitting up, lying on her tummy, back and side, being held by arms and legs and moving at slow, medium and, now, faster speeds.

Begin Boomerang by sitting your baby on the bolster, facing you. Grasp her lower legs and rock her slowly backward, letting her lean forward to maintain balance. You may be amazed how far down baby can keep her balance. Bring her forward to a standing position. Repeat this several times to strengthen abdominal and thigh muscles as well as to stimulate the righting reflex and put the balancing mechanism to work.

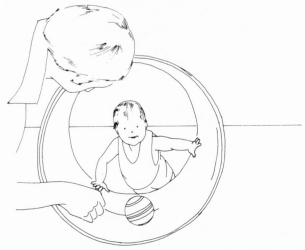

Ball and Barrel. Chasing a ball will someday be a favorite pastime. Chasing a ball rolled through the barrel helps your merry one develop awareness of moving in a confined space and addresses goal orientation. Give your resounding approval when your baby understands the verbal command, "Please get the ball." Two or three trips a day through the barrel should satisfy her.

Big Dipper. Let's play Washing Machine in the big dipper to utilize balance and body control. Sit your little star in the bowl and vary the speeds at which you tip and spin him. For the wash cycle, spin slowly to the left, slowly to the right, then make quick little tipping motions from side to side. Rinse cycle—fast spin to the left, fast spin to the right, then slow tipping motions from front to back. Dry cycle—spin your baby round and round at medium speed, then lift him out.

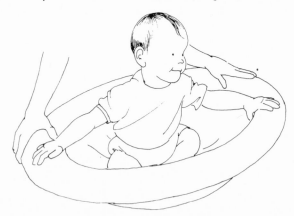

Your might concoct your own version of "Here We Go Round the Mulberry Bush," making the rhythm of the words match the tempo of the motions.

Two to Tee. Pulling out the Teeter-Totter brings your baby scurrying! In fact, he may cheerfully try to climb up on his own. Your little one can grasp the handles tightly as he uses tummy, back and leg muscles to maintain balance while moving up and down. This may be played slowly, moderately or to the full

speed of the Teeter-Totter for one to three minutes, accompanied by a rhyme such as "Hey, Diddle, Diddle, the Cat and the Fiddle."

MOVING OUT

Partner Movements

SEE-SAW

Value: Playing and sharing with your fast-growing baby is a joy, and this exercise helps keep both of you physically fit by increasing back and leg flexibility.

Here's How: Sit on the floor facing your baby and place your legs over her knees, which are spread slightly. Have her grasp your fingers, and see-saw back and forth. The further you lean in each direction, the more beneficial the movement is. Grasp her upper arms until she gets the idea to move back and forth. Singing "See-saw Margery Daw" gives a merry beat to the movement. For variety, do it while you both kneel.

> *See-saw Margery Daw,* [baby's name] *shall have a new master,*
> [Baby's name] *shall earn but a penny a day,*
> *Because (s)he can't work any faster.*

How Many: Move until the rhyme is over, or eight times; may be repeated daily.

Assistive Movements

THE ANGEL

Value: Your little angel will enjoy watching himself do this movement, which builds neck, back, bottom and abdominal muscles, in front of a mirror!

Here's How: Hold your baby's back close against you and face a mirror. Place one hand in front of his chest and lock his knees together with your other hand wrapped around them. Together, bend your upper torsos slightly forward, then

lean back and he will lean forward on stiffened legs. Take your hand away from his chest and see how nicely he holds the position for a slow count of three. (We overheard one parent tell his baby, "Okay, be an angel for me. Hold your wings up high.")

How Many: One balancing movement; may be repeated daily. If your baby still droops after two or three tries, go on to the next exercise and come back to this another day.

FORWARD, HO!

Value: "Determination" and "persistence" are two words that have been used to describe the wagon-train leaders of the old West. Nine- and ten-month-olds are likewise courageous in their desire and drive to stand and be on the go.

Here's How: Stand behind your partner and grasp her upper arms. Gently pull one arm forward at a time; she will rotate her hips and step forward. Steady praise will encourage your little one to walk a good distance across a room.

How Many: Walk baby two or three times daily.

THE SWING

Value: This splendid swaying movement develops neck and back strength and increases spatial awareness and trust in you.

Here's How: Lay baby on her back, facing you, and bend over her with your feet wide apart. Grasp her lower arms near the wrists with your thumb and first two fingers, while you grasp her ankles with your other hand. Be sure you have a good hold and that her head is tucked forward before you swing her back and forth between your legs. Begin with a gentle swing and broad smiles to make her

feel secure and, as she becomes accustomed to the movement, swing her waist-high.

How Many: Three or four swings, once a day.

CRUISING

Value: Your baby is putting relentless energy toward walking. Cruising helps her develop posture control and allows her to practice walking while holding out one hand.

Here's How: Stand your go-getter next to a couch. Let her hold onto the couch with one hand and take her other hand for support. As you move slowly forward, she will keep hold of your hand but will have to let go with the other to balance between you and the couch. Encourage her with endearing words and place interesting toys at each end of the couch.

How Many: One cruise, up and back. May be repeated daily.

PPT (Parents' Pep Talk): You should be thrilled to watch your baby's progress. Take a moment to pat yourself on the back, because *you* are doing something very special for your baby—you are allowing him to use his whole body to learn about himself and his surroundings. You are entitled to feel quite smug, because this early movement is important for your baby today and for all his tomorrows.

CHIPMUNK CLIMB

Value: In this movement your baby learns how to use his arms, hands, legs and feet to climb like a chipmunk up a ladder.

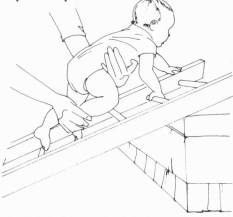

Here's How: Tilt the little ladder against the front of a couch, about 18 inches high. Have someone hold it securely. Call for your baby to crawl toward the ladder and pull up. As he grabs with his hands and puts his weight on one foot, guide his free foot onto the next rung. You may need to assist him by holding him around the waist with one arm—and move his hands, too—until he gets the idea. A toy placed at the top will stimulate your amazing nine- or ten-month-old, but climbing singlehandedly to the summit may still take several months of practice.

How Many: One climb; may be repeated daily.

WALKWAY ONE

Value: Your child is ready to try a movement that challenges her to balance while adjusting to gravity, moving both uphill and down.

Here's How: Place baby at the bottom of the ramp. Hold her under her arms

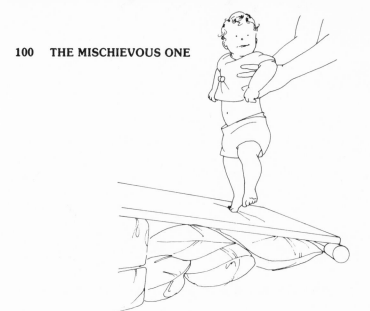

and walk her up and down the ramp. Walking down is more difficult, because she must transfer body weight as she experiences a gravitational change.

How Many: Two complete walks up and down; may be repeated daily.

Active Movements

MOMMY AND ME

Value: This is a movement variation that a parent showed *us* in class. We had been urging babies to crawl over ladder rungs after a toy, and this mother encouraged her baby to go after her. Baby thought it was great fun, and so do we!

Here's How: Place the big ladder on the floor and set your baby at one end. Crawl backward over the rungs, calling to your baby to chase you. She will crawl forward over the rungs, greatly anticipating a big hug and kiss when she catches you.

How Many: One chase, may be repeated daily.

EXPLORING

Silly Pool

Have a camera ready for this one: *whipped cream!* This is one of our babies' favorite media and one of the messiest. Your baby may not dive in enthusiastically at first, but, encouraged by your smiles and participation, he will undoubtedly come around to tasting it and smearing it all over his body and the pool. A portable mirror that you can place in the pool is a wonderful addition to the experience. He will busy himself pasting whipped cream all over the baby in the mirror and will enjoy the pleasure of pushing, patting and moving the cream around the smooth surface.

Other media that will fascinate your nine- or ten-month-old are squeezable, smashable *angel-food cake*; *rice paper*; *peanut butter*; *cooked pasta* and *mashed potatoes*. Enjoy!

ALL AROUND

"Playful" and "calm" are two key words to remember when presenting sensorimotor experiences now. Your baby is becoming more and more capable, and sometimes you are tempted to push activities that you see another baby doing or that you think your baby *should* be doing. Your child has his own beautiful pattern, and forcing will most likely create a balker. If you are relaxed and patient, your baby will make his own choices and find his own way.

Smelling and Tasting

Your baby will want to try *drinking from a cup* alone. Fill a cup with a little liquid and, if necessary, help him grasp the cup with both hands, raise it to his mouth, then place it back on the table. He will let you know with gestures and sounds when he doesn't want any more assistance.

Share *smells* with your baby: fresh lilacs, turnips, strawberries. Allow him to fondle and explore them at his pace, under your supervision. Call his attention to everyday fragrances: baking bread, ocean air, fields of hay, pine trees, spices, popping popcorn or a crackling log fire.

Seeing, Touching and Manipulating

Your baby's world is opening up quickly because of increased mobility and sharpened sensory skills. She is discriminating among qualities of objects—size, weight, texture—and hands are becoming wonderful manipulating tools.

She is also understanding and expressing more emotion. Now when you give your baby something to explore, think about its emotional impact. Her feelings will often be related to your mood by the special tone in your voice and the expression in your eyes and on your face. You can describe an object's characteristics, but until you give it an emotional quality, that object will not be nearly as alive or interesting. When your baby touches a bunny, make it feel soft by the tone of your voice. Likewise, make a puppy *feel* warm; soap feel slippery and coffee cup feel hot.

Let your baby get the feel of *using a spoon* by dipping it into peanut butter and putting it into her mouth to taste and feel the stickiness. You might ask her, "Do you like the peanut butter? It's sticky, but it tastes mmmm . . . good!"

Give your baby a hand towel to help *dry off after a bath* and play Let's Dry Off the body parts.

Your baby is using more *objects as play instruments*. Show him how to push a block with a wooden spoon, and let him experiment with other blunt kitchen tools.

Your baby loves the feel of soft *play dough* to smash, squeeze, stretch, roll, and so on. (See recipe in Appendix.) But *prickly things* must be handled carefully. Let your baby daintily feel a rose stem, hairbrush, cactus pear or teeth on a comb.

Nine- and ten-month-olds find endless amounts of curious objects while exploring. Give your baby *an old purse* to investigate, and she will spend hours putting things in and taking them out of its pockets.

Show your baby how to push the off button on an *alarm clock* when it rings to demonstrate cause and effect. Or show your curious one how to turn the handle on a noisemaking toy, such as a *jack-in-the-box*.

When the temperatures soar, your adventurer will enjoy *playing with a hose* that is running gently. He can move it, feel the cool water, listen to its gurgle and watch it sprinkle.

Hearing, Seeing and Language

If you take your baby's lead, you can expand everyday events into spontaneous happenings. As you are unbagging groceries, for example, your explorer may become intrigued by a small paper sack. Let him shake, crush and wave it, then show him how it bends, opens and closes. Talk about its stiff, smooth feel and crunchy sound while your little one discovers more possibilities! Language is the bonding agent in the following experiences.

Sing *silly jingles* that you invent or repeat from the television or radio to increase your baby's attention span. Change or dress him while you sing and he'll be more playful and cooperative.

A small *music box*, by itself or inside a toy, is a nice way to keep your baby happily occupied while you change a diaper. Watch him listen to the clicking noise as you show him how to turn the handle.

Listen to your pal's jabbering and try to interpret the sounds. *Converse* as though you understood every word, which adds to his vocabulary. If he is saying, "ba, ba, ba," add "be" to form "baby" phonetically.

Give your baby a pan with a lid and a few small items to play the *pan game*. He will drop objects into the pan and become absorbed by the noises. *Drumming and banging* pans, spoons and cups is another pastime for your nine- or ten-month-old. This can be nerve-racking for the rest of the family, but it's important play to him.

Imitating and Language

Show your baby how to *clap* hands to a rhyme. Try "Clap with me, one, two, three, clap, clap, clap!" Pat or pound on a table, a floor, your legs or a drum, and encourage your baby to imitate you. *Pat* softly and see if he pats the same way, or pound loudly and see if he pounds with his entire arm. Make this a silly game with lots of giggles.

Hug one of your child's stuffed animals, then tell him to give it a squeeze. Follow by lots of hugging between you and your baby. Ask him to give Grandma and Grandpa a big hug, too. They will be thrilled if their grandchild does and understanding if he doesn't.

Babies are adorable when they first *smell a flower*. They usually blow their cheeks out instead of inhaling, but it makes a memorable picture.

Body Positioning

Throughout this book we attempt to minimize or eliminate the risk of injury to your baby through adequate preparation, watchful supervision and assistance. As your baby becomes more aggressive in activities, you should expect minor mishaps. In fact, Dr. Jaroslav Koch, in *Total Baby Development*, writes,

> All exercises to train crawling entail a degree of risk of skin scraping or other minor hurt. But much more serious dangers can be avoided through these slight calculated risks: babies who early acquire good motor abilities, and positive and negative experiences are better protected against serious accidents than children who lack experience and exercise.

Chasing is a delightful and favorite activity. Squat down on all fours on the floor near your baby, and as he starts to crawl away, grab his legs and pull him back. He will crawl away again, and as you grab him again, laugh and bring him back for hugs and kisses.

Tossing is another activity that has probably been going on since time began. Many dads just love to toss babies into the air, and most babies love every thrilling moment.

Begin with a very small toss to instill confidence, then graduate to whatever height you both feel comfortable with. Your baby may even like a series of tosses and bounces on the bed to the tune of a favorite rhyme.

Gliding is great fun for your baby—and good exercise for you. Sit on the floor, hold your baby's hands and place your feet on his pelvic bones. Roll back onto the floor and pull and lift him into the air with your feet. Straightening and bending your legs will give him a teetering feeling: he will arch his back and raise his feet, strengthening back and leg muscles.

Your baby will probably try to fashion a little *fort* under a card table or dinette. Place pillows around it to make it more secluded. Later, throw a sheet over the entire table for a real hideaway.

Visiting a park is a special treat. Your little adventurer will enjoy exploring the grass, walkways, steps, slopes, leaves and sand. Try holding her on low sliding boards or a small merry-go-round. The best entertainment of all is to watch the quacking, wing-flapping ducks in a pond or cooing, strutting pigeons near the playground.

Socializing

According to Dr. Stephen Lehand,

> Babies develop hand signals or body language during this period to show that they recognize different objects, because they do not yet have spoken language. Initially, the gestures may all look the same or appear to be a code that is hard to break. But, if you zero in on your baby's gestures, it will be evident that he has a clear and definite system for representing different objects. He will greet you one way, the dog another, handle bath time in a different way, etc. His body language is extremely important, for it serves the foundation upon which he builds his verbal language. He is trying to communicate.

What a fascinating, complex person your baby is!

Seat baby on your lap and *play So Big!* Ask her, "How big are you?" Then sweep your arms through the air and say, "Soooo big!" See if your baby stretches her arms up high to communicate that she is "big."

Teach your child to *respond to frowns.* When he does something he shouldn't, frown, shake your head and say, "Please don't do that," then *prevent* him from doing it. Follow with some simple redirection, and he will happily go his way. He will gradually understand that he must stop when corrected.

Going stroller riding, biking or backpacking in a *caravan* with friends is fun for your little one. During these jaunts she always has company to listen to her jabbering and explain the scenery. Doing the playful parenting *program in the park* is a nice change for you and your eager beaver. You may even find friends among onlookers.

Chapter 10

SO PROUD
Eleven and Twelve Months

HOW DO YOU DO?

Besides awaiting your baby's all-important first birthday, you are probably anticipating the unforgettable moment when he takes that first staggering step. For months you have watched his daily preparations. When his muscles are ready, he will take off with great gusto. He will be so proud—and you will, too!

In the meantime your baby may be concentrating so much on being upright that you must dress him standing! He still climbs up and down stairs, over obstacles and even out of his crib or stroller. If he is walking a bit already, he may try to sit on a small chair. He is such a busy little charmer!

His grasp is stronger and firmer, and he may enjoy hanging from a dowel or bar on his own. Since he is becoming more proficient at controlling his grasp, he can more easily drop objects into a container, perhaps putting blocks into a box and taking them out or nesting boxes and bowls.

In fact, sometimes you think there's no end to your baby's dexterity. He can hold a crayon to attempt to scribble, take lids off containers, point with his index finger and reach accurately for an object, adjusting his grip to its size, shape and position. His hands are developing more steadiness and precision, and he may be able to insert a key into a lock.

Your bright-eyes may group some objects by shape and color, too. He can do one thing with one hand while the other does something else: watch him remove a bright red ring from the spindle with his left hand and replace it with the right.

As his personality matures, your live wire's ability to imitate increases accordingly. Persistence and the desire to imitate show clearly in his language development. He may produce specific sounds from your everyday language. He may say two to eight words besides "mama" and "dada," imitate the environmental sounds of objects around him—such as "bow-wow" when he sees a dog—and even babble short sentences.

By the end of the twelfth month, your powerhouse may be walking full tilt. Once he can reach people and objects easier and faster, his world is more exciting. The expression, You've come a long way, baby! was never more true! For as you reflect on all the events and challenges of the first year, you cannot now imagine what life would be like without the beautiful baby who smiles and laughs with you, hugs you, becomes angry, cries when you leave and shows joy and love of learning. He has reason to be so proud, and so do you.

SUPPLIES

> parachute
> big bolster
> barrel of fun
> big dipper
> Teeter-Totter
> poles—two 48-inch dowels, 1 inch in diameter (broom or mop handles may be used)
> dowel
> big ladder
> ramp
> little ladder
> beam—6′ × 6″ × 2″ board, painted with three layers of nontoxic enamel paint, placed between blocks or bricks
> box—low, sturdy cardboard box (from a grocery store or moving company), laundry basket or milk crate
> tires—two old car tires without rims, wash and spray with clear plastic.
> silly pool—pudding, birdseed, dry coffee grounds, uncooked cereal

GETTING READY

Your baby is becoming more independent as he steps out into the walking world, but he still needs attention and assurance to progress in total development. Playing the following warm-ups will foster a secure, loving and supportive relationship between you.

Cuddles and Chitchat. These games may be likened to good old-fashioned rug play, where you and your scamp tumble, roll, tickle and play together on the floor with much dialogue, laughter, hugging and kissing.

Start with a knee ride as you sing this rhyme:

> *To market, to market, to buy a fat pig;*
> *Home again, home again, jiggety, jig.*
> *To market, to market, to buy a fat hog;*
> *Home again, home again, jiggety, jog.*

Listening requires the ability to associate sounds and language. This old-time favorite will teach your baby to listen for specific stimuli:

> *Knock at the door,* [Gently knock on baby's forehead.]
> *Pull the bell,* [Lightly pull a lock of hair.]
> *Lift the latch,* [Lightly pinch baby's nose.]
> *And walk right in!* [Walk your fingertips up chin and into baby's mouth.]

Bubbles. By now your baby may be attempting to say "Bubbles," for she *loves* to play with the parachute—crawling under and over the big or little waves, rolling and unrolling like a hot dog, shaking it like a windstorm, swinging in it

like a boat afloat or watching it billow into the air and float down. She probably has her own ideas for relaxing on it, pulling it or playing night-night or Peek-a-boo. Three to five minutes pass very quickly.

Big Bolster. Your roustabout enjoys pushing the bolster along the floor as you help control it. Once he becomes proficient on his feet, let him push it all by himself.

Add rhythm as you rock on the bolster to round out the three to five minutes. Play "Touching toes, one, two, three. Touching hands, one, two, three," while you rock your baby on his tummy so that his feet, then his hands, touch three times in a row. Use your imagination—think of some more!

Barrel of Fun. During the eleventh and twelfth months, we often see babies having grand times with the barrel on their own "baby power." Your baby may crawl inside the barrel and roll over and over on her own.

Many mothers invent their own games. Our favorite creation is to stand the barrel on end, lower baby into it and play Peek-a-boo, then tip it over carefully and let giggly crawl out the bottom. After three to five minutes of this, you may have to swoop your little one away to get her interested in the next warm-up!

Big Dipper. Baby will laugh out loud at your craziness and funny faces while you wiggle the big dipper all around, playing Jiggles. Follow this with spinning and tipping games—fast, jerky quick dips from side to side mingled with slow, gentle rocking.

Leave the big bowl in the playroom and encourage your baby to explore other climbing movements. Ask what she is doing; she'll have a grand time explaining in her own little language.

Two to Tee. This toy is especially nice to share when another little someone visits. Once he climbs on, call to his pal to come and join the fun. (Or have your child fetch a doll.) He will teeter happily, balancing by pushing and pulling with his arms, until *your* arms totter out!

MOVING OUT

Partner Movements

LIFT OFF

Value: Your baby is off to an early start in counting backward while strengthening hand, arm, trunk and abdominal muscles that will someday help him maneuver a sled, bicycle—perhaps even a space shuttle.

Here's How: Seat your baby on the launchpad (floor) and kneel behind him. While you both grasp the dowel, count down: "Ten, nine, eight, seven, six, five,

four, three, two, one, zero . . . *lift off*!" Slowly raise the dowel and pull your baby to his feet. Continue to lift until he is about two inches off the floor. Hold for a few seconds, then return him to earth.

Begin this movement over a bed, couch or pillow until your astronaut understands it, so he will have cushioning if he lets go.

How Many: Two lifts; may be repeated daily.

Assistive Movements

THE POLES

Value: Your little investigator will check out the poles carefully—moving and

twisting them, rolling them on the floor and, perhaps, biting them, before letting you start this movement!

Here's How: Have your baby grasp two poles while you stand behind him with your hands over his. Keeping the ends on the ground, move the tips of the poles back and forth to build confidence. Gradually, move the right pole forward and your baby will step forward. Move the left pole forward and he will take another step. Once he follows this pattern with ease (perhaps in several weeks), raise your hands above his for a minute and let him handle the poles alone. Of course, once he is walking well, he will be bored by the poles!

How Many: Eight forward steps, using an interesting rhythm. May be repeated daily.

FOAL WALK

Value: A father in one of our classes named this movement. He said that his daughter reminded him of a newborn colt just finding its legs when she did this walk.

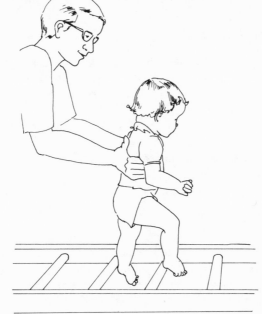

Here's How: Place the big ladder flat on the floor. Start baby at one end and encourage her to walk the length of the ladder while you hold her under the arms. Even wobbly movements deserve much praise at the finish.

How Many: One walk; may be repeated daily.

WALKWAY TWO

Value: This movement gives your baby the feeling of moving with gravity. Share it with him in the grassy knolls at the park.

Here's How: Stand your baby at the bottom of a grassy incline (or the ramp) while you hold one hand for assitance. Cheer him to walk to the top, turn around and walk down. Tell your little one how nicely he is growing and how much you love him.

How Many: One walk up and down; may be repeated daily.

SUPER CHIPMUNK CLIMB

Value: Your bright and capable baby has progressed from fun activities to truly challenging tasks. She senses your excitement as you stimulate her to climb the ladder at a steeper angle, developing confidence, more balance and body control.

Here's How: Move the ladder from its original angle to a steeper slope against a chair back, about 25 inches high. Have a helper hold it securely. As your climber begins to swing up onto a rung with one foot, guide her free foot onto the next rung. Like before, up she goes!

How Many: One climb; may be repeated daily.

WHIZ WALK

Value: Beginning to work on the beam is an exciting event. By her graduating from the wide ramp to a more narrow surface, you can see your little one's progress in balance, eye-foot coordination and space awareness.

Here's How: Place the beam between two chairs or, if you are outside, use a low retaining wall or brick planter. Stand baby at one end of the beam, holding her under the arms for steadiness. Let her carry her own weight; your hands only help her stay on the beam.

Some babies begin very cautiously, while others charge full speed into this exercise. Whatever her tempo, your baby will gobble up your smiles and raves. Say a little rhyme for her, something like this:

> *Walking, walking, feel your toes go walking,*
> *Walking, walking, all along the beam.*

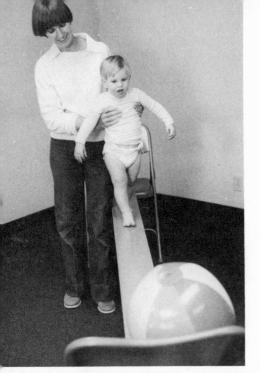

Singing, singing, Tania's toes are singing,
Happy, happy little Tania's toes.

How Many: One walk, across and back; may be repeated daily.

Active Movements

OUT YOU GO

Value: How many times have you heard, "He doesn't even play with that toy. We should have just given him the box." Babies and boxes go together like ice cream and cake!

Here's How: Seat your baby in the box. Place a toy in plain view, shake it and coax baby to climb after it. When he does, cheerfully rub his arms and legs, then give him several minutes to investigate the toy.

How many: One climb; may be repeated daily.

TIRE CRAWL

Value: Rolling out *two* old tires will certainly arouse your baby's curiosity!

Here's How: Lay the tires flat on the floor, side by side. While singing "The Bear Went over the Mountain," jangle a sparkly toy and see if your baby will climb in sequence up and over the tires. Then stack the tires one on top of the

other, place your climber inside and see if she can crawl out. Finally, stand the tires on end side by side and see if your little bear will scoot through them after a favorite toy.

How Many: Each setup may take some time. Do just one variation a day.

EXPLORING

Silly Pool

Moving the silly pool outside on a sunny day is a pleasant change. Your little rascal can work with eyes and hands to explore *pudding, birdseed, dry coffee grounds* and *dry uncooked cereal*. Your baby will even have a great time mixing two media, such as birdseed and peanut butter. You, other siblings and neighborhood friends should join in the play.

Verbal exchange is essential for success. Tune into your baby's sounds and repeat them. Add your own descriptions: "sticky," "smooth," "rough," "bumpy," "grainy," "lumpy" and so on. Once your baby is bored with the pool, gently hosing him off can be an *extra* sensory treat!

ALL AROUND

Whether you and your baby are new to the program or old pros, we want you to feel good and be successful. Select one activity from each category to work into your daily schedule, keeping in mind that once each activity is presented, your baby will alert you to her preferences. She will show her appreciation of your efforts and patience with smiles and responsiveness to each activity. Your proud one is saying, "Thanks, Mom and Dad. I love you!"

Smelling and Tasting

Eating out is a stimulating experience for an eleven or twelve-month-old. He may not eat much, but he will drink in all the interesting aromas, different colors and textures and extra attention! Select a restaurant that is prepared to serve young children, and go armed with finger foods to occupy your squirmer. One mother we know gives her baby ice chips, which are cool and soothing if baby is teething.

Call your playmate's attention to *smells in shopping places*: the fish market, cleaners, drugstore and supermarket.

Seeing, Touching and Manipulating

Your sprinter is now struggling to escape while you feed him, change his diaper, bathe him and dress him. Give him lots of love, space and, perhaps, a picnic bench or parson's table while he continues to develop that crucial eye-hand control.

Let your baby *scribble* with an oversize crayon on a large sheet of paper taped down to a table. (Remember that any way he holds the crayon at this age is okay.)

Sponges teach children about properties of air and water, even though they may not realize that while they squeeze out the water. Add a squirt of mild liquid soap in the bathtub and plastic tub to make the play even more interesting.

Make a small slice in a tennis ball and tie a knot at the end of a soft rope and insert it into the ball. Suspend it from a tree limb, patio cover or the top of a door frame. Your baby will have a marvelous time *striking the swinging ball* with his hands or a rolled-up newspaper. This activity provides stimulation time after time over the next five or six years.

Your industrious one loves to *turn the pages* of old magazines. Make a game of pointing to pictures and naming the objects. Offer her the magazine upside down and see if she turns it around.

Your little one will be a study in concentration while she *inserts* small, safe objects such as circular cereal bits into an empty plastic bottle. And all family members can enjoy *building blocks* together. Try using plastic containers with lids, boxes with lids or pieces of foam.

Using shaped beads and coffee cans, cut a circle, square and triangle in the plastic lids and show your baby how to match the *geometric beads* to the right cans.

Along with her collection of personal belongings, your baby will enjoy having her own *cupboard*. She'll find and keep boxes, jar lids, soap wrappers, tissue paper, old magazines, sticky tape and blunt kitchen utensils in her own cabinet.

Finally, don't forget to let your baby *feel* bricks, walls, tile, wood, clean rags, twigs, rocks and other safe surfaces.

Hearing, Seeing and Language

Give your baby a toy *xylophone* to play with. Your little musician can bang, pull, push and make his own kind of music on it. You can *make* rhythm instruments, too, from empty juice cans. Fill them partially with different objects, such as rice, beans, pebbles or paper clips. Secure the top with masking tape, then cover the whole can with contact paper. Later, your toddler will enjoy naming the different sounds.

Talk pleasantly but firmly to your companion, using eye-to-eye contact, when you give him *directions for simple tasks*, such as, "Please put the doll on the couch." Praise him when he follows your directions. Ask simple questions, like, "Where is mommy's purse?" When he brings it to you, reward him with a kiss. Use *simple statements* for everyday happenings: "Time for lunch," "let's play," or "Father's coming home!"

Now is a good time to sort through your *feely bag*, perhaps keeping a few samples and adding a long, soft sock that your baby can put his hand and arm into, an old nylon, soft knit hats, a clam shell, a sculptured rock, old placemats, a small basket, an old 45-RPM record and the like.

Imitating and Language

Genevieve Painter explains in *Teach Your Baby* that gestures used in everyday situations act as learning clues for children. She writes:

> If you say to your baby while he is, say, standing in the living room, "Open your mouth," he may very well not understand you. If you say the same words while he is in his high chair and you have a spoon in your hand, he will very likely understand . . . And it is through imitating your actions that he is eventually encouraged to imitate your speech as well.

Wave a toy airplane in the air and see if your baby does the same, then show your mimic how to *blow air through a straw*. Once he can accomplish the latter task, show him how to blow bubbles through a straw in water and with a wire wand and store-bought bubble liquid. Your baby will be absolutely enchanted with his discovery!

See if your *copycat* will follow any of these movements: open and close your fist, drum your fingers on a table, flex your index finger, rub your eyes, yawn, blink your eyes and put your finger in your ear. Hide and Seek is also a perennial favorite. Laugh and smile with your baby when he imitates you and tell him how clever he is.

Self-Awareness

Your baby is beginning to learn about her body and all its parts: how they work individually and how they go together to function as a whole.

When you are *dressing up* for an evening out on the town, your little one will usually stand right in the path to see what you are doing. Keep him happily occupied with items in your dressing area. As you're deciding what jewelry to wear, hang a necklace on his ear and see if he fingers it or takes it off. Put a tie around his neck and see if he removes it, or let him play with a handkerchief. He will have a good time while allowing you a few uninterrupted moments to primp.

When looking at pictures of *animals*, ask your baby to point to the animal's eye, then to his own. Do this, gently, with the pets in your house, too.

Problem Solving

Here's an exciting new category presenting both simple problems and fun solutions to stretch your little one's ability to concentrate, watch and remember events.

Does your baby like to get into the action while you fold diapers? *Cover a favorite toy* with a diaper, then see if he pulls the diaper off to find the toy. When your baby has mastered this game, make it more difficult: use a diaper and tea towel. While your baby watches, hide a toy under the diaper a few times and let him find it. Then hide it under the towel and see what he does. When he goes directly to the second cover and removes it, he understands that the toy is separate from the hiding action. What a clever fellow!

Place a toy on a diaper, blanket or newspaper just out of your baby's reach. Hold her firmly and ask her to get the toy. She will not be able to reach it, so show her how to *pull the diaper* to retrieve it. Ask her, again, to get the toy and see if she uses the diaper.

Body Positioning

Once your rascal learns to walk with confidence, offer him *different walkings surfaces*, like grass, sand, leaves and dirt. Have him *walk atop objects*, such as cardboard blocks, carpet squares and throw pillows. Hold his hand—for reassurance more than physical support—as he steps on the irregularly placed objects. His balance and eye-foot coordination will markedly improve with irregular rhythmic steps.

Teach your eleven- or twelve-month-old to *sit on a stool*. Show her a small stool, then turn her away from it and gently press her bottom into the seat. With practice, she will proudly seat herself. Ask your cuddler to *carry* a large object, such as a stuffed animal. When she lifts it, her center of gravity will tilt and she will assume a different body position than when she walks empty-handed. Give your scamp a *push toy* with wheels and a long, wooden handle to help her orient herself while her attention is distracted, thus making walking more automatic.

Socializing

Take your baby *swimming* and swish her in a circle, zigzag from side to side or bob gently up and down. Beside the pool, sit with legs apart, roll a *beach ball* to your baby and ask her to roll it back. Show her how to stop the ball with her hands. Other children will quickly join the giggles and good time.

Part III

TODDLER PLAY

Thirteen Months to Two Years

INTRODUCTION

Congratulations! You have completed the first part of Playful Parenting and are ready for Toddler Play—where the "big kids" are! You are also celebrating a big event: your baby's first birthday. This is probably the one celebrated with the most preparation, excitement and happiness. Many parents in our classes talk for weeks about the big family get-togethers they have planned for the occasion.

Now brace yourself for a packed, exciting second year. Your toddler wants to walk, to talk, to imitate adults and to explore the whole bloomin' world. She is blessed with insatiable curiosity and is open to all kinds of learning. Movements that were once awkward are now accomplished smoothly and easily. Your toddler is moving from garbled sounds to coherent language, acquiring a system that helps control her environment. And she is testing her power. If she is to become satisfied with herself and learn to direct her life, she must learn what control is all about.

Your child's fresh approach to life will leave *you* breathless and enriched. And even though the coming twelve months may have their difficulties, you will treasure the memories from this period. Your child is developing a mind of her own, has a desire for more challenging stimulation, needs protection (since she has no understanding of danger) and requires a suitable degree of discipline.

With these thoughts in mind, we have designed the second part of the program in a format that fits a toddler's unlimited energy and driving independence. Toddler Play offers your child abundant opportunities to be successful while developing motor skills and self-assurance, as well as learning more about her wondrous world.

Many child-development specialists maintain that a child's self-concept is directly related to motor-skill development, so the program now helps you provide stimulating activities and a planned environment of toys, equipment and furnishings scaled to her size and capabilities. Through continued support for efforts and accomplishments, you will share many positive experiences with your birthday child.

Toddler Play includes new GETTING READY categories of Loosening Up, Body Awareness, Finger Play, Rhythms, Pretending and Locomotion, and two new pretend character puppets, Rocky Robot and Winnie Wedo, are introduced. Choose or create a hand puppet for each character to assist you in acting out activities. Let's elaborate a little:

> *Loosening* teaches your toddler the difference between tension and relaxation by engaging in silly, fun games.
>
> *Body Awareness* enables your mover to "sort out" one part of her body from another in order to be aware of the relationship of her body to space. Rocky Robot asks simple questions and gives imitative suggestions.
>
> *Finger Play* builds hand-muscle control for activities that involve individual finger strength and finger coordination, such as writing, drawing, brushing teeth or playing a musical instrument.
>
> *Rhythms* aid your busy bee's abilities to move smoothly and respond with precise movements to external rhythms. Winnie Wedo gives your toddler simple directions for walking, running, dancing, jumping and rhythmic sequences.
>
> *Pretending* is a big, new bag of imaginative tricks for large-muscle development.
>
> *Locomotion* addresses the ways your toddler can travel from here to there: including rolling, crawling, creeping, walking, jumping and climbing.

Other categories continue to offer tried-and-true games while adapting the emphasis to your growing child's deepening needs. MOVING OUT remains essentially constant, but the developmental movements progress in difficulty, improving and refining your toddler's growing capabilities. EXPLORING takes on the delightful addition of Super Stuff while continuing favorite Silly Pool activities. Finally, exciting new sensory suggestions are given in ALL

AROUND. (If you are new to the program, this may be a good time to read Diaper Play for background information.)

Try one suggestion from each GETTING READY category and from Super Stuff and Silly Pool daily. Use the structured ideas as springboards for your own inventions—games you know your tot will enjoy.

As your toddler begins the second year, remember that there is no "correct" way to parent. In fact, be prepared for some friction, because even beautifully developing children go through balky periods. When your toddler becomes moody, stubborn or resistant, remind yourself that negative attitudes do not last forever. If you remain self-assured, loving and optimistic, you will cope more easily with the inevitable frustrations of childrearing.

By the time your curious learner reaches age two, she will express herself verbally and feel secure and satisfied. As she plays, she will be developing her ideas, using her imagination, concentrating, role-playing and imitating grown-up social behavior. Through play she will be sharing, cooperating, and loving and respecting others, traits that will endure throughout her life. Her personality will have expanded twofold, making this second twelve months one of the most magical and rewarding periods of childhood.

Let's get started!

Chapter 11

THE ASSERTIVE ONE
Thirteen Months

HOW DO YOU DO?

"Beautiful" is the word to describe your thirteen-month-old toddler! He has bright, clear eyes and is full of smiles. He snuggles and hugs, tugs at and clings to your skirt and hides behind your slacks. He gives kisses, plays patty-cake and waves bye-bye. He happily goes anywhere, is the center of attention at an outing and falls asleep easily after a rousing day.

Your thirteen-month-old's curiosity seems endless. His drive reminds you of the weeks when he started to crawl, only now your zealous adventurer needs an environment to move freely and safely while exploring to the maximum. We'll create such an atmosphere in Toddler Play, because you don't want to say no too often or your trailblazer may think you love him more when he isn't learning.

When laughter and good feelings abound, your mover has wonderful times. He climbs low steps, pushes boxes, pulls toys, empties drawers and laundry baskets and scatters tissues, napkins and toilet paper. He industriously peels off socks and hats, fetches magazines and waters flowers with a hose. Everything within reach eventually becomes prey to his hands and mouth, so you need to keep a watchful eye—not an easy task!

If your toddler is not yet walking, don't despair. Enjoy each moment for itself. Once he begins to walk, you may yearn for the slower pace of crawling.

Walking or not, your thirteen-month-old wants to do whatever he wants to do without restraint. He often demands your attention, as though *you* make play happen. Consider this a compliment, for structured play is his major educator. Play helps develop large and small muscles, solve problems, stretch the attention span, enhance self-awareness.

Playful exchanges with your child stretch his language ability, too. Though passive language still dominates, your child is reaching out to understand and piece together the language around him. He tries to imitate your speech by pointing, gesturing and mimicking your sounds and cadences. Imitation is more noticeable during play situations in parks, in church nurseries or in toddler classes. One thirteen-month-old may spark a whole group to repeat a movement, particularly when he is applauded for the effort.

Unfortunately, temper tantrums may also be part of your toddler's assertiveness at this age. If and when one occurs, try to discern the cause. Maybe your tot is running into an impenetrable wall of "no's." Perhaps he's finding that he can manipulate you. Whatever the reason, your youngster will be learning to express and control emotion for quite some time. Your firmness now will help him find emotional stability.

In the meantime, let's give your assertive one some opportunities to expend some of that immense energy and curiosity.

SUPPLIES

> Hula-Hoop
> parachute
> big bolster
> beam
> railroad track—6' × 6" × 2" base with 6' × 4" × 2" board nailed and glued perpendicular to base, painted with three layers of nontoxic enamel paint
> big ladder
> little ladder
> ramp
> box
> tires—two
> super stuff—shakers, foam blocks, rhythm instruments, yarn balls, cloth diapers
> silly pool—thick and thin dry spaghetti, whipped soap suds, sticky textures, fresh fruit

GETTING READY

Turn on some peppy background music and your happy, curious thirteen-month-old will be eager to play games. Each game you play is a learning experience. Muscles flex and strengthen, vocabulary ability increases, self-awareness expands and, most important of all, the interaction between you and your assertive one fosters a closer relationship.

Loosening up

"Ring Around the Rosy": A wonderful way to begin play is to sing and act out this familiar rhyme. The pulling, circling and flopping down reduces muscle tension and sets a happy, giggly atmosphere. Getting up and circling to the opposite direction teaches your child the concept of "down and up."

> *Ring around the rosy,*
> *A pocket full of posies,*
> *Ashes, ashes,*
> *We all fall down.*

A variation of this is to hold a Hula-Hoop and play. In our classes several toddlers hold onto a hoop as they sidestep around. The element of surprise is great fun, and the movement connects large-muscle use with hearing.

Body Awareness

Wiggles. This movement is most appropriate when you are sitting on the floor opposite each other or while baby sits in front of a mirror. Go through the motions slowly. Your toddler may be fascinated just to watch you at first, but before long he will have the routine down pat.

> *Wiggles, wiggles are after me,* [Wiggle on bottom]
> *My fingers, my toes and even my nose.* [Wiggle fingers, toes and wiggle nose with finger]
> *I'll chase them, chase them all away* [Do push-away motion with arms.]
> *And be very still for the rest of the day.*

Rocky Robot Says While your wiggle worm is sitting in the bathtub or on your lap, try this new game. Let your hand puppet help act out the role.
"Touch your eyes. Make them blink."
"Touch your ears. Can you move them?"
"Touch Mama's cheeks. Watch Mama puff them up."
"Show Daddy where your mouth is. Open your mouth wide."

Finger Play

As your toddler becomes more aware of body parts and how they move, she also begins to notice size differences. Compare hand sizes—big and little, or, if brother plays, small, medium and large. Talk about how hands and fingers feel, clap, and so on. Kiss each of your child's fingers and play this game to "Two Little Dickey Birds":

Two little dickey birds, [Hold index fingers up.]
Sitting on a wall.
One named Peter, [Wiggle on finger.]
One named Paul. [Wiggle other finger.]
Fly away Peter, [Put one finger behind back.]
Fly away Paul. [Put other finger behind back.]
Come back Peter, [Return one finger.]
Come back Paul. [Return other finger.]

Rhythms

All along, *you* have been initiating rhythm. Now watch your thirteen-month-old generate his own body rhythms while playing this classic in a bus or on the patio swing.

Pat-a-cake, pat-a-cake, Baker man, [Clap toddler's hands.]
Bake me a cake as fast as you can. [Continue to clap hands.]
Roll it and roll it and mark it with a B, [Roll his arms around and
   use his initial.]
Shoot it in the oven for [toddler's name] *and me.* [Stretch arms out
   and above head.]

Winnie Wedo. This new pretend friend has suggestions for rhythmic sequences:

"Nod your head yes and no."
"Pat your knees soft, hard, slow, fast."
"Kick your legs while lying on the floor, on your tummy, on your back . . . little kicks, big kicks, slow, fast."

Pretending

Toddlers like to play with familiar things, and at this age dogs and cats are favorite animals. The following large-muscle games offer great goofiness and easy success in a crawling position.

DOGGIE CHASE

Ask your child to crawl forward and backward on hands and knees, making barking sounds, while you give chase.

KITTY POUNCE

Have her crawl in a circle as fast as she can, then lunge down on to her tummy as if pouncing on a mouse!

Locomotion

Logroll. Logrolling lets your energetic one develop large-muscle control while moving from one place to another. Show him how to bend in at the elbow and roll over and over. He may need your help to get started; then you can chase each other, rolling over and over and humming "Puff the Magic Dragon."

Bubbles. We don't want to forget our special, silky-smooth companion, the parachute. If several helpers are around, have them billow it high while you hold hands and walk or run under it . . . crawl under it together and slink out . . . play hide 'n' seek and pop out . . . shake balloons on it till they bob and dart.

After these merry games, take a moment to cuddle and love your growing play partner, who is surely warmed up and ready to move out.

MOVING OUT

Partner Movements

TOMMY TIPPY

Value: This movement allows your toddler to move forward and backward in rhythm while keeping feet stationary, strengthening arm and leg muscles.

Here's How: Have your toddler stand on the floor in front of you. Sit down and gently place your feet on his. Holding his hands in yours, rock him back and forth to the rhyme, "Hickory, Dickory, Dock":

> *Hickory, Dickory, Dock.*
> *The mouse ran up the clock.*
> *The clock struck one,*
> *The mouse ran down.*
> *Hickory, Dickory, Dock.*

How Many: Rock for length of song; may be repeated daily.

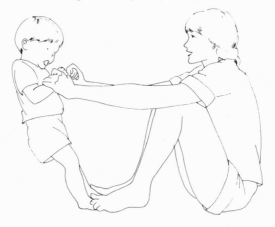

Assistive Movements

BOLSTER WALK-OFF

Value: This simple but intriguing movement strengthens arm, shoulder, back and tummy muscles, while preparing your toddler for a forward somersault on the bolster.

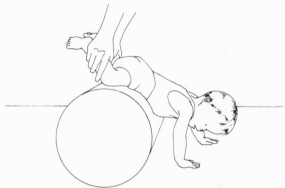

Here's How: Stand your child behind the bolster. Grasp his lower legs and begin to roll him forward onto the bolster. When his hands reach the ground, allow him to keep walking on his hands until he walks off the bolster and his feet flop onto the floor.

How Many: Two walk-offs; may be repeated daily.

HANDY DANDY HANDWALK

Value: How your tot is progressing! From the floor to a tabletop, from a wide ramp to the beam.

Here's How: Place the beam between two chairs. Position your dandy's hands on the beam, holding legs parallel to it. Using a noisy toy for encouragement, let her handwalk the full length of the beam. Say a cheerful, popular nursery rhyme as she walks.

How Many: One handwalk across the beam; may be repeated daily.

ENGINEER WALK #1

Value: Almost every toddler is curious about trains. The next walk—on a piece of equipment we call a railroad track—helps your engineer develop balance, spatial awareness and eye-foot coordination.

Here's How: Place the railroad track on the floor and have your toddler stand at one end while you support him under the arms. A favorite toy held by Dad at the other end of the line will give him incentive to walk the full length of the raised track, then return to starting position.

How Many: One or two trips a day.

LITTLE BIRD WALK #1

Value: The Little Bird Walk is named after Big Bird on "Sesame Street," who shows trust, persistence and the courage to try new things—just like your tot!

Here's How: Hold your "little bird" under the arms and encourage her to walk across the beam, saying, "How nicely your walking feet are moving across the beam! Listen to them go 'pat, pat, pat.' Let's go get the toy!"

How Many: Walk the length of the beam and return to start once daily.

I THINK I CAN

Value: Your thirteen-month-old may be stepping smoothly along the flat ladder now or she may be doing a somewhat comical, staggering walk. Praise her as she regains balance after each step and uses eyes and feet together.

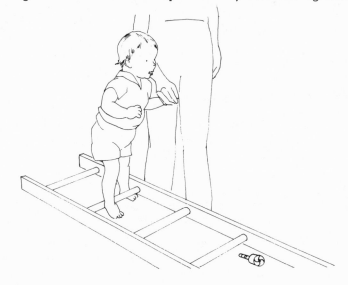

Here's How: Place the ladder flat on the floor. Starting your toddler at one end and giving one-handed assistance, walk to the other end for a toy. Have her tote it back with her free hand. Scoop her up at the finish for a roaring bear hug.

How Many: One complete walk; may be repeated daily.

FIREMAN'S LADDER CLIMB

Value: Your child will enjoy practicing the Fireman's Ladder Climb, learning not to be afraid of heights—just like a real fire fighter—as he develops balance, body control and strong arm muscles.

Here's How: Place the ladder against the back of a couch or a wall in a steeper position than baby is used to. Anchor it securely. As your fire fighter grabs hold of the rungs and puts weight on a rung with one foot, guide his free foot onto the next rung. He will climb to the top of the ladder with more confidence and ease than in the previous months and increase his skill level even more with continued practice.

How Many: One climb; may be repeated daily.

Active Movements

Whew! This has been a lively twenty to thirty minutes! Take a well-deserved break while your still-bustling thirteen-month-old does the next two movements more on her own.

WALKWAY THREE

Value: Going up the incline is still easier than going down, but your walker is learning to cope with gravity.

Here's How: Place pillows on each side to catch her if she tumbles and be watchful of her movements, especially the first few times, but encourage her to climb from the bottom to the top of the ramp on her own. Your outstretched arms at the bottom are great cheerleaders for the trip down.

How Many: One complete climb; may be repeated daily.

IN AND OUT

Value: If your assertive thirteen-month-old sees an opportunity to climb in and out of an obstacle, she will.

Here's How: Place a toy inside the box and coax your adventurer to climb in after it. Once she has played with the toy, encourage her to climb out after

another toy. Let her solve the problem of how to get out! Once she learns how to get in and out easily, experiment with different size boxes.

How Many: One crawl in and out. Leave the box(es) out so your explorer may crawl at her leisure in and out and also on top of box(es).

EXPLORING

Exploratory play is like a breath of fresh air for a child, a time for free movement and experimentation. You may playfully demonstrate to get the ball rolling, but, for the most part, just sit back and be a good listener and applauder. Offer your assertive tot a different activity each day while you play some festive music.

Super Stuff

Create *shakers* of all sizes. Plastic milk or juice bottles can be filled with dried beans. Large containers with handles are perfect to shake, roll, drop, throw and push. Your shaker may help decorate them, and she will have fine times dancing with them to a musical beat.

Foam pieces can usually be purchased from an upholsterer's shop for next to nothing. These are fantastic for stacking, lining in a row, plopping on, knocking down, throwing, pushing, dragging—the possibilities are endless! Be sure your toddler doesn't take any bites out of the foam, though.

Yarn balls are easily made from yarn scraps fashioned into loose, floppy balls or tight, small ones. You may have used these for massaging when your toddler was smaller; just make a few more—six or eight will suffice. These help your thirteen-month-old develop eye-hand coordination and large arm muscles.

Cloth diapers are almost obsolete in many homes, but these have many uses besides blanketing baby's bottom. Just the right size to promote manual dexterity, they can be folded, gathered, thrown, caught and worn as scarves or capes.

Silly Pool

Wading-pool activities continue to be a highlight of your toddler's day. Encourage company and chatter while he breaks long, *dry spaghetti* and dumps it into assorted containers. Whipped *soap flakes* are another highly satisfying medium. Add a dash of food coloring to transfix your toddler for some time.

Assorted *sticky textures*—stickers, cloth adhesives, plastic gauze strips and masking tape—interest and amuse your youngster. Ask him to place a sticker on certain body parts, both yours and his.

Your investigator enjoys nearly every kind of *fruit*. Start with a whole fruit, then peel and section or cut it up, showing him the skin, seeds and core. Let him have a feel, smell, taste and drink—just a small amount if it's a first-time taste. Introduce rarer fruits, too: persimmons, pomegranates, guavas.

ALL AROUND

Smelling and Tasting

When your toddler tries to smell, he usually blows out through his nostrils instead of inhaling—a funny, adorable sight. The conscious effort tells you that he is becoming aware of this important sensation.

Offer your toddler a variety of interesting, nutritious *snacks*, such as cheese, peas, green beans, fish-shaped crackers, melon balls and homemade fruit rolls. Have meals outside when the weather is nice. Take a lunch to the park, lake or beach and make it a happy, social time. *Share a taste and smell* of fun-time foods: frozen bananas, popcorn, ice cream, cotton candy.

Your toddler likes to feed himself because he feels independent. *Finger feeding* develops finger dexterity, too. Peeled apple wedges, raisins and ribs are good finger foods. Ribs are also good to exercise teeth and jaw muscles.

Call your explorer's attention to *smells* around him that are not related to food: burning leaves, car wash, fertilizer, garbage, damp cellar and so on. Talk about nice smells and unpleasant odors.

Seeing and Manipulating

Emptying drawers is a favorite pastime of toddlers at this age. Your monkey may also enjoy emptying ashtrays, dumping shoes out of boxes, taking small plastic sandwich bags out of a carton or spilling dry dog food out of a box. To prevent short tempers, give him a low drawer filled with odds 'n' ends that he may empty at his leisure.

Stacking toys graduated in size prepare your toddler to count and measure. Your zealous learner can practice eye-hand coordination and finger dexterity when you show him *how to thread* curtain rings onto a dowel or place large beads on a thin plastic straw.

Let your toddler discover how to unroll, curl and drape a *ribbon* around his shoulders. Give him the *cardboard* roll from inside toilet paper or paper towels to roll, drop objects through or jabber into.

Now that your child has learned to grasp objects rather well, she must learn to *release* them. Offer her objects of different weights and sizes to pick up and drop. A favorite practice place is the high chair, where she can watch feathers, small blocks, plastic and metal lids and balloons fall.

Hearing and Language

Good *listening skills* can help your toddler become more sensitive to the language spoken around him. Call his attention to noises, such as a car's engine starting, water sprinkling, windshield wipers, garage door opening. When Dad calls on the telephone, let your listener say hi.

Name everything your toddler touches. Her vocabulary will grow and grammar will improve without any special training.

When you and your companion read a book, *talk about the pictures*: "This is a kitty and it sleeps in a basket." Then ask questions: "Where is the kitty? Where does it sleep?"

Imitating and Language

Dr. Roger A. Webb writes, "Imitating people and reaching for things are more related than they seem. Both are major ways by which a toddler adds to his 'intellectual bag of tricks.' "

Give your toddler a wrapped object and show him how to *unwrap* it. Try using foil, tissue, flocking, scented stationery, wallpaper, newspaper and the like. Hide a small object in a zippered makeup bag and let him *open and close* the zipper. Let him open and close an empty matchbox.

Your toddler loves to imitate kitchen actions as you prepare a meal. Give her a saucepan with water and a wooden spoon. Let her roll and flatten a little pastry dough with a rolling pin, don't forget to name her actions and the utensils and thank her for being such a good helper. Your pal may offer you a piece of her concoction. While she watches, *chew and swallow* it so she learns how people eat.

Self-Awareness

Play games that involve your child's eyes, nose, mouth, ears, hands, feet and toes to help him picture himself in his mind. Let him compare his *body parts* with those of a pet. Encourage him to touch his and your facial features as you say:

> *Little eyes see pretty things*
> *Little nose smells something good*
> *Little ears hear someone sing*
> *Little mouth tastes luscious food.*

Show your mimic how to wink and watch his amusing attempts. *Open and close your mouth*, making a smacking sound. He will giggle at the sound and try to do the same. Place *funny hats* on your toddler and let him see himself in a mirror. Put some old hats on your head and make silly faces. Your mimic will delight in imitating your movements.

Problem Solving

Caplan states that the most important skill a child can acquire is learning how to learn. Adults too often give children answers to recite rather than problems to solve. Let your toddler tackle these problem-solving situations.

Ask your thirteen-month-old to *retrieve a toy* from under the couch. After he tries, unsuccessfully, to reach it with his hands, give him a tool—such as a wooden spoon—to use. Try again the next day and see if your toddler looks for the spoon or finds another tool. Praise him for this good "thinking."

Place a toy on a flat surface where your explorer can *reach* for it. While she's looking, put your hand between the toy and your tot. See if she pushes your hand out of the way to find the toy. (One parent told us that her daughter went after a cookie, but ignored the toy!)

Give your toddler *locks* and latches to explore. Explain the more complex ones. Give him an assortment of *containers with lids* unattached. Let him learn to press, snap and screw on the different tops.

Add a *third cloth* when hiding the toy under the cloths. Switch the materials in random order and see how often she goes to the right cloth. Praise her good tries.

Body Positioning

Your toddler's world is full of movement; help her *express the movements* descriptively. How much more alive is waking up "slowly," "quietly"; yawning "lazily," "heavily"; kissing "tenderly," "playfully"; running "gleefully," "recklessly"; stepping "uncertainly," "impatiently." Think about labeling these movements for your inquisitive learner.

Allow your toddler to *walk barefoot over smooth pebbles* and sand, which will develop her arches. Encourage her to tackle *low obstacles*: wooden logs or driftwood, shoes, pillows, and the like. By learning to adjust her body position, she will develop eye-foot coordination. Talk about walking "slowly, gingerly."

Now is the time to encourage your tot to step down from a low step to a sidewalk. He may ask to hold your hand at first, but soon he'll step out confidently.

Do *bottom spins* with your goer. Sit on the floor and propel your bodies by sidestepping and balancing with your hands as you pivot around on your bottoms. Cheer him on, saying, "Round and round I go. Where I stop, nobody knows!"

Give your toddler a heavier, more advanced *pull toy*. She will learn to walk and glance back and to maneuver around corners. Don't forget your toddler's *old playmates*: big ball, big dish, big dipper, barrel of fun, Teeter-Totter and cuddles materials. Your child's growing intellect will spark new ways to play with the old equipment. Other fun pastimes are *climbing and sliding*. Allow your monkey to climb stairs any which way; and just wait till he discovers all the fun ways to climb up and slide down the ramp!

Socializing

What a social bug your toddler is! He likes to be with other little people in familiar surroundings, where they take toys away from each other, show affection, imitate each other and communicate through body language. He may even play "drop the napkin" with a dinner guest, then carry toys to that person to display friendship.

Show your thirteen-month-old how to "throw" a *farewell kiss* to Grandma and Grandpa or to big sister as she goes off to school. Your toddler likes the game of *throwing* stuffed animals and toys out of the crib for someone to retrieve, too.

Your tot may be enthusiastic about *animals*, especially if you own a friendly pet. Be sure to supervise your child's eagerness, because he may innocently think it's fun to pull an animal's hair, poke its eyes, pull its tail and try to climb on its back for a ride.

Your social bug likes to *imitate* your cough, laughter, nose-blowing and telephone talking—anything for attention! She *returns toys* to the giver now as a social game. Hide one behind you and see if she looks for it.

Your thirteen-month-old is beginning to consider you a kind resource who gets books from a shelf, reads to him, pushes the swing in the playground, holds his hand while he walks, pushes him in the stroller and just plain gives tender loving care.

Chapter 12

THE SHOW-OFF
*Fourteen and Fifteen
Months*

HOW DO YOU DO?

Living with a fourteen- or fifteen-month-old is exciting, but exhausting! Your toddler discovers something every moment, and she loves a range of activity, from interacting and playing with you to showing her independence.

With a surge of walking power comes a new image of herself as a "big person." Suddenly you can't find hairbrushes, a shower cap or slippers. Guess who has them—your toddler, who wants a piece of the adult world.

With her fantastically improved walking and climbing abilities, you may find her standing on countertops, tables or your dresser. She wants you to find her hiding behind drapes and chairs, under the bed or inside the closet or pantry. She may slip away without warning, now that she can turn the doorknob.

Toddlers this age are famous for emptying trash cans and ashtrays and for shredding favorite magazines. They are fascinated with mechanisms: stereo knobs, TV tuners, radios, electric toothbrushes. Your child's intense curiosity and boundless energy may cause you a few headaches, but let her know that you approve of her desire to learn about her new, walking world.

Understandably, your fourteen- or fifteen-month-old needs constant supervision, but you *can* teach her that some objects are not playthings. Instead of saying no to a forbidden item, allow her to touch and hold it while you watch. When she begins to lose interest, redirect her attention elsewhere. This method often satisfies a child's curiosity while eliminating the repetitive use of "no."

Your "so big" youngster can take off shoes, socks and other items of clothing by herself, so buy outfits with big buttons, large zippers, wide armholes and sleeves and oversize collars. Purchase simple rugged clothing and allow her to get dirty and wear them out with her explorations.

Your toddler is also more and more alert to conversations and uses jargon and gestures to get a point across. She can repeat words, put sounds together and amuse herself with vocal play. She can point to and name familiar persons and objects, and enjoys jabbering about the view from the stroller. When *you* stop to chat with someone, though, she will be gone before you know it! What a little dickens she is.

Your tot is learning that she has social power—power to affect people. She practices different techniques, too: she may pull your hair to see your reaction. She may discover that hitting upsets you but makes Daddy laugh; that if she cries, Grandma will rescue her but Dad won't. Your social bug is always ready to show off, so try not to restrain her good nature and skills. Channel them into play!

SUPPLIES

> wedge—crib mattress leaned against stack of pillows
> parachute
> dowel
> railroad track
> ramp
> big ladder
> tires—three
> super stuff—tubes and balls, small brooms and large balls, ribbons, net balls
> silly pool—cooked rice, yarn or string, gelatin

GETTING READY

Watching your fourteen- or fifteen-month-old's zesty explorations is very exciting. Playing learning games arouses your tot's interest in unstructured play and deepens affection between you.

Loosening Up

SPINNING TOP

> *I am a spinning top* [Stand up and spin.]
> *I whirl and whirl until I stop.*
> *I am blue and green*
> *And make this sound:* [Make sound and fall down]
> *"Wheeee," until I fall onto the ground.*

Body Awareness

Your scamp now recognizes the names of major body parts and may point to them when named. These two games emphasize that knowledge, though it may take many repetitions before she can follow you all the way through.

Rocky Robot Says: "Let's play . . ."

SNEEZE GAME

> *Touch your eyes that let you see,*
> *Touch your nose that makes you sneeze.*
> *Touch your ears that let you hear,*
> *Touch your lips and kiss me here.*

Finger Play

While your toddler is nestled in your lap, play this game slowly, helping him form the hand positions.

> *Here is a boat for* [child's name], [Cup both hands.]
> *Here is a house for him, too.* [Fingertips together for roof.]
> *Here is a ball for him to play with,* [Fingers and thumbs make a circle.]
> *And here is a kiss for him, too.*

Rhythms

Winnie Wedo wants your tot to respond to the magic of music while developing coordination, improving posture and expanding language skills. Play one game until your child knows it, then begin the other one. His smiles tell you, "This is fun!"

Winnie Wedo Says: "Let's do . . ."

> *Down and up*
> *Down and up*
> *Nod your head and turn around.*
> *Down and up*
> *Down and up*
> *Nod your head and lie down.*

ONE, TWO, THREE

One, two, three,
Clap with me,
Clap, clap, clap
One, two, three,
Roll with me,
Roll, roll, roll
One, two, three,
Shake with me,
Shake, shake, shake.

Pretending

Your fourteen- or fifteen-month-old uses his *entire* body to investigate his world.

Monkey Walk. You and your monkey squat on the floor on your hands and feet and walk forward on them. The challenge (and silliness!) of a chase-me game makes your rascal move faster and builds stamina.

Scooting. Both of you sit on the floor with your hands behind you and your knees bent. Push off with your feet and scoot your body back between your hands. Continue, while your little mimic follows you. (She may have a different style of scooting, but that's okay.) Try scooting forward, too, and sing, "Michael, Row the Boat Ashore."

Locomotion

Mountain Rolling. Even though your tot does not yet know left from right and is too young to learn, we encourage you to do activities in both directions. This movement helps your toddler get a good start on learning laterality—the awareness that her body has two distinct sides.

Using the wedge or a slope in your backyard or park, have your toddler stretch out and roll down the hill. Make sure you have her roll facing in each direction. Roll down after her, saying, "I'm going to get you," and give her lots of affectionate squeezes and strokes.

Woggling. What's this? A combination of walking and jogging, and one of the exercises your roustabout can do best. Since this makes good use of large arm and leg muscles and is an excellent cardiovascular exercise, join your child for a stimulating session! While outside, play a game of "chase" and ask your toddler to run after you until he catches you. Then you chase him.

Bubbles. Last but not least on the warm-up roster is parachute play. Play Hide and Seek and show your pal how to pop out on her hands and knees shouting, "Boo!" Bring out two or three inflated balloons and make them float, bob and dart. Then wrap up your tot, cuddle a minute, and tell her it's time to play with the dowel.

MOVING OUT

One reminder before we go on: for reasons of progression of difficulty or more independent movement, some exercises will be repeated from here on out. Less physical assistance, however, does not mean less participation on your part. As your youngster masters the skills, she needs your support, encouragement and companionship.

DOWEL HANG

Value: Your monkey likes to feel weightlessness, and this movement also strengthens hand, arm and torso muscles. If he lifts his legs while hanging, your toddler will also strengthen thigh and abdominal muscles.

Here's How: Stand facing each other. Hold onto the dowel, placing your hands over your toddler's to prevent his grip from slipping. Lift him about four inches off the floor. Let him hang for a count of eight, then return him to the floor. Once he learns to hold the dowel on his own, eliminate your hand support.

How Many: Two lifts in succession; may be repeated daily.

ROWING

Value: Stretching, tugging and pulling strengthen your youngster's arm, back and leg muscles, preparing her, perhaps, to row a boat at sea someday.

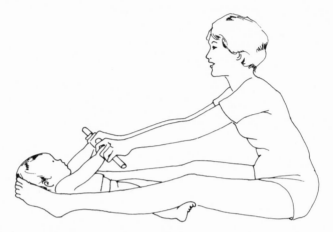

Here's How: Tell your little skipper, "Let's play boats," as you sit down facing each other. Spread her knees slightly and place your legs over them. Grasp the dowel together and begin to pull back and forth. Lean forward until her back touches the floor, and let her do the same. Sing this rhyme to add salt-air enjoyment to your rowing:

> *Two little boats are on the sea,*
> *All is calm as calm can be.*
> *Gently the wind begins to blow,*
> *Two little boats rock to and fro.*

How Many: Row slowly until nursery rhyme is over; may be repeated daily.

Assistive Movements

BACKWARD SHOULDER ROLL

Value: Set a circus mood for the next two movements with lively background music and tell your toddler to step into the center ring to perform! He will develop flexibility and body control.

Here's How: Have your acrobat lie on his back while you kneel by his feet. Place both hands on his upper thighs and lift upward, carrying his legs all the way over as he rolls on his back, until he lands on his hands and knees. Ta-da!

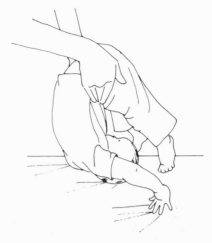

(Applause!) As you are rolling him over, make sure that he turns his head to the side to protect his neck.

How Many: One roll; may be repeated daily.

FORWARD SOMERSAULT

Value: There is nothing more adorable than watching your growing wonder try a forward somersault. She will strengthen back and abdominal muscles.

Here's How: Ask your little clown to scamper to the top of the wedge. Kneel behind and help her squat on hands and knees. Get her to put her head down by asking her to look at her tummy or belly button, then gently move her head toward her chest, hold her hips and lift her up slightly as you turn her over. Her back should be rounded and her chin as close to her chest as possible. Remember, it may take months before your child can complete a forward somersault by herself on the floor. *Any* effort she makes now is terrific!

How Many: One or two somersaults; may be repeated daily.

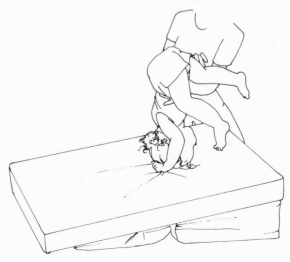

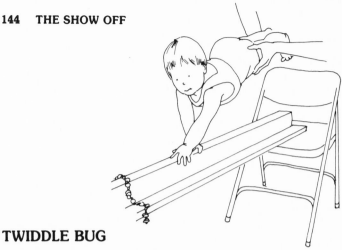

TWIDDLE BUG

Value: Toddlers are fascinated by bugs: caterpillars that roll up when touched, crickets that jump across narrow twigs and moths that flutter about in the air. With this movement—your toddler refines his arm strength, body control, eye-hand coordination and spatial awareness.

Here's How: Place the railroad track between two chairs with a favorite toy at one end. Cuddle your toddler and have him place his hands on the track. Continue to hold onto his thighs and knees so that they are parallel to the track and encourage him to walk along the rail to get the toy. What a love bug he is!

How Many: One walk; may be repeated daily.

ENGINEER WALK #2

Value: Your confident engineer may keep his eyes on the wiggly prize at the end of the track as he toots along with one-handed assistance.

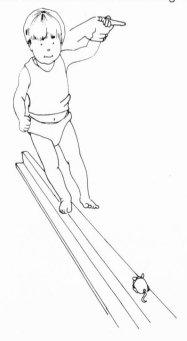

Here's How: With the track on the floor, stand your walker on the raised portion and place an enticing toy at the other end. Holding one hand, give him the signal to go, "Toot, toot!" as he walks along the track.

How Many: One walk; may be repeated daily.

Active Movements

Time out to swish and swirl your superstar around the room. He's been playing and concentrating so nicely that a little snuggle time is well deserved! When you've caught your breath, begin again with . . .

SQUARE WALK

Value: Watch the concentration on your walker's face as she works to walk over the big ladder rungs into the square spaces.

Here's How: Stand your toddler at one end of the ladder and encourage her to step *over* the rungs and *into* the squares. Be prepared to help her if she loses her balance or confidence. When she finishes, hug her for completing a difficult task.

How Many: Walk length of ladder once; may be repeated daily.

CHIMP CLIMB

Value: This movement develops arm and leg strength and body and space awareness for chimplike tree-climbing.

Here's How: Place your toddler at the bottom of the ramp (or a small slide at the park). Tell her to be a chimp and climb up using hands and feet. Your monkey will climb up, turn around and slide down. Catch her on the way down!

How Many: One or two climbs; may be repeated daily.

DOUGHNUT HOLES

Value: Learning to manage his body is a big part of your toddler's daily lifestyle. Walking, crawling and climbing through tires develop agility, body control and space and body awareness.

Here's How: Turn on pleasant background music, such as "Mary Poppins," and place three tires in a zigzag pattern. See if your explorer will step or climb in when you ask, "Please show me what good stepping legs you have. Step into the tires," or "Please sit down in the tire."

Next, place a tire upright, throw a ball through it and ask him to crawl through the hole to retrieve it. What a clever crawler!

How Many: Give three or four verbal requests each time you bring out the tires.

EXPLORING

Time to hang loose and have fun watching your toddler show off with new mediums. Your child will explore at his own pace, stimulating senses and developing creativity and imagination. You can learn a lot about your little magician by observing this play.

Super Stuff

Collect a variety of *tubes*—orange juice or other plastic cans without lids, paper-towel rolls or photocopy machine tubes—and small balls, such as Ping-Pong balls. Watch your imaginative tot push the balls through the tubes with a tool, drop them through and stack them inside. The tubes themselves can be rolled down the ramp, tapped on tabletops, tooted through, peeked through and blown along the floor. Just for fun, keep a record of the different ways your child uses the tubes and balls over a two-month period. We think you'll be amazed!

Hitting a beach or sponge ball *with a small broom* is great fun! Your child develops eye-hand coordination as she sweeps the ball around the floor or into a confined area—through a Hula-Hoop, into a box, through a tunnel. She is learning how to manage an object in play.

Turn on some nice dancing music, then offer your show-off different sizes and styles of *ribbon*: some that curl up when you pull and let them go, wide ones that can be split in half, brightly colored and shiny ones to twirl with.

Make attractive, interesting *net balls*. Cut out 6-inch circles of small mesh nylon fabric. Stack circles and gather together across the middle with a strong yarn and puff material out. They are safe to use inside the house and your toddler enjoys playing with them because they don't hurt when they hit him. Net balls are also great because they are easy to store and can be used frequently over the next six or seven years.

Silly Pool

As your curious one probes the following media, talk about what she is doing, how it feels, the texture, color, odor, sound and taste.

Cook some rice, cool it and place it in the wading pool or tub. Cups, spoons and other household items make this texture fun to explore, and food coloring adds color interest.

Expose your child to the vast variety of *yarns and strings*: different weights, colors, strengths and lengths. Show him how to pull apart the fibers, wiggle them, roll them around a tube and even paste them on paper. This activity requires your supervision.

What's this? *Gelatin?* Yes, it's the *best* fun! Your fourteen- or fifteen-month-old can squeeze it through her fingers, poke holes in it, jiggle it, smear it on herself and lick it off her fingers. This is a perfect outdoor medium on a warm day, when you can wash down your scientist with the hose. Where's the camera?

ALL AROUND

Your enthusiasm makes these sensorimotor experiences mentally and physically invigorating for your tot.

Smelling and Tasting

Smelling different odors helps your toddler learn to distinguish many substances and situations and can strengthen love through pleasant smell associations. Your little scamp tells you with smacking sounds, smiles, wiggles and jibberish when she smells her favorite food. She also grows excited when you near the beach, since she can smell the salt air, or the mountains, where she can smell the unique crispness of snow.

Stimulating the sense of taste also can be a happy game as you let your child taste a new food from a spoon. Take your time, and let her experience the texture with her tongue. Your encouraging look will go a long way to bolster her sense of adventure.

After you bathe your toddler, pat some sweet-smelling *lotion* on her body and gently massage her. Put some on her hand and tell her to rub your arm with it. Talk about its pretty smell.

Introduce your toddler to those wonderful *cooking* and *baking* ingredients, such as vanilla, nutmeg, cinnamon and allspice. Let him smell onions, garlic, celery salt—whatever you cook with.

We've suggested before that you take time to smell the flowers. Now we literally mean for you to give your toddler *flowers to smell*: sweet peas, orange blossoms, roses, geraniums and the like. Talk about their shapes, colors and sizes. Pick some, and let him help you arrange them in a vase. Some plants also have interesting odors—strawberry plants, eucalyptus and so on. Watch to see that your child *doesn't eat* the flowers or leaves, though.

Try adding sour-cream *dip and raw vegetables* to the repertoire of snacks for your fourteen- or fifteen-month-old. Cucumbers, tomatoes, green onions, cauliflower and radishes have distinct tastes, smells and textures.

Seeing and Manipulating

Your toddler loves to finger his environment. Set up special "touchable" areas in your home to eliminate some "no's" from your vocabulary and let him feel worthwhile learning about his world.

Now that your toddler can *release* an object, ask her to roll a Ping-Pong ball down an incline. She will learn to place it on top and release it so that it rolls down.

Your child can learn about the concepts of *pulling apart and putting together* if you give her large toy pop beads to play with. She may not be able to put them together by herself for some time, though.

Give your tot an assortment of *small and large items* to put inside a small-necked bottle. He will learn that some objects, such as Ping-Pong balls, are too large to fit into the bottle, while small cereal bits are just right.

Give your toddler *push toys*. While he maneuvers them along the floor, he is practicing total body coordination.

Cut out pictures of familiar objects, then show your youngster two *real objects and their corresponding pictures* and name the objects. Lay everything in front of him and ask him to "put the balls together, put the books together" and so on. Use everyday objects, such as a cup, a ball, a toothbrush, a banana, an apple and a cracker, and choose pictures that are very clear. Give him your assistance if he needs it, and if he doesn't understand the game, come back to it another day.

Show your tot how to *insert and pull out* a cork while you hold the bottle. Give her a large *button* and a coat with large buttonholes. Show her how to button by grasping the edge of the coat with one hand and pushing the button through the hole with the other. Before you know it, she'll be buttoning and unbuttoning her own clothing. A *pegboard* with large pegs also stretches your industrious one's eye-hand coordination and space awareness.

The ability to distinguish geometric forms leads directly to the development of thinking skills for reading, writing and arithmetic. The *postal station* toy has three forms children usually learn first: the circle, square and triangle. Isn't it exciting that your child is ready for this? Praise him for correct matches, and help only if needed. A very simple *jigsaw puzzle* (only three or four pieces) also utilizes eye-hand coordination and space awareness.

Show your toddler how to screw and unscrew large plastic *nuts and bolts*. At first she may only be able to turn them one way, but eventually she will be adept at putting together and taking apart large metal ones.

Continue to use the *supermarket* as an environment for additional stimuli. Buy a box of crackers and let your child sample one. Tell him it is "salty." Give him an apple and ask him to put it in the bag. Tell him the color of the apple and its shape. Let him touch frozen boxes and tell him what is inside while showing the picture on the label. Give him something light, like a bag of potato chips, and heavy, like a pound of spaghetti. Let him touch the softness of a loaf of bread and the hardness of a can. With patience you'll get home with everything on your list—and no extras due to his improved reach!

Hearing and Language

The more your toddler hears, the fuller his vocabulary will be when he starts to construct phrases and sentences.

Give your fourteen- or fifteen-month-old new *rhythm instruments*, such as sticks, a triangle, bells, a music box or a stuffed musical animal. When teaching *jingles and songs*, add special movements using your hands, fingers, arms and other body parts. *Encourage babbling* by imitating your little squirt. Laugh with him so he thinks it is funny. Say "Goo," and see if he imitates *you!*

Talk to your companion while you are doing everyday chores, while outdoors or while watching interesting situations: a boy washing his dog, road workers digging, telephone repairmen on ladders and so on.

Imitating, Imagining and Language

Help your tot learn to imitate his environment by letting him observe the movements of animals, machines and people. You are preparing your child for what Dr. Koch calls task games, where he acts to express a role, like playing doctor. Acting out a task will begin during the third year.

Also allow your bright one to stretch his imagination by giving him various household items during playtime: little broom, rag, dustpan, plastic cup and saucer. His capabilities will surprise and delight you.

Show your toddler how to *imitate pictures* in a magazine, such as that of a person yawning. Ask, "Can you do that?" If not, demonstrate and see if he imitates you.

When you *dust*, give your little shadow a diaper or cloth and ask him to help you. He will happily imitate your chores.

Give your budding writer one color crayon and large sheets of paper for scribbling, which utilizes arm movements. Someday she will be able to focus her muscle movements onto smaller pieces of paper. Learning how to *handle a shovel* and how to pour sand or dirt from the shovel into a bucket or truck is another delightful eye-hand coordination experience.

Let your little friend pretend to *feed a stuffed animal*. Demonstrate how a teddy bear jumps, waves bye-bye with its paws, hides behind a box and blows a kiss. Ask him what teddy is doing, and see if he repeats some of these activities. When you see *live animals*, talk about them and imitate their movements. Later, ask your tot about how birds fly. See if he waves his arms and hug and kiss him for his good memory.

Tell your toddler to *"drive Daddy's car."* He will move his arms from left to right, pretending he is turning the steering wheel. Add sound to his movements and see if he follows you around the room while you both drive pretend cars.

Self-Awareness

Play *Who's this, Who's that?* in front of a mirror. Ask your tot, "Who's that?" when she sees her reflection in the mirror. If she does not answer, say her name. Then ask, "Who is this?" and point to yourself. See if she will say Mama or Dada and kiss her for the effort.

Problem Solving

Your fourteen- or fifteen-month-old is ready to solve easy problems. Let him try alone first. Then, if he comes to you for help, let him watch you complete the task. Smile and share the answer with him.

While your toddler is seated at his table, show him a favorite toy. Tie a string to it and lower it over the side or place it out of reach on the tabletop. Stretch the string near his hand and ask him to retrieve the toy. If he does not *pull the string*, show him how to do it. Repeat this several times, slowly, until he understands.

Catching small, floating objects in the bathtub or at the sink is a great sport and develops eye-hand coordination, as well. Use a small strainer or goldfish net.

Cover a toy with *three overlapping cloths* placed in such a way that your detective cannot take them off all at once. Watch as he takes off the top cloth and finds another one, and see if he works until he finds the toy. Pick up a small toy while your curious one watches, then put your hand under a white handkerchief.

Leave the toy under the handkerchief, pull out your hand and show him your closed fist. If he does not pry open your hand, open it yourself and show him that the toy is gone. See if he looks under the handkerchief.

Ask your space expert to insert a small hair roller into a larger one. See if he can also push a small wad of paper through a roller.

Body Positioning

Every toddler should exercise muscles daily to improve posture. These activities teach your little one to correctly push, pull, lift and carry objects.

Tie a rope to a cardboard box so that your little shopper can *pull the box* behind her.

Now is the time to purchase or make an indoor *climbing gym* that has steps, a platform with a single railing, a small slide or slant board with rungs and perhaps a tunnel. Your adventurer will enjoy it for years.

Give your live wire a toy that he can *ride and propel himself* that is specially designed for this age level. He will improve balance and strengthen large muscles while tearing around the kitchen floor, making loud car noises or riding down gentle grassy slopes.

Place toys of different weights and sizes in front of your tot and ask him to *lift* them. If he needs help, offer a hand for support. He is learning to control his balance.

Socializing

Your clever child is learning to move in response to oral requests. As you play, create your own solicitations: "Come give Father a hug," "How big are you?" These become unique to your family.

When relatives or friends visit, show your toddler how to offer his hand and *shake Grandpa's hand*. Grandpa will be so proud of his talented, polite grandchild!

Teach your toddler to shake his hand and wag his finger to say, "*No-no!*" Show your mimic how to *applaud* after a fun activity. Our students like to clap after completing a game or song.

Nothing is more relaxing than seating your toddler in your lap to *share a book*. Not only will her vocabulary increase and her attentiveness deepen as you read, but you'll feel each other's warmth and tenderness. She will snuggle close and love it—and so will you!

Now that your toddler is more mobile and independent, he likes to *play side by side* with another peer. He'll not yet make any real efforts to interact, although he will enjoy being approached by and babbling to other children. Once a week take him to a park or play group where other children are present and let him enjoy the social atmosphere.

Chapter 13

THE IMITATOR
Sixteen and
Seventeen Months

HOW DO YOU DO?

Your sixteen- or seventeen-month-old is adorably alive. He loves to clown, laugh and dance, and he feels good about his accomplishments. His speed has increased to a trot, and everything around the house intrigues him: light switches, keys and locks, lipsticks, pens, telephones, wallets, tools. Nothing goes unnoticed. Make another safety check from floor to ceiling, since your energetic adventurer can now push chairs and climb onto countertops, tables, shelves and toilet seats to reach high cupboards. And let your toddler know that certain areas are *off limits*.

There is no resisting your sixteen- or seventeen-month-old, though, when he wants to roughhouse, play Hide 'n' Seek or chase. He unzips zippers, undresses, clops around in "big people's" shoes, carries a purseful of treasures, tries to comb his hair and brushes his teeth. His wonderful ability to mimic allows him to enjoy simple music games, finger plays and puppets. A children's television show may become a favorite. Encourage good listening habits, which lead to language development, and continue to label everything, using descriptive words.

Your child is still generally happiest in familiar surroundings and routines. He decides what to wear, what snack to eat and what toy to take to Grandma's. He can hurl a ball, climb up and down stairs, walk on a low board, take a few steps backward, walk sideways, push a cart and pull a small wagon. He likes to play with stiff books, pour water, play in a sandbox and fiddle with toys. Taking walks, touching, listening and sharing are lovely ways to spend time together, and you'll often be rewarded with some short sentences, such as "Mommy up," when he is tuckered out and wants to be carried.

Now is a wonderful, important stage for your toddler to express feelings of love, disappointment, anger and happiness in the company of young playmates. Your little one is learning how to give and take and how to cope better with frustrations and delays. He wants to do things by himself, but since he likes

Mom and Dad's approval, he sometimes accepts your help with a smile and a hug. Redirect him when necessary, and reward correct behavior with strokes, smiles and praise. Let's see what your little imitator can do!

SUPPLIES

> parachute
> big bolster
> box
> railroad track
> tires—three
> little ladder
> beam
> big ladder
> super stuff—liquid bubbles, bean bags, balls and (if available) a baseball pitchback (a tubular frame with nylon net that rebounds objects when thrown at it)
> silly pool—pudding, all-purpose flour, uncooked rice
> wedge
> flannel board

GETTING READY

Now is the perfect time to foster your imitator's talent for mimickry. Choose from the following games, and use your imagination and resources to vary the activities. Your scamp will sometimes demand the repetition of her favorite games, even though you have long since tired of them. Be patient and respect her desire to choose and her ability to remember sequences. Sharing her enthusiasm will lead to joyful interaction.

Loosening Up

I'm A Funny Little Puppet Clown. This charming game lets your sixteen- or seventeen-month-old touch, be silly and feel the difference between tight and floppy muscles.

I'm a funny, little, puppet clown, [Hold hands standing up.]
When my strings move up and down, [Move arms up and down together.]
First I'll stand up, [Drop hands and stand straight.]
Then I'll fall down,
I'm a funny, little, puppet clown.

—LOUISE SCOTT AND J. J. THOMPSON

Body Awareness

Your toddler loves to identify body parts and to discover what each can do. This is important; as he learns more about his body, he will be able to integrate all bodily sensations. Then he can relate with ease to his surroundings and judge distances, sizes and relative positions of objects.

I HAVE

I have two eyes to see with, [Touch both eyes with hands.]
I have two feet to run, [Run in place.]
I have two hands to wave with, [Wave both hands.]
And nose I have but one. [Touch nose.]
I have two ears to hear with, [Touch both ears with hands.]
And tongue to say good day. [Point to tongue.]
And two red cheeks for you to pinch, [You pinch his cheeks.]
And then I'll run away. [Run around room.]

Rocky Robot Says: Sit with your playmate and help her learn that her body has a top, bottom, front, back and two sides.

"Pat the top of your head."

"Where are your feet? Can you wiggle your toes? Your feet are on the bottom of your body."

"Mama rubs Tommy's back. Tommy put your back on the floor."

"I like the sides of your body. I'll tickle them."

Finger Play

Your child has progressed a long way in using his hands. Now is an appropriate time for him to work on individual finger strength, coordination and the simultaneous use of both hands. He may only get a few simple movements at first, but you can see the sparkle in his eyes as he watches your movements and listens to your voice.

OPEN, SHUT THEM

> *Open, shut them, open, shut them,*
> *Give a little clap.*
> *Open, shut them, open, shut them,*
> *Lay them in your lap.*

Rhythms

Essential for your toddler's eventual success at play and in the classroom is the ability to hear and follow directions in sequence. Help your mimic develop these abilities by playing repetitive, rhythmic games to singing, chanting or music.

Taxi Ride. Your child will happily play this body rhythm game. Sing and move your arms in appropriate motions:

> *The taxi on the street goes bump, bump, bump,*
> *Bump, bump, bump, bump, bump, bump.* [Bounce on bottom.]
> *The taxi on the street goes bump, bump, bump,*
> *All around the town.* [Move arms in large circular motion.]

Other verses might include:

> *The meter on the taxi goes flip, flip, flip.* [Bend wrist up and down.]
> *The doors on the taxi open and close.* [Arms swing out from chest.]
> *The windows on the taxi go up and down.* [Move body up and down.]

Winnie Wedo Says: Take turns leading a succession of body rhythms, varying the tempo and body positions to add to the gaiety.

"Clap your hands high; low; side to side."

"Pat your tummy, head, legs; softly or firmly; while standing, sitting or lying down."

"Walk at different speeds around the room."

Pretending

Laughter, tickling, cuddling and rolling with your look-alike teach her to love and trust you and prepare her for large-muscle-movement adventures.

Half Moon Swing. Play slow, swaying music or hum as you grasp her upper arm and upper leg on the same side. Swing her gently from side to side, facing you. Change sides, and sway her back and forth, saying, "Wheee," or "Tick-tock, tick-tock." Soothe any initial tenseness with easy motions and soft words of encouragement. Later, be brave and do it hanging upside down.

Locomotion

Choo-Choo Train. You have joyfully watched your child mature into a super-charger who can walk on two feet (bipedal). Choo-Choo Train involves bipedal posture and forward and backward motions.

THE TRAIN

> *Choo-choo train with wheels so round,* [Bring arms together to form a circle.]
> *Chug-chug forward, up and down,* [Move forward, bending up and down.]
> *Chug-chug backward, into town.* [Move backward.]
>
> *What a lot of noise it makes,*
> *What a lot of steam it takes,*
> *To make the train go round and round.* [Move in circles.]

Bubbles. Bringing out the parachute always brings smiles.

MUSHROOM

Round up a few friends or family members for this game. Have several people grab the parachute, billow it high and bring it down behind them as they sit down, tucking it under their bottoms. This will make a giant mushroom for your toddler to run around under, look at, wonder about, and punch at when it finally floats down.

FLYING

Next, have everyone grab the parachute, lift it high and, on the count of three, release it. As it falls to the floor, your playmate can watch it change shape, ripple, fly and fall.

MOVING OUT

Partner Movements

CYCLONE

Value: Grandpas, dads and big brothers have exhilarated toddlers for generations with this exciting movement, which strengthens chest, tummy, back and leg muscles.

Here's How: Ask your toddler to stand tall and tight like a soldier or stick. (Demonstrate, if necessary.) Grasp her upper tummy and chest area, lift her over your head, hold and spin with her, then lower her back to her feet. Try saying this rhyme, faster and faster:

> *Round and round the rugged rock*
> *The ragged rascal ran.*
> *How many r's are there in that?*
> *Now tell me if you can.*

How Many: Spin for duration of rhyme, or five or six turns. If toddler asks for more, be sure to stop before you (or she) become dizzy.

Assistive Movements

TUCK 'N' ROLL

Value: Your playmate is now ready to do a forward roll over the big bolster, combining the locomotor skills of pushing, transferring weight and rolling.

Here's How: Stand or kneel next to the end of the bolster. As your toddler lies across it, instruct her, "Put your hands down, tuck your head, push with your toes and over you go." You may also roll the bolster forward slightly for added momentum.

In the beginning you may need to help your gymnast go through the motions. Your touch and encouragement will make her feel more secure.

How Many: Two or three rolls.

BOX JUMP

Value: Your toddler's ability to become airborne is a direct extension of walking and requires strength, balance, coordination and agility. This movement can build a lifesaving trust. Every year, children are lost in fires because they are afraid to jump, even to their waiting parents. Practice this movement so your toddler will have the confidence to jump freely in an emergency.

Here's How: Make a great production of your toddler's jump off the box: have him climb onto it, stand or kneel in front of him, take both his hands in yours and count loudly, "One, two, three, JUMP!" Assist him onto a carpet, blanket or other soft surface. Your arms should be shoulder high to him, so that he lands with his own weight and balance. He will love it and will scramble up for another go.

How Many: Two or three jumps is a grand performance! May be repeated daily.

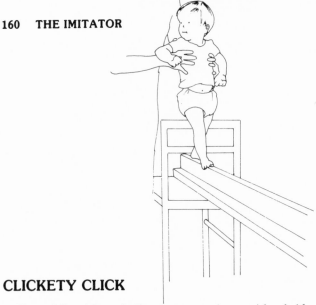

CLICKETY CLICK

Value: We wish to challenge your engineer with a bridge crossing by placing the railroad track between two chairs.

Here's How: Have your scrambler climb onto the chair by himself (mount), if possible, or lift him up. Walk beside him, assisting him under his arms as he toots along the track. If he doesn't voluntarily make train sounds, add a steady "clickety click" for interest. He may like to jump down (dismount) with your two-handed assistance, after receiving a scrumptious hug and praise for his safe crossing.

How Many: Two crossings; may be repeated daily.

CHARLEY HANDWALK

Value: Earlier, your brave engineer crossed the bridge on his feet; now, his arms, back and neck muscles get a workout. Sharpened ability to control body

and balance while consciously moving forward prepares him to read and compute in school.

Here's How: Have your agile one mount the chair, then instruct him to bend over and grasp the track while you lift his legs, holding them securely around the knees. A favorite stuffed toy at the other end will hasten his crossing as you recite a favorite rhyme.

How Many: Two crosses; may be repeated daily.

CIRCLE WALK

Value: Which of your toddler's favorite characters likes circles? Cookie Monster, of course! Here is a funny circle walk that stimulates body control, balance and eye-foot control.

Here's How: Place three tires flat on the floor, touching and slightly staggered. Offer your toddler one-finger assistance to step onto the tire wall. Help her walk all the way around one tire, then encourage her to walk in an S-pattern on the others. Singing a favorite song will add to the fun.

How Many: One walk; may be repeated daily.

NICE AS CAN BE

Value: Your little gymnast has been building up to this movement: a backward somersault. You will find that she can perform it "nice as can be," while learning about body control and flexibility.

Here's How: Seat your toddler up on top of the wedge, her head facing down the wedge. Smile and chat with her as you stand or kneel beside her, grasp her pelvic area and lift and roll her at the same time from her back to land her on hands and knees. If she is just beginning the program, go back to Chapter 12 and

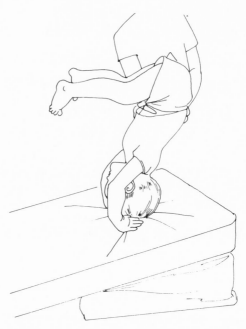

practice the Backward Shoulder Roll until she knows how to turn her head to the side. Exclaiming, "What a good tumbler you are!" will enhance your tot's feeling of accomplishment.

How Many: Two somersaults; may be repeated daily.

PPT (Parents' Pep Talk): How are you doing? Feeling a bit frazzled? Are you wondering, "How in the world am I supposed to do all these activities when I am so busy feeding, diapering, bathing, dressing, safeguarding and picking up after my toddler—not to mention handling a career and/or other children?"

Relax. You're right. You cannot possibly do every activity every day. Just do the best you can. The most important element to give your toddler is a variety of meaningful exchanges throughout your day together, whether bathing, dressing, picking up or playing. Frank Caplan writes,

> A toddler who lives in an environment charged with frequent, exuberant expressions of the good feelings of caring, laughter, and encouragement, as well as lots of face-to-face socializing with loved ones, is going to have far more than the average share of social initiative and get-up-and-go.

So turn on some quieting music and put your feet up. Let your toddler snuggle up; stroke her head and back, perhaps share a book, let her touch your facial features, kiss her nose and ears and let her kiss yours. You are doing a great job—her smiles tell you so.

Active Movements

FIREMAN'S LADDER CLIMB

Value: You may now proudly stand one step to the side of the ladder and watch your able firefighter maneuver on her own. She is feeling very competent, thanks to her good climbing arms and legs. Be alert for a possible misstep, but cheer her on with compliments and fire-fighter phrases.

Here's How: Slant the little ladder against the back of a couch or a wall and secure it. Usually your climber will reach up with one hand, then step up, putting both feet on the same rung before she moves the other hand. You may lift her down from the top, but it's preferable now that she climb up and onto something else or she can climb down by herself.

How Many: Two climbs; if a small indoor slide with a ladder (available in any toy store) is handy, leave it out so your adventurer can climb the ladder and sweep down the slide.

LITTLE BIRD WALK #2

Value: Let's see if your youngster will follow you across the beam, holding arms out to his sides, to develop posture control and self-confidence.

Here's How: Elevate the beam between two bricks or books. Mount the beam, walk to the other end and dismount, holding your arms out shoulder high. Smile

and call to your tot to follow you. You might sing one of your child's favorite "Sesame Street" songs.

How Many: Two walks; may be repeated daily.

WASHBOARD ROW

Value: For the most part, washboards are only seen in homes as antique decorations, but they can be terrific toddler entertainers—play boards to make music by running a stick or spoon over the rungs. This ladder walk may remind you of a washboard, because your trickster steps *on* the rungs.

Here's How: Lay the big ladder on the floor and call to your doer to walk on the "bumps." You may demonstrate the first few times so he sees as well as hears what you want him to do. Or, tap each rung as he approaches it and ask him to step on it. Even if he succeeds in stepping on only part of the rungs, that is wonderful progress. Praise him each time he steps successfully.

How Many: One ladder walk; may be repeated daily.

EXPLORING

Super Stuff

Free-movement time is a special time for you to relax, and watch your beautiful offspring experiment with the media: *bubbles, balls and bean bags*. He can shake, throw, blow and follow them and feel softness, fuzziness, furriness, lightness and heaviness. These observations are added to the reserve of knowledge on which he builds creativity.

Pop *liquid bubbles* with one finger, a whole hand, or both hands smacked together. Sit on, roll on, punch, twirl, blow, hold and watch them.

Balls of all sizes, weights and materials can be rolled back and forth, flung, thrown against a pitchback, bounced and dropped. *Bean bags* are also fun to carry, toss, stack, step over and on, throw over the shoulder and between the legs and drop into pans. Bean bags are simple to make, too. Use sturdy fabrics, filling them with dry beans or dry popcorn. One parent numbers her bean bags to teach her youngster her numbers. Another parent uses the primary colors for her fabrics. Still another weighs the beans before she fills the bags and uses different shapes and sizes to correspond to the different weights.

Silly Pool

Let your toddler help make some instant *pudding*, then let him play in it, smear it, smush it, squeeze it, slap and smack it! Licking it off each finger will take several yummy minutes.

All-purpose flour is another cool, soft medium, though very different from pudding. Use flour with plastic dishes, cups and funnels so your child can pack it, pat it, swiggle his hands in it, spread it out and trace patterns in it. Give him a mirror for added excitement.

Pour uncooked *rice* into bowls and watch the tiny pieces slip through fingers; dump it into tin cups and listen to it ping; and mix it with flour to see and feel what happens to the texture. Add it to play dough for a stickier, bumpier texture. Really soft dough, used with rice, looks entirely different when rolled out and stamped with cookie cutters. Your toddler may just be thinking, "Mom sure is good at finding fun things for me to explore. I like playing with Mom."

ALL AROUND

Though your sixteen- or seventeen-month-old toddler has many skills, his attention span is short and his tempo is slow. Try to maintain a relaxed, pleasant atmosphere so he can explore at his own pace.

Smelling and Tasting

Your happy-go-lucky companion likes to help *in the kitchen*—making cookies, adding marshmallows to fruit salad, dumping premixed spices in the casserole and taking a tiny sampling of everything! This sharpens his awareness of food textures, colors and odors and gives *you* great company!

Visiting friends and relatives is a smelling and tasting treat. Your tot may smell coffee, roast chicken, herb tea, a flower garden or a fish tank, or taste cinnamon or garlic for the first time. As she grows up, she will associate certain smells and tastes with loved ones.

A *workshop or hobby store* can be filled with interesting odors: wood, glue, oil, nails, metal, sawdust, plastic, fabrics, yarns. Daddy's or Mommy's *work place* is another world of sensory adventures.

Seeing and Manipulating

When you go out-of-doors, your toddler can carry precious "finds" in a *nature basket*: stones, seed pods, twigs, leaves, grass, flowers, pebbles and shells. Talk about and share what these feel like, where they come from and how they work.

Putting things inside other things—all shapes and sizes—is a favorite pursuit. A box with different *geometric shapes* is a real challenge and may require help. Also try using kitchen measuring cups for *nesting toys*.

Painting with *water colors* is a wonderful bath-time game. Wet a piece of paper and stick it to the side of the tub. Your toddler will discover how to blend colors and make marvelous things happen with the brush on the wet paper. *Finger painting* is another good bathtub activity.

A *sandbox and water* rate high in popularity with your tot. Sand and water, are fun to pour into containers and to dig in or splash in with utensils.

Hearing and Language

Looking at the family *photo album* together allows your toddler to recognize himself and to learn his name and those of other family members—siblings, pets, cousins. Pasting pictures into a *scrapbook* is another nice activity to share. Your toddler will be proud of his new achievement.

Musical instruments can demonstrate the difference between *high and low sounds*. Your toddler will delight in making noises on an instrument such as a piano.

Sing to your little one when you're driving and see if she picks out certain words, such as "Baa" in "Baa! Baa! Black Sheep." Your music buff can also recognize and insist on hearing certain *records* over and over. She often dances and claps her hands to these familiar tunes.

You may be surprised at how much *TV commercials* catch and hold your toddler's attention—especially those with children or animals. Encourage him with pats and smiles if you hear him repeating two or three words from a jingle. And join in!

Imitating, Imagining and Language

Show your toddler how to *set the table*—where to place the dish, glass, napkin and silverware at his place setting. See if he can repeat the names of each item and, perhaps, put his spoon in place.

Your little mechanic will be proud to help work on the family care with her own durable plastic *tools*. Watch her surprise Dad by handing him the screwdriver upon his request!

Show your mimic pictures of people in action, and see if he can imitate what they're doing. Richard Scarry's book, *Best Word Book Ever*, is an excellent source for this activity.

Doll play is recommended for both boys and girls. Dolls can be hugged, put night-night, fed, talked to, taken to the store, put in the bathtub, taken for walks—the duplicates of your child's activities.

Your assistant will come running when he hears you dragging out the *vacuum*. He likes to help turn it on and push it around.

Self-Awareness

Placing a *mirror near a play area* allows your playmate to watch himself build with blocks, nest cups or scribble. Now is also a good time to let him again observe his eating manners.

Your child may come to you tugging at her pants to let you know her diaper is wet. Respond with *"Are you wet?"* and promptly change her to reinforce her effort to communicate.

Place a box of facial tissues low enough for your toddler to reach; she will get a tissue and attempt to *blow her own nose*. She still needs your help, but her willingness to care for herself is wonderful!

Let your bather use *his own soap* in the tub. He can lather his hands and rub soap all over himself, but watch to see that he doesn't get any in his eyes.

Problem Solving

A flannel board is a pleasurable pastime for the present and in the future. It may be purchased in an educational aid store or may be made. To make one buy a piece of wood or use sturdy 18" X 24" cardboard and stretch flannel material over it. Glue or staple material. Start with animals made out of flannel and see if she can place the shapes on the board. This activity should be unstructured; simply let your partner mimic you or try things out on her own.

Place *toys in brown grocery or lunch-sized bags* and let your investigator have the fun of searching for and discovering them.

Toddlers seem to like to play with a *quantity of the same item*, such as a large can of spools, big buttons or jar lids. Jar rings used for canning make beautiful bracelets, too.

Body Positioning

Your toddler now likes to be more the *stroller pusher* than the rider. Lower the bar and let him push. *Piggy-back* is a good way to carry your youngster in a crowd or at a parade. Have him hop on your back with his legs spread around you, and grasp your hands under his bottom. He can see all the merriment around him and, when he is tired, he'll just lay his head against your shoulders. Swaying back and forth with your toddler in a *hammock* is another wonderful way to snuggle.

Making a *tunnel* with chairs and a big blanket is a super rainy-day activity. Your toddler may like to lug and tug at bed *pillows*, too, stacking them to fall on, jump on and walk on.

Stairs are a fascinating challenge for toddlers and a real concern for parents. In our opinion, at sixteen or seventeen months you can let your child satisfy his curiosity, under your supervision. A small flight of carpeted stairs is desirable to start, or just move your safety gate up two stairs. He will begin to climb them, holding the rail and leading with one foot. He may come down the same way or scramble down. Once he has made several successful trips up and down, let him manage on his own.

Big boxes used to pack washing machines, dryers or other large appliances are great to create a house for your toddler to walk and crawl through. Cut out some doors and windows and give your artist a paintbrush and poster paint or crayons to decorate.

If you have stashed away *old pieces of equipment* such as the big ball, Teeter-Totter, barrel of fun or big dipper, your imitator may spot them in a cupboard and ask for them. Rotate the pieces so she can continue the beneficial activities. Because of her progress, they will seem fresh and new.

Socializing

Toddler classes at preschools are becoming more popular. These provide nice opportunities for you and your toddler to explore new activities, make new friends and enjoy each other's company in different surroundings. Visit several facilities first to check their programs and find an environment suited to your toddler. Most classes have some activities for motor development, and you could help expand their program with input from this book.

If you have not already considered it, a *mommy-and-toddler swimming class* is a wonderful experience. Your little frog will most likely paddle with progress because he is so used to working with his body and with you. Knowing that he can handle himself should he fall into water certainly will make a summer more relaxing for *you*. And splashing in the water and watching other toddlers is such fun!

Playing outdoors near other children is a marvelous pastime. Now is also a time to begin teaching your toddler respect for the street. You may have to try many approaches, from spankings to removal to the house, before finding one that works with your child. Whatever your choice, be persistent.

Toddlerhood is a special time for all *family* members, particularly older siblings. Everyone loves to carry, play with and care for the youngest in the house. Toddlers adore older children and learn love and respect from them. Trips to the pizza house, campground or beach are special treats when big brother or sister comes, too. And, if there is no older sibling in your family, a sensitive teenage baby-sitter can often fill this place in your toddler's world.

Chapter 14

"DO IT MYSELF"
Eighteen and Nineteen Months

HOW DO YOU DO?

Your eighteen- or nineteen-month-old is a full-fledged toddler on the go. He is growing in many directions, with a very strong drive toward independence. The keen look in his eye lets you know he is always thinking, and his statement, "Do self," shows that he is striving to become self-reliant. His energy and determination often leave you breathless and exasperated, but his smile melts you, his giggles and antics lift your heart and love swells up inside you when you see him sleeping peacefully at the end of the day.

At this age, a toddler can be full of surprises. He may call himself by name, ask for favorite foods and use two-word sentences, such as "All gone," "Thank you," and "Oh, my!" though "no" is probably still the most-used word. His range of capabilities is astounding. Most children this age are very physical with expanding, but still limited, vocabularies. Others work quietly on fine motor skills; still others are little chatterboxes. *All* are lovable and amusing to watch.

Your eighteen- or nineteen-month-old may put away a toy at your request, much to your amazement. You will likewise be shocked the first morning you awaken to find him peering at you from beside the bed! He can help dress himself by holding out his arms for sweaters, lifting his legs for pants and retrieving his shoes to be laced. He may also be displaying a hand preference when using a spoon or a small glass.

Your toddler also likes to pretend and role-play; he sweeps with a small broom, fills a lunch pail for a picnic on the patio, and climbs into a big chair to "read" a magazine. Playing catch with a cloth diaper or large foam ball is a fun activity to do with Dad. And favorite playthings might include a drum; large beads to string; a low, sturdy tyke bike; a cuddly stuffed animal; boxes; a rocking horse; a sandbox; a climber or a doll.

An eighteen- or nineteen-month-old thoroughly enjoys adult attention and, therefore, becomes a terrific assistant. He may help unload grocery bags, put fruit into an open refrigerator bin, wash the car, dust and garden. Praise his efforts during these activities to elicit feelings of worth and accomplishment. The compliment, "Look how clean and pretty the car is because *you* helped clean it," makes your toddler feel like a million dollars.

A spirit of sunniness and kindness at home is important to stimulate your toddler's physical *and* mental growth. Your child will be successful most of the time if you keep calm, listen to him, place some limits on his freedom and remember to smile and reassure him during play. Older siblings need to understand this, too. No family can be cheerful and calm 100 percent of the time, but a family's steady encouragement will help your exuberant child better enjoy activities.

Keep your spirits high. You are doing a great job! Think about your toddler's needs. Be creative. And, if you haven't already done so, find a competent baby-sitter and treat yourself to some leisure time. You deserve it, and a free evening will allow you to return to your "do it myselfer" with renewed vigor.

Ready to play?

SUPPLIES

> parachute
> rings
> box
> beam
> railroad track
> chairs—two sturdy, high-backed wooden or metal chairs (dinette or card-table size are perfect) of equal size
> rope—4- to 6-foot strand
> big ladder
> ramp
> big bolster
> super stuff—feathers, streamers, Hula-Hoop, decorator beads
> silly pool—cooked spaghetti, cold objects, dry cereals

GETTING READY

Movement time is an exciting occasion for your eighteen- or nineteen-month-old. Your toddler likes to show off to an enthusiastic admirer.

You may wish to mix up your game routine just a little to capture his curiosity. His attention span is short, so keep the overall tempo lively. Your warmth and friendly enthusiasm will deter any balkiness.

Loosening Up

I'm a Funny Little Puppet Gay. Turn on some lively music, swoop up your little athlete, dance around the room and go right into this loosening-up game.

I'm a funny little puppet gay, [Stand up with tot.]
Move my strings and watch me play, [Move legs up and down.]
Now I'm stiff, [Stand like a stick.]
Now I'm tall, [Stretch arms overhead, stand on tiptoes.]
Let go of my strings and I will fall. [Collapse onto the floor.]

Body Awareness

Sticker Game. Most eighteen- or nineteen-month-old toddlers love to run nude, especially after a bath. Take advantage of this opportunity to play several body-awareness games with him.

Purchase some self-adhesive stickers such as happy faces and animals, or use a small piece of masking tape. Give one to your tot, and keep one. Show him how it sticks, then ask him to put it on his tummy and make his tummy go in and out; put it on his cheek and puff it in and out; or put it on his ankle and wiggle it about. Ask him to put it on your forehead, and let him watch you wrinkle it. Put yours on the tip of his finger or behind his knee and ask where it is. Let him experiment.

Rocky Robot Says: Continue to have your talented playmate touch different body parts to objects, allowing him to orient himself in space and to develop good listening skills.

"Show me how you touch your nose to the sofa."

"Put your elbow on the table."

"Walk your toes up the wall." (Lie on back and walk feet up a wood-paneled wall.)

Head, Shoulders, Knees and Toes. Sing the following song slowly, keeping in mind that your tot's body awareness matures from head to foot and midline outward. Remember, too, that he will do all the actions quickly only after many repetitions.

Stand and touch the parts as you sing:

Head, shoulders, knees and toes,
Knees and toes, knees and toes.
Head, shoulders, knees and toes,
Eyes, ears, mouth and nose.

Finger Play

These games develop finger dexterity and the ability to concentrate on and remember a sequence of movements, which are important for the everyday skills of handling eating utensils, dressing, stringing toy beads, painting and making cookies.

Finger Puppets. Crocheted or vinyl animal finger puppets will charm your toddler, since she can do a simple finger wiggle and imitate some animal noises. Or teach her this rhyme:

> *Put your finger in Kitty's hole.* [Clench hand, put finger through.]
> *Kitty's not at home.*
> *Kitty's out at the back door,*
> *A-picking at a bone.*

Rhythms

Your tot needs to develop an awareness of rhythm to move easily and gracefully and to cope with variables of space, time and force. Drs. Arnheim and Pestolesi write:

> The rhythmic child is able to move smoothly and with regularity equally well in small and in large spaces, can move fast or slow, can engage in short bouts or sustained movement patterns and is able to move lightly or heavily.

Winnie Wedo Says: Do these activities while sitting or lying on the floor. And invent some of your own!

"Bend feet up and down . . . pointing toes."

"Pound on the floor with open palms, loudly and softly."

"Kick feet while in a seated position, slowly and fast."

"Hug yourselves, twisting at the waist, and exclaim, 'Ooooo, I like myself!' "

Jogging. Have your toddler trot around obstacles while you beat out a rhythm on a drum or pan. Recruit big brother or sister for an even sillier time.

Pretending

We now wish to bring continuity of movement into focus. Your toddler must be able to move without abrupt interruptions while walking, running, climbing and jumping. Games using the large muscles inspire your wiggler to practice continuity. She will learn and apply the concepts of slow versus fast, rhythmic versus arhythmic, controlled versus uncontrolled, straight versus angular and angular versus zigzag, and abrupt stop versus follow-through.

Two Little Monkeys Jumping on the Bed. Stand up and hop in place, fast or slow, while singing this rhyme.

> *Two little monkeys jumping on the bed,*
> *One fell down and broke his head.*
> *The mama called the doctor, and the doctor said,*
> *No more monkeys jumping on the bed.*
>
> *One little monkey, etc.*

Helicopter. Here's one for Dad. Tell your child that he is going for a helicopter ride! Grasp him above the elbows, facing you, and spin him around and around like a blade or in a wavelike motion: starting, stopping, changing directions, making helicopter sounds of "shoooo" or "woooosh," circling smoothly about the room, then crash-land gently on the couch with lots of tickles and giggles.

Locomotion

Your tot, just like an adult, sometimes needs to play to use up energy, to become revitalized if tired, or to relax and enjoy social contact. He will find that these activities expand his energy—perfect for a relaxing change of pace. Because of your togetherness, tons of good feelings will flow, too!

Rolling Pin. Spread out the parachute. Both of you lie down and roll with arms overhead or tucked in to help push yourselves over. See if your roller can roll fast and slow, first to one side, then the other.

Fox. Creep facedown on tummy in a big circle, like a baby fox chasing its tail. Then your foxy little creature will be ready to venture out of his den for some developmental movements!

MOVING OUT

Partner Movements

PEDALING

Value: This traditional exercise develops strength in your toddler's upper-leg, lower-back and tummy muscles.

Here's How: Lie on the floor and place your toddler on her back, on your tummy, with your legs in the same direction. While humming "A Bicycle Built

for Two," lift your legs and rotate them in a circular motion, "pedaling." Encourage your tot to do the same. If necessary, get her started by grasping her upper legs and moving them in the circular motion. She may only kick her legs at first, but that's a start.

How Many: Eight rotations with each leg; may be repeated daily.

RING SWING

Value: Watching monkeys swing on rings will fascinate your monkey after she

does this movement, which strengthens arm, shoulder, chest and tummy muscles for future rope swinging.

Here's How: Have your tot stand on a chair near a mat or couch. Let her grasp a ring in each hand and swing her down onto the mat or couch. Make the distance short until you and your swinger feel confident.

How Many: Two or three swings.

Assistive Movements

ZIPPER

Value: If you haven't had the camera out for a while, bring it out while your little ham shows off in this sideways beam walk. Though she may already know her front and back, this walk helps her distinguish among her front, back and two sides.

Here's How: Elevate the beam slightly between two bricks or books. Have your tot mount it, turn and face you. Grasp her hand and begin sidestepping on the floor in front of her. She will mimic your feet movements and across the beam she'll go. Let her use her good jumping legs for the dismount.

How Many: Two sidestep crosses, leading first with one foot, then the other.

CLICKETY CLICK

Value: This movement calls upon your tot's body control, balance and eye-foot coordination and demonstrates how nicely his capabilities are progressing.

Here's How: Place the railroad track between two chairs, and have your engineer mount it. Offer him one hand or finger and hold it at his waist level, letting him balance on top of the track. Assist him from both sides of his body, alternating with each trip across, and sing "Piggy on the Railway" (making up your own tune).

> *Piggy on the railway, Picking up stones;*
> *Along came an engine, And broke poor Piggy's bones.*
> *"Oh!" said Piggy, "That's not fair."*
> *"Oh!" said the engine driver, "I don't care!"*

How Many: Complete walk back and forth; may be repeated daily.

BLAST OFF

Value: Each time your toddler completes this movement, proclaim her the "Winner!" She is combining running, balancing and jumping skills while maneuvering in a narrow space at a fast pace . . . terrific cardiovascular exercise and sports preparation.

Here's How: Stand with your sprinter at the bottom of the ramp, holding hands. Say, "Ready, set, go!" and run alongside her as she dashes up the ramp and jumps off the end onto a soft surface. She'll want to race again and again!

In the coming months, continue to cultivate your child's enthusiasm for climb-

ing and jumping, but don't let her try to jump from dangerous heights. Some children seem to have built-in good sense; others are a bit more daredevilish in nature. Give your child ample opportunity to jump, but direct her jumping eyes to heights that are safe for her.

How Many: Two jumps now, plus as many more as interest and time permit later in the day.

CHAIRS AND ROPE STEP-OVER

Value: This fun visual-motor game challenges your toddler to perceive lateral and horizontal space limitations while maintaining her balance—fancy talk for stepping over a rope strung between two chairs. The immediate muscle-movement feedback of knocking down the rope tells your child that she needs to step higher.

Here's How: Lay the rope across the legs of two chairs, about one inch off the ground. Allow your tot to check the setup, then show her how to step over the rope. After she has successfully stepped over the rope at this height, with your help, raise it a bit. If she should knock the rope down, simply say, "Oops, let's try again!"

How Many: Step over two or three times; may be repeated daily.

WEDGE WALK SOMERSAULT

Value: Once your scamp gets the hang of turning somersaults, you will find her attempting them in the craziest places.

Here's How: Have your tot follow this series of movements: walk up the

wedge, lie down on her tummy, extend her arms over the edge toward the floor, touch the floor, tuck her head and roll into a somersault. For at least the first few times, she will need your help to reach her hands to the floor and, perhaps, to push a little on her bottom or legs to get her rolling.

How Many: Two somersaults.

FLAPJACKS

Value: Pancakes or flapjacks are favorite foods because toddlers can watch you flip them in the pan. Your "do-it-myselfer" will relate to this movement when you tell her that she is going to flip just like a flapjack!

Here's How: Have your tot back up to the bolster until she bumps into it. Stand in front of her and, as she touches the bolster with her back, steady it and place your hands on her pelvic area, rolling her backward on the bolster slightly. As she starts to roll onto her back, tell her to reach over her head toward the floor with her arms. As her hands touch, she will automatically tuck her knees and over she'll flip, landing on her hands and knees.

How Many: Two flips.

Active Movements

Did you ever think there would be so many movements for your eighteen- or nineteen-month-old? Are you finding it hard to get her to follow your lead? Take a breather and let her do what she wants for a while. She may be more receptive to the next movements, which she can do on her own.

KNEE BENDS

Value: This movement is a takeoff on a toddler's ability to squat and stand up, which most do whenever picking up a toy.

Here's How: Have your tot stand beside you with his feet slightly apart and his hands on his hips. Bend your knees, then stand up straight, and let your mimic follow you. After some practice, he will be able to balance easily and keep his back nice and straight. Synchronize this song with the motions:

> *Have you ever seen a Tommy pop, a Tommy pop, a Tommy pop?*
> *Have you ever seen a Tommy, pop this way and that?*

How Many: Six or eight bends—good for parents' legs, too.

INSIDE OUT

Value: This motor activity stresses the concepts of under, between, through and around by having your eighteen- or nineteen-month-old weave in and out of structured spaces.

Here's How: Stand the big ladder on its side. Steady it with one hand, and encourage your toddler to crawl in and out of the spaces. Have him trail older brother or sister for more excitement. Crawling the length of the ladder is quite a feat. Sing this appropriate song:

Go in and out the window,
Go in and out the window,
Go in and out the window,
This bright and sunny day.

How Many: One weaving crawl daily.

RESCUE CLIMB

Value: By now your mountain climber can go up the big ladder and onto a surface with ease. Time for him to learn to come down, using his strong climbing arms and legs.

Here's How: Place the ladder at a fairly steep angle against a couch or wall and secure it. Call to your toddler to climb it, and once he reaches the top, tell him to turn around and come down. (Coming down face forward is easier for toddlers at this age, since they can see where they're going.) Reassure him, saying, "That's the way to do it, one foot at a time." It will take some time, remember, before he can come down the ladder as quickly as he can scamper up.

How Many: One climb, up and down; may be repeated daily.

EXPLORING

Nothing is more beautiful than watching an exuberant child discover something new. So switch on some favorite background music, and enjoy!

Super Stuff

Feathers are soft, fluffy, slender, smooth and colorful. They can tickle toes, chins, ears, necks, arms and knees. Small feathers may be thrown, blown and dropped to float silently to the ground. See if your tot can race a feather to the floor, twist with it and catch it. Her eyes shine as a fan, an air conditioner or a breeze catches her feather and dips and turns it.

Streamers may be long, short, stiff, curly, brightly colored, silky—a whole kaleidoscope. A three-foot strip of crepe paper makes a good streamer for an eighteen- or nineteen-month-old to shake, run with, twirl, hop with, lie down on and jump over. Tie streamers to tree limbs, too, and hold them up in the wind. What fun!

Your toddler may recognize the shape of a circle; now he may experience the shape by playing with a *Hula-Hoop*. Do you remember how to jump in and out of it, lift, drop, shake, push, pull and roll it? Play Tug-of-War, ball or bean-bag toss and horsey or walk through several in a row for an interesting tunnel. And we know that you are dying to twist with it, so go ahead!

Decorator beads are perhaps the most popular medium of all, except for liquid bubbles. Purchase strings of beads in hardware or department stores or through catalog shops. Cut them into manageable lengths—about three feet—and give your curious one several strands to drag, curl, wiggle, drop into containers, bunch in his hands, drape around his neck or arm, carry in a purse, and on and on and on! Their interesting sounds add to their mystique, and they have wonderful staying power: even five-year-olds enjoy them.

Silly Pool

Isn't it fun to watch your child's anticipation? She knows that something crazy is about to happen, and she is eager for adventure.

This is a relaxing time. There is no right, wrong, good, or bad way to explore in the silly pool. Encourage her to explore. Messiness is the rule. Watch and wonder what she is thinking.

Your explorer may be curious enough about *cooked spaghetti* to squeeze, pull, smash or wiggle it. She may also find it "yucky," in which case you can laugh together.

To expand her exploration of *cold objects*, use cold cans, refrigerated fruits and vegetables, crushed and block ice, frozen vegetable packages or ice cubes—plain, flavored, colored or frozen around "surprises" that appear when the cube melts. And this is the perfect place to put a toddler with a big ice cream cone!

Cereal sorting is a nice activity for a play group. Each parent may contribute a portion of a different kind of dry cereal to the pile. Toddlers may pick up pieces, smash them, sort them, stack them, scoop them, break them, drop them into containers, taste them and eat them.

Sawdust is another material for your tot to play in. And review past silly-pool

activities to reintroduce other materials. Your eighteen- or nineteen-month-old experimenter's refined skills bring new meaning to already-tested materials.

ALL AROUND

As your child grows, the list of experiences could become endless. Continue with puzzles, balls, sand and water play and include your child's favorites. Our suggestions should stimulate you to invent your own interesting and beneficial play happenings.

Now is also a good time to begin talking about purchasing toys. Since hundreds are available, choose wisely. Cost is an important consideration. To get the most for your money, follow these basic guidelines. The toy should be (1) durable, (2) versatile, (3) safe, (4) workable and (5) attractive. Organize your selections into categories: role-playing, building, arts and crafts, exploration and discovery, physical skills, and music and rhythms. Try to balance your choices with at least one from each group, and try to update your child's supply several times a year.

Smelling and Tasting

Eighteen- and nineteen-month-olds are really into eating, especially by themselves. They can handle a spoon pretty well and drink from a glass without help. Eating is time for socialization.

Show your toddler how to blow on hot food to cool it off. Or, on a hot day, your toddler will love to sit in her high chair to savor a homemade juice popsicle. Not only is it a delicious treat, but it develops her finger dexterity and eye-hand coordination.

Get into a festive mood at holiday times by *baking cookies*, and let your helper play in some of the frosting and dough, lick the mixing spoons and taste and smell the yummy treats.

Seeing and Manipulating

At this age, most tots only put edible items into their mouths, and some of the activities in this section are based on this assumption. We still advise watching your toddler, however, when she is using small items.

Continue to collect touchables for her *nature basket*: pinecones and needles, acorns, bark, smooth rocks and so on. Talk about how they feel and smell, how much they weigh and how they look. *Sewing baskets* also hold fascinating items: fabric swatches, trims, spools of thread, buttons, measuring tapes and the like. This activity requires supervision because of pins and needles, but a few minutes letting your tot try on your thimble and feel pieces of lace is lovely.

Your toddler can have a marvelous time with a set of *plastic milk bottles*, filling them with sand, water, pebbles, cereal or raisins, then emptying them.

Continue *crayon play*, and vary colors and textures of paper. Supervise your budding artist so he does not get carried away and mark furniture and walls.

Hold up a piece of newspaper for some *paper play*. See if your muscle man can punch a hole in it. Tearing and wadding paper is also great for finger dexterity.

Let your curious one hold a *prism* up to the sunlight and watch the colors dance. Knobs, keys and buttons on *old machines*—telephones, typewriters, adding machines—are a gold mine for a toddler's inquisitive nature.

Squeeze bottles of all shapes and sizes are great companions for the bathtub or for a bucket of water. Your toddler will feel so grown-up when you go on a picnic and he gets to use the *Thermos bottle*.

Hearing and Language

Play a *question-and-answer game* with your pal. Let her point and ask, "Whatsat?" while you label everything. Enjoy *verbal exchanges* with your child, too. Ask her questions like, "Where's Father?" or "Where's Mother?" Expand her answers of "work" or "bye-bye" by adding, "Dad drove the car to work." Your toddler is trying very hard to talk, so don't correct her attempts. If she says, "Doggie pretty," you might respond with, "Yes, the dog is pretty." Compliment her efforts, and expand on them with more questions to plant the seeds of conversation.

Roll two sheets of 8-by-10-inch paper separately into tight rolls. Tape them so they stay rolled, and you have two paper *sticks* for your musician. Fold two more sheets of paper lengthwise separately into three folds. Wrap them around each hand and your toddler has two paper *instruments* that he can brush past each other to make noise. A little tape will help hold them together. See what other paper instruments you can invent.

Play *counting games* on your toddler's toes and fingers. He may surprise you by counting, "One, two, three," with you. He may also line up objects and count them by touching them and jabbering in his own language. Show your little pupil *opposites*, and describe them: "more" and "all gone," "full" and "empty," "big" and "little," "tall" and "short."

Take *short trips* to places that have interesting, noisy activities: an airport, zoo, building site, dairy. There should be *quiet times*, too, in your child's day. Read to your tot in a room where there is no TV or radio.

Use the word *"now,"* with emphasis, if necessary. Your toddler is beginning to understand it.

Imitating, Imagining and Language

Your toddler is beginning to imitate adult activities, and these are spilling over into pretend, role-play games with a pinch of childish imagination.

Pull the stepstool up to the sink and let your youngster play in the water while you *wash the dishes*. Let him wash small plastic cups or bowls.

Show your child how to use the *flyswatter*, then look out! She will work very diligently to get rid of all the flies.

Let your toddler have his own *hairbrush, comb* and, of course, *toothbrush*. Let him have a go at using all three before you do the finishing touches. Show him how to use a *lint brush* or a roll of masking tape to remove lint from couch or clothing.

Continue to provide your look-alike with lots of clothes for *dress-up*. Give him an assortment of hats and shoes and a long mirror to admire himself.

Self-Awareness

Bath bubbles are great to stick on different body parts: the top of your toddler's head, shoulders, elbows. Hold up a hand mirror so she can see herself. Since your independent one likes to take care of herself, let her *wash and dry her hands*.

Allow your toddler to *flush the toilet*. He will probably find the action and noise of the water interesting. Give your rascal a *sponge* to help mop up his spills, too!

Visit a department store and let your tyke see herself in a *three-way mirror*— upside down, too!

Problem Solving

A homemade *"do it myself"* board or box with all kinds of knobs, hinges and locks is terrific fun for your little mechanic. Show your handyman how to turn on and off different types of *water faucets*, too. He will show off this new skill at the drinking fountain in the park.

Your toddler will give his all trying to *blow up a balloon*, and what fun she will have swatting it once it's inflated! Supervise her efforts so she doesn't put the balloon completely into her mouth and chew it.

Body Positioning

Your toddler feels very important sitting in her own *chair or rocker*. She will push it around to be close to other family members, or drag it to her small table for snacks or for arts-and-crafts play.

Lower the crib bar on your big guy's bed now so he can climb in and out. He is going to try this eventually; lowering the bar now can avoid a serious fall.

A small wagon provides hours of fun for your toddler. He can sit in it, pull it, be pulled or turn it over and spin its wheels. Cutting the grass is a breeze, too, when your helper pushes his *toy lawnmower* beside you.

Show your pal how to *walk along the curb* with one foot on and one foot off. See if she can *kneel and roll* a ball or throw a bean bag. And the *big blanket* is worth mentioning again. Your child loves to be swung in and pulled on it.

Socializing

Escalators make toddlers' eyes widen the first time or two they ride with Mom or Dad. While you're at a shopping mall, take your youngster to a *pet store* to look at the fish, birds, turtles and puppies. Other lookers may visit with your child and chat with him about the animals. Often, attendants will let him feel tiny tame animals.

Fairs of all types are great occasions for eighteen- or nineteen-month-olds. They like all the happenings, especially the animals, small train rides and snow cones! *Parks* with pigeons, fountains, flower beds, trees, baseball diamonds, stairs, dirt paths, bushes and play equipment are also adventurelands for children.

Eighteen- or nineteen-month-olds need to be near *other children*. They enjoy playing beside others their own age, but they adore older children and like to hug and kiss babies.

These were two months to remember. The world is opening up fast to your youngster. She has such character, such zest, such ease in giving and receiving affection. Don't you just love her?

Chapter 15

PRACTICE, PRACTICE, PRACTICE
Twenty and Twenty-one Months

HOW DO YOU DO?

Most parents will look back on the twentieth and twenty-first months with memories of a two-fisted, cookie-totin' tot who loves to run, jump, throw and climb; who peers down your throat to see where the food has gone or down the end of the hose to see where the water went; who notices and is transfixed by her shadow; who chatters on the phone; whose favorite word is "mine," and who kisses her own hurts as she pushes toward independence.

She is a delightful companion who laughs easily. She likes thinking activities: playing grown-up Hide 'n' Seek, where you cover your eyes while she hides, and playing finger and rhyming games. She wants you to play night-night, to "pretend" eat, and to let her pat you and kiss your boo-boos. She pretends, too: to shave, ride a motorcycle, be an airplane, vacuum, cook and walk her baby in her own stroller.

Photographs of your twenty- or twenty-one-month-old at play are studies in total concentration and contentment. You are gratified to see things taking shape that you've worked on together for months: smoother movements, verbal responses, completion of more difficult tasks, greater ability to follow directions, greater ease in selecting clothes and in dressing and undressing, greater success in self-feeding and, perhaps nicest of all, an understanding of desirable behavior. With improved skill levels, your child has more resources to handle frustration, and is therefore more amiable. Her cooperation is wonderful!

Your tot's attention span is still fairly short, and she still does best in familiar surroundings. Temper tantrums, whining, throwing objects, hitting and running away are usually signs of overloading. Advance planning, diversion, redirection or removal remedy most unpleasant situations, and your calmness and consistent firmness teach your tot control. She will be happier and healthier for your strong guidance.

Your rascal is becoming very capable, but she needs your support and concern more than ever. Often, her abilities cause her some difficulties: climbing too high on the jungle gym, wanting to swing but not realizing the danger of other swings in motion, climbing to the top of the big slide and becoming afraid to slide down. She needs your assistance to build confidence, your watchfulness to ward off danger, and your love and laughter to take tumbles in stride.

Along with physical advances comes progress in language growth. All the time spent talking to your child—saying simple sentences, giving simple explanations, labeling—comes back to you now through increased vocabulary, two-word phrases, completion of gaps in songs and rhymes, and an understanding of some personal pronouns. With your encouragement, she may even try to verbalize her daily adventures.

From our experience, parents begin to show real signs of concern at this point if they notice delays in their child's development—other than problems already diagnosed by a doctor. Let us mention that it is often difficult for a doctor to observe developmental problems in the brief encounters they have with children during checkups. You know your child better than anyone; if you are suspicious of a problem for an obvious reason—your child makes no attempt to walk or climb, does not respond to your verbal requests or does not repeat familiar words—call this to your doctor's attention. Persist until you are satisfied with the answers. Otherwise, valuable time can be lost. Children make wonderful strides and overcome tremendous problems when they are properly diagnosed and given help and loving attention.

Continue to use the program to your child's advantage. Find the level at which she best responds and work with her at her pace. After practice and more practice, she will show off admirably and delight in being part of the "big" world.

SUPPLIES

rug squares—carpet samples

parachute

rings

tube—large truck tire inflated inner tube with cloth tape wrapped around stem and tube

tilt board—wide, flat board with a narrower, flat board projecting from it

wedge

big bolster

beam

big ladder

ramp

railroad track

super stuff—ropes, pinwheels, balloons and paddles, giant scoops and balls

silly pool—dry, uncooked cereal; crisp, plain cereal; pea gravel, shaving cream, food coloring

GETTING READY

The twinkle in your tot's eyes lets you know she is ready when she comes running at the sound of familiar warm-up music. We want your child to feel relaxed and to develop her sense of humor through play. She is discovering new traits and, through practice, building skills for more efficient movement.

Loosening Up

One need only hold an infant to feel her potentially unlimited flexibility. However, it is amazing just how fast toddlers' movements can begin to seem restricted. We want your tot to bend, twist and stretch with ease, so the following games emphasize flexibility.

FLOWERS GROW LIKE THIS

> *Flowers grow like this,* [Cup hands.]
> *Trees grow like this,* [Spread arms and raise up on toes.]
> *I grow* [Jump up and stretch.]
> *Just like that!*

HOW DOES A CATERPILLAR GO?

> *How does a caterpillar go?* [Walk fingers slowly down legs
>   to toes in sitting position.]
> *Dear me, does anybody know?*
> *How does a caterpillar go?*
> *On a cabbage leaf the whole day long.*
>
> *How does a little froggie go?* [Hop fingers back up legs.]
> *Dear me, does anybody know?*
> *How does a little froggie go?*
> *By a lily pond the whole day long.*
>
> *How does a fluffy duckling go?* [Stand up, bend over at waist,
>   touch floor, wiggle fingers.]
> *Dear me, does anybody know?*
> *How does a fluffy duckling go?*
> *A-searching worms the whole day long.*

Body Awareness

As your tot plays and shares with you, he learns who he is through sensory feedback: seeing, hearing, touching and moving. He redefines his position in space—establishes his own "launch pad."

THIS IS THE WAY WE CLAP OUR HANDS

This is the way we clap our hands,
Clap our hands, clap our hands.
This is the way we clap our hands.
So early in the morning.

This is the way we jump our feet; swing our arms; smack our lips;
etc.

Rocky Robot Says: See if your quick learner will move specific body parts at your request while standing in front of a mirror. Or mirror each other's action, while you lead or stand by her side.

"Show me how you move your arms."
"Move your head . . . shake it, or move it up and down [nod]."
"Can you move your knees from side to side?"
"Show me how you move your hands together; twist them."

Finger Play

By now, finger play may be a good way to show off your toddler's alertness and listening ears. Grandparents will adore holding her and whispering that she has very good storytelling fingers. Remember to work on one game until your tot knows it well before venturing forth to successive exercises.

Here Is My Family. This charming finger game will amuse your munchkin as it has others in our classes. Begin with the first verse; over the coming months, add the remaining verses:

Here is my sister, [Hold up one thumb.]
Here is my brother, [Hold other thumb up.]
Watch her hide, [Hide behind back.]
Watch him hide, [Hide behind back.]
Bring them back together
Bring them back together
Oh, so nice, oh, so nice. [Rub fingers together.]

Here is Mother, Here is Father, etc. [Hold index fingers up.]
Here is Grandma, Here is Grandpa, etc. [Hold middle fingers up.]

Rhythms

Winnie Wedo Says:

Speeds. "Let's see if we can get your jogger to run around the room with you." Make two slow circles, then increase to a medium running speed and, for the last loop, really take off! Whoop it up! Call his attention to shifts in speed and praise him for his good balance, strong heart and running legs.

Tickle Bee. What child doesn't just love to frolic on the floor while Mom or Dad gently tickles her tummy, toes or legs? Tickle in a pattern, saying,

> *Tickle, tickle, over here,*
> *Tickle, tickle me;*
> *Tickle, tickle, over here,*
> *Tickle, tickle, one, two, three.*

Let her get you with her tickle fingers.

Pretending

Gorilla Walk. Think gorilla—bananas, jungle music, hairy chest, long arms— and start with feet apart, trunk bent forward slightly, arms hanging freely. Walk forward and backward, taking slow, lumbering steps while swinging arms from side to side. Make gorilla sounds and call to your tot to be a little gorilla. What a crazy way to practice moving at yet another body level (slightly bent) while balancing.

Squares. Playing with rug squares can help warm up your jumper's muscles and imagination on any given day. Spread them on the floor and pretend to be rock hoppers, jumping from one to another. Place them in a circle, square or triangle and let your little alligator cruise along them on his belly. Also try to put them in a straight, curved or hodgepodge sequence.

Locomotion

Your tot's large-muscle movements are becoming more rhythmic and, eventually, he will not even think about them when moving. These games reach toward that goal. Constantly reviewing the same old large-muscle motor activities would soon bore your child, so use your creativity freely when you present these.

Levels. Set up the chairs with the rope at its highest point, and ask your child to walk under it, like an old man stooped over and slow. Then ask your child to be a wiggly, playful puppy and crawl under a medium-high rope on hands and knees. Finally, lower the rope almost to the ground and ask him how he will get under it—maybe like a snake, s-s-s-sliding on his tummy, or like a log rolling over and over. When you show your toddler a high, medium, then low rope, see if he can say, "high," "medium" and "low."

Bubbles. A scrumptious hug and a whisper of "Let's play bubbles!" prompts your tot to squirm right out of your arms, running for the cupboard where you keep the parachute.

BILLOWS

Gather some helpers to make the chute billow high and fast while your youngster runs in and out.

WAVES

Together, you and your playmate can be the wave machine, reaching on tiptoes and bending down to the floor to make slow, rolling waves. She may like to roll on them, too.

POPCORN

This is a lively game, so watch out! Place small foam balls or Ping-Pong balls on the chute and hold it tightly. Shake it up and down together with all your might, using quick, jerky motions. Let your tot hop on and try to catch the balls. Her flushed cheeks and laughter tell you what a great time she's having!

MOVING OUT

Partner Movements

RING KICK

Value: If we could only bottle a toddler's verve, we would never have to worry about the energy crisis! This movement lets your child spend any pent-up energy through play. And your tyke will like to strengthen arm, chest, back, tummy and leg muscles this way.

Here's How: Stand behind your tot, holding a ring in each hand. Let him reach up and grab the rings, then say, "One, two, three, up," and lift him off the ground. Give him the go-ahead to kick, kick, kick with all his might. Practice in front of a mirror, if possible, so he can see his body and facial expressions as he kicks his hardest.

How Many: Kick for ten seconds, or however long your arms will hold out, until his interest wanes.

Assistive Movements

WIBBLE WOBBLE

Value: The Wibble Wobble introduces your carefree toddler to the tilt board. This sport gives her sensitive inner-ear balancing mechanism a workout, so she'll someday master roller skates, ice skates, a bicycle or a tricycle.

Here's How: First let your prober check out the tilt board while you demonstrate its motion. Then place it on the floor and help her sit on it. She'll quickly try to shift her bottom and upper body to maintain balance. Congratulate her for a new endeavor well done.

How Many: One good balance; may be repeated daily.

OVER EASY

Value: Your toddler is now ready for a challenging gymnastics combination: walking up the wedge, then sliding into a forward roll over the bolster. This sequence will boost her self-confidence and her interest in practicing motor skills.

Here's How: Place the bolster at the thick end of the wedge. Spot her as she walks up the wedge, lies on her stomach, extends her arms over the top of the bolster, reaches for the floor, pushes with her toes, rolls onto the bolster slightly, tucks her head and rolls over onto her back. She'll go over easily—so easily she'll come back for more!

How Many: Two or three rolls; may be repeated daily.

HUG-A-BUG

Value: This movement requires your child to place one foot behind the other on the beam.

Here's How: Place the beam between several thick books. Place your hands under her arms, and encourage her to begin walking backward. If she tries to rely on looking at the beam, have a friendly chat with her so she looks up and learns to search for the beam just by placing her feet. Give your champ a loving squeeze when she completes this walk.

How Many: One walk; may be repeated daily.

BOTTOMS UP

Value: Your tot's Flapjacks practice has led to this exercise. All the lessons about backward motion are providing greater versatility in everyday situations: maneuvering in and around furniture, sitting on the potty chair and climbing onto swings. Here's another exciting step backward!

Here's How: Ask your child to walk up the wedge backward, and lie on his back. As he extends his hands toward the floor and tucks his legs, grasp his pelvic area and help him flip over onto his feet and knees. He will pop up with a grin and a look that says, "I can do that again!"

How Many: Two flips.

FIDDLE FINGERS

Value: Walking on her hands on or over the rungs of the big ladder is a real challenge for eye-hand coordination and upper-body strength, and prepares your tyke for activities like cutting paper and fabric with scissors.

Here's How: Place the big ladder flat on the floor or on another interesting

surface: ceramic tile, grass, brick. Place a bright, noisy toy at one end, then grasp your tot's legs in a wheelbarrow position and tell her to get that toy!

How Many: One walk; may be repeated daily.

Active Movements

JENNY POP (Use your child's name)

Value: There is something magical about watching a tot sit and play with a jack-in-the-box. Her eyes twinkle every time Jack makes his surprising appearance. She will demonstrate the ability to mimic actions and shows her understanding of timing and good humor.

Here's How: Sit on the floor facing your tot. Bend your knees out, soles together, and hold your ankles. Bury your face against your ankles and say, "One, two, three, Jenny pop!" while you thrust out your arms and legs.

How Many: Two pops; may be repeated daily.

BUG BOUNCE

Value: This crazy, fun movement strengthens your child's legs and tests his balance. The spice of chase may be added, too, to make it a grand time for several players.

Here's How: Place the tube flat on the floor and straddle it, one foot inside the tube and one out. Say, "Ready, set, go!" and bounce forward, pushing off with legs as you move around the tube. Pretend to be hop bugs, trains, cars, donkeys—whatever!

How Many: One bounce around the tube; may be repeated daily.

MONKEY CLIMB

Value: Your tot really gets up in the world when she does this climbing movement!

Here's How: Slant the railroad track against a couch or chair and secure it. Help your tot mount the track with feet on either side of the raised portion of the track, hands on the raised part. Watch her scramble up as you stand by to lend a helping hand. When she reaches the top, help her hop down and give her a pat on the back as you tell her, "Well done."

How Many: One climb.

RESCUE CLIMB

Value: Climbing the ladder assimilates many of the traits you have been nurturing for months: concentration, balance, confidence, eye-hand and eye-foot coordination, body awareness, body control and strength. Take pleasure now in watching your climber coordinate these abilities.

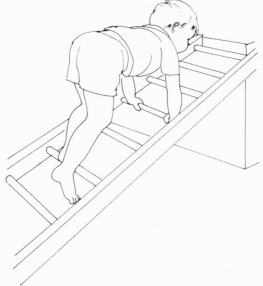

Here's How: Find a new place, perhaps outdoors, to prop the big ladder in a steeper position, and secure it. Make siren sounds and call your little fire fighter to hurry and rescue his favorite stuffed toy at the top of the ladder. Once he reaches it, have him "save" the toy by tossing it to you, then ask him to turn around and climb down. Snuggle him and praise him for his safe rescue.

How Many: One climb and retreat; may be repeated daily.

EXPLORING
Super Stuff

Like the snake charmer with his magic, your toddler will have an enchanting time with a three-foot piece of soft nylon *rope*. He can twirl, drag, drape, wiggle, wrap around or pull something with it—even a make-believe something! Give him several pieces of rope for more magic tricks.

A little breeze, a pinwheel and your tot make a happy combination. Find a grassy hill where he can hold it up high, down low and move it from side to side while running, walking and turning in circles. Indoors, use a fan to create a helpful breeze, and set the mood with music—percussion, marching, flamingo, soft shoe. Share his wide-eyed enthusiasm with much encouragement and end with a *grand finale*: blowing on it to make it spin.

Balloons have long been special play treats for your mischievous one. Now, let's add a *Ping-Pong paddle* for diversity. Show your pal how to bat the balloon into the air, then play a game of bouncing it back and forth. Keep a lighhearted tempo while pushing, swatting, hitting, pounding and swinging at the balloon, keeping it low enough for his reach. You may see a bit of a baseball, tennis, racketball, football, volleyball or all-around athlete in him, but for now, encourage just the enjoyment of the game.

Fashion a *giant scoop* from a large, clean, plastic bleach bottle and round up several old tennis balls. Place these before your inventor and see what happens. He can put a ball into the scoop and dump it out, toss one up or carry five or six balls and pour them out. You can roll a ball slowly toward him and see if he lines up the scoop to catch it. Sometime, just for fun, roll a whole bunch of balls at once and see what he does. Laugh with your squirt and tell him what a good player he'll be during school recess!

Silly Pool

What a great place to enjoy conversations with your tot while you needlepoint with other mothers or chat with neighborhood youngsters. You can enjoy doing something with your hands while visiting with your explorer. She will repeat phrases and learn new words and, in return, you can listen to her, repeat her words and laugh and smile with her while sharing new materials, such as *uncooked cereal*. This is a good medium for scoops, funnels and containers of all sizes because it pours easily. Once your tot experiments with it alone, try mixing it with another medium, such as all-purpose flour. Give her the pleasure of mixing by placing the media side by side on a cookie sheet with a lip. Place the entire sheet inside the wading pool to provide a smooth spreading surface to make handprints and cookie-cutter designs.

Crisp, plain cereal is another new texture to explore. Your child can crunch it, eat it, add water to it and listen to the popping noises, mix it with a spoon in a bowl, smash it wet and dry to see the difference, pound on it with a mallet and walk on it, like a giant stomping through thick underbrush.

Pea gravel, often found on pathways at nurseries, is the best fun for little truck drivers and steam shovelers. A bagful in a wading pool makes for interesting sounds when placed in different containers—tin, plastic, cardboard—and its weight is an important learning factor.

We have used pea gravel successfully in our classes, but with the understanding that if a child is still putting everything in his mouth, this medium should either be well supervised or saved until he is older.

The last but certainly not least popular texture is *whipped soap suds*. Though we have mentioned this briefly before, now let your little artist mix in a few drops of food coloring. Your tot will have fun forming designs and blending colors on a cookie sheet—a study in total concentration. Your little helper is good when it comes to cleaning up, too. Let him wash his hands and dry them. How grown-up he is becoming!

ALL AROUND

Smelling and Tasting

Your little helper will like rummaging through the *garden* to pick vegetables, smell them, and talk about their colors, shapes, sizes and weights. While you are in the garden, talk to him about the odor of the soil and plants themselves, when dry and damp. Inside, he will think shelling peas is play, and he can even help prepare green beans.

Allow your energetic one to *assist in preparing food*. Push a chair to the counter and let her help you wash fruits and vegetables and add raisins, crumbled bacon or dressing to a salad, smelling and tasting as you go. She will like being with you, chatting and, perhaps, saying rhymes as you clean up.

Next time you pass a *fruit and vegetable stand*, stop and purchase some and let your explorer look, touch and smell them. Visit nearby *factories* where cheese is made, chocolate is cooked or peanuts are roasted. Even nonfood factories are fascinating places for little people to observe machinery for a short time, though places with highly toxic smells should, of course, be avoided.

When you enter a library, large apartment house, elevator, post office or Laundromat, call your little sniffer's attention to the *building smell*.

Seeing and Manipulating

Your child's eyes are becoming increasingly important. They tell him how to best manipulate his muscles to accomplish a task, such as what puzzle piece to pick up and move into place. You may now notice a definite preference for one hand over the other.

Tiny creatures attract your toddler's attention when you are out for a walk or playing in the grass. Ants working industriously in a homemade *ant farm* are visual wonders. Fill an old mayonnaise jar with dirt and ants and keep it somewhere he can view them without reaching them. *Goldfish* in a bowl aquarium introduce your tot to fish life. He will enjoy seeing them from all angles.

Your tot's eyes and fingers are becoming more adept at working with small details. Allow her to finish *peeling a banana* or to unwrap a cube of butter or a square of baker's chocolate. For a real "ten" on a tot's list, pile sand, water or good ol' dirt to make *mud pies*. She can make crude balls and patties and will love patting, squeezing and smashing the mud—especially if there is a puddle large enough for her toes, too.

Playing a simple *lotto* game gives your tot a chance to use his eyes and hands to match pictures and have pleasant verbal exchanges with you. Give your toddler a small, bouncing *ball in the bathtub*. Let him bounce it off the back of the tub, grab it as it floats by, place it in floating bowls and the like.

A piece of one-inch-thick *styrofoam*, some short nails with large heads and a small hammer will set your little carpenter up in business. Start the nails for him and they will go in very easily. Now is also a good time to purchase a *basic block set* for your little builder. Older siblings and Dad can get very involved, too, while your tot puts miniature people and cars into the block building creations.

A variety of torn pieces of paper, bits of yarn, popped popcorn and fabric scraps gives your tot an ample selection for her first *simple collage*. Run a squiggly line of glue all over a piece of stiff paper and let her go to town. She will be completely engrossed in placing her strips and bits. Designing a collage will make her feel very grown-up, especially if she sees older siblings working on one, too. Hang the finished art on her bedroom door where she can show it off. She will be so proud!

Hearing and Language

Fostering your toddler's language development is even more exciting at this point, because he reacts to situations more verbally and communicates more needs and feelings. Sometime soon your child will probably shock you with the ability to speak in sentences, which he seems to have acquired almost overnight. Take heart, and continue to talk with him, read, play rhyming games, use simple sentences, give simple instructions, ask simple questions and label *everything*. Most of all, *listen* intently.

Use a *hand puppet* and change your voice to read a story to your tot. She will want to feel it and try to move it. Show your toddler how to blow into a *noisemaker* that toots or beeps. Some shoot thin paper tubes, much to the delight of your party-goer. Some even make sounds when turned upside down, or imitate animals!

Fill thick *water glasses* with different amounts of water and tap them with a spoon to show her the different sounds. Help her tap them gently. See if your drummer can march around a room hitting a *drum on a strap*, draped around her neck. Play loud marching music and ask everyone within hearing distance to join the parade. Give your tot pie tins to bang for *cymbals*.

Act out words in books with your child: yawn, scratch, tap, hop, tickle, draw, blink. Make it a fun game by picking out new action words for him to learn. He will love your antics.

Share sounds that are *unique to certain environments*: the quiet of a mountain road, chiming of a clock shop at the hour, peeping of young chickens and turkeys in a feed-supply store, clicking of a computer shop.

Imitating, Imagining and Language

Dr. Fredelle Maynard, Ph.D., in her book *Guiding Your Child to a More Creative Life*, writes that there are two kinds of creativity: "the special talent variety, which depends upon genes and chromosomes, and the instinctive urge to learn, grow and develop, which exists in every individual." You can foster your twenty- or twenty-one-month-old's "zest for life" by responding to his questions and statements with interest and enthusiasm and by providing daily opportunities for free exploration, imitation and expression.

Your tot will gladly pick up and put away toys upon request, as long as you don't make the tasks too rigid. Let her have her way in helping with other *daily chores*: watering plants, fetching the newspaper, taking out trash, picking flowers for the table and bringing in the mail.

Play the *naming game* when dressing, undressing, bathing and maintaining personal hygiene: toes, toenails, clippers, comb, hair, barrette, pants, pocket, snap and so on. He will watch intently as you put on makeup and will want polish on his toenails, too.

Your toddler will feel very important if you give her a bowl with a small amount of *baby powder* and a few cotton balls and let her powder her baby. She will have a wonderful time powdering herself, too (a beautiful picture memento!).

With his own small set of *yard tools* or the small ones you use on houseplants, your tot will eagerly help plant flowers, rake leaves, and mow grass. Talk about the worms you find, the color and shapes of leaves, seed pods and the like. Some jobs take twice as long and are ten times as messy because you involve your child, but before you know it, he will be a capable and cheerful assistant. And otherwise he may never learn some of the skills you take for granted.

Your mimic may also want to try his hand at your sports activities. Many tiny-tot sports sets are available, and *bowling* is one he can be successful with at this age. Encourage everyone in the family to take part.

All of a sudden, a pet may have special new meaning for your toddler, especially a friendly dog. Your child wants to follow it around, share snacks with it and play night-night. He will also throw a ball for the dog, brush it and help walk it.

Self-Awareness

The often-heard word "mine" tells you that your toddler is working hard to organize his surroundings. Encourage his drive toward independence, give him personal items and places to keep them, and allow him to fend for himself as much as possible.

Let your tot pull his *freshly laundered clothing* out of the dryer and sort it with you. Thank him for helping carry it to his room and see if he can identify other family members' clothing.

Your capable one may run for a tissue, try to *blow his nose*, then, very grown-uplike, put the tissue in the trash. Thank him for being a good clean-up bug; he won't want to be a litterbug.

Your feeling-good tot may like to run nude in a *sheltered backyard*, fill a wading pool with water from a hose or run through a low sprinkler on a warm, sunny day.

Your tot may be managing a cup and spoon well now, but this is also the time many parents find it necessary to begin teaching *table manners*: no more playing in the food or making loud noises at the table. Your child may seem hurt at first, because playing in food is such fun. But he wants to please you, so a frown and a firm reminder will usually turn the tide. If he persists, remember: redirection or removal.

Ice cubes are a popular cure for bumps and bangs, followed by close inspection and, sometimes, medical attention. You will often find your toddler going to the refrigerator in an attempt to "fix" his hurt with ice. Greet him with calm and comforting words and praise for his efforts to make his bump better.

Problem Solving

Allow your twenty- or twenty-one-month-old to *make simple decisions*. Giving her a choice—such as which of two outfits to wear, which fruit to eat or which shoes to wear—makes her feel grown-up. Once you have allowed her a choice, though, don't try to dissuade her from the decision.

Your enthusiastic helper will take great pride in helping *make his bed*. This job presents some difficult tugging and pulling predicaments. And then there are all those stuffed animals to stack! Give him a big hug for his help.

If big sister is painting at an easel, give number-two child a *long-handled brush* and one can or bottle of paint to dabble on the other side of the easel—preferably in an outdoor location, where spills don't matter.

Toys with *hidden parts* that appear and disappear when knobs are turned or compartments are opened will captivate your child. Make cloth toys that have pockets with *different types of closings*, such as zippers, snaps or flaps with double-stick tape, to test your tot's determination and ingenuity. As he gets older, add more difficult closings, such as hooks and eyes or ribbon ties.

Large dump trucks with simple moving parts make your construction worker use the *handles* to dump sand and pebbles. Other toys allow him to drop little people down chutes, push them on swings, put them on vehicles and the like. Ask your tot what he is doing, and enjoy his long, demonstrative explanation.

Body Positioning

There are many character *Bop Bags* on the market. These are made out of vinyl, their bottoms weighed with sand. Select one of your child's favorite characters and let him help you blow it up. Once you show him how to punch it, your child will have a great time using his muscle power.

The *Sit 'n' Spin* toy is another toddler tickler. Twist your bottom in the opposite direction you move your arms. Your tot may need a few tries to get used to it, but once he has the idea, he will spin himself into the giggles.

Purchase a *child's patio swing* with a safety bar across it or make one if you are handy with a hammer and saw. These can be easily attached to a patio roof or support beam. A *sack hammock* swing is another great sensation for your tot to experience.

Obstacle courses made from boxes, tires, chair tunnels, mattresses and card tables make good games for your rambunctious one—especially on a rainy day. Set one up so that he has to crawl under a bed, and for ultraexcitement, let him use a flashlight!

Your mover may now be able to drive a *tyke bike* or similar riding toy like crazy, even down a small slope. She may also enjoy propelling a *kiddie car* in all directions. Give her a race helmet, and look out!

Socializing

Playing tag with older brothers and sisters can be a very silly game. Your runner will move as fast as her legs can carry her.

Visits to the *seashore* may now include jaunts to find sea creatures, such as starfish and crabs; a walk along the boardwalk to watch boats; collecting seashells; perhaps taking a ferry ride or eating a corn dog. The new smells, tastes and faces are wonderful stimulants.

Shopping malls often feature visiting *petting zoos*. Take your twenty- or twenty-one-month-old to one, if possible. Not only will she enjoy the animals—llamas, lambs, calves, bunnies and goats—but she will love the happy atmosphere, crowded with other parents and children.

Chapter 16

GROWING WITH GUSTO
Twenty-two and Twenty-three Months

HOW DO YOU DO?

Each day you have watched your moppet grow with gusto into a more self-assured, independent little person. At the same time, you have found yourself needing more patience to handle your happy, yet sometimes frustrated, child. Good childrearing does not happen by accident; it requires planning by both parents. Stimulate play, encourage further exploration of his world and teach him to cope with anxiety.

Since your learner is trying to master many basic skills, he may become rattled when trying to pull on socks and shoes or to dress and undress. Understand that his accomplishments will eventually make your life easier and give him time to practice these skills before you complete the job.

Your go-getter continues to demonstrate physical agility: he can throw a ball overhead more accurately, perhaps even through a basket or Hula-Hoop. He enjoys kicking a ball and chasing it, and sometimes runs so fast that he tumbles over himself. Good thing children are built so close to the ground! As coordination improves, he will slow his momentum, turn sharp corners and stop quickly.

During the twenty-third month your adventurer will travel up and down stairs without grasping the railing, still leading with one particular foot. He walks sideways and backward, and climbing is still a favorite. When you least expect it, he may be standing on a chair like a superhero, ready to jump, so make sure he isn't close to obstacles that could injure him during his leap.

Your curious creature has greater coordination than ever. He pushes and pulls, tugs and lugs, piles up cubes, turns pages one at a time, folds pieces of paper and strings beads. He shows a hand preference while scribbling. He has simple skills, like dropping and throwing objects, opening and closing doors and drawers, swinging hinged objects back and forth, knocking down and replacing small objects, putting together and taking apart toys and puzzles, putting objects through openings and pouring materials in and out of containers. Your twenty-two- or twenty-three-month-old is also beginning to recognize quantitative attributes: that there are one or many objects, that they are empty or full, big or small, heavy or light.

By now some toddlers know many words and love to chatter, while others show no desire to talk. Judge your child by the vocabulary he understands rather than by the words and phrases he can speak. You can expand his language ability by talking to him without putting words into his mouth. Remember, parents are the models for their children's proper speech patterns.

Many of the parents in our classes claim that they become exhausted during these two months, because their youngsters demand so much of their time and energy. Be honest with your child. Remember that the *quality* of time you spend together is more important than the *quantity,* and tell him when you have reached your limit. Teach your toddler to play by himself for at least an hour in the morning and one in the afternoon. Find a special outdoors place or a room where he can be free and safe to play as he pleases. He will become more self-reliant while you take time to sit back, relax and pursue your own favorite hobby. Our EXPLORING section has many ideas to keep your busybody happy and occupied.

Your growing tot cannot help but feel secure and confident after all these months of loving interaction. Keep his developing personality in mind as you update a stimulating, challenging, rich environment with opportunities to learn, to foster curiosity, to develop language and to become a competent and independent person.

SUPPLIES

tires—two
parachute
inner tube trampoline—large inner tube with canvas top stretched taut
    over it (to be purchased)
big bolster
beam
railroad track
tilt board
wedge
big ladder
ramp
tube
super stuff—Ping-Pong balls, plastic tops, tennis balls; plastic, tin or
    paper dishes; plastic or cardboard numbers
silly pool—flour, macaroni, fideo

GETTING READY

During these two months your toddler is trying to understand that he is an individual. Don't push him into independence; just encourage him toward it. Play the following games to make life more challenging as your child develops his "self."

Loosening Up

Roly-Poly. Our little students love this symmetrical game, which teaches the concepts of up, down, in and out. Practice these each day for a few minutes.

> *Roly-poly, roly-poly, up, up, up;* [Roll hands around each other, moving upward.]
> *Roly-poly, roly-poly, down, down, down.* [Roll hands downward.]
> *Roly-poly, roly-poly, out, out, out,* [Roll hands away from you.]
> *Roly-poly, roly-poly, in, in, in.* [Roll hands toward you.]

Here's another to stretch your muscles while he learns different body parts. Perform the actions suggested:

> *Up I stretch on tippy toe,*
> *Down to touch my heels I go.*
> *Up again my arms I send,*
> *Down again my knees I bend.*

Rocky Robot Says: Children always need reinforcement about what they've learned. Facing a mirror, help your imitator review the following movements to improve her body image.

"Roll hands together going up and down and in and out."
"Clap hands over head."
"Bend your knees."
"Jump slowly, then fast."
"Kick the right foot, now your left."
"Nod your head, up and down, right and left."

Rhythms

Toddlers enjoy moving freely to music. Play a record and ask your child to dance.

Galloping. Ask your toddler to be a horse and to gallop around the house. Give him a small broom or stick and invent a story to set the rhythm. Or use this:

Galloping horses, galloping through town.
So many different colors, some are white, and some are brown.
Some are galloping up the mountain, some are galloping down.
Galloping horses, galloping through town.

Winnie Wedo Says: Time to learn more about regulated movements. Let's see if you can do the following:

"Lie down on your side and raise your right leg [count one, two, three, . . .]."

"Turn to your left side and raise your left leg [repeat counting]."

"Raise both feet over your head."

"Come forward into a seated position and bounce toward your feet four times."

"Rock side to side [bring feet together and hold ankles]."

Finger Play

Your toddler learns language through imitation. Finger Play gives him a chance to copy you—his best teacher—as best he can, to exercise the little fingers for improved dexterity and to expand vocabulary. Wiggle your fingers as suggested in this rhyme:

My fingers like to shake about,
Shake about, shake about,
My fingers like to shake about,
All around the room.
Second verse: *My fingers like to wave about.*
Third verse: *My fingers like to wiggle about.*
Fourth verse: *My fingers like to clap about.*

Pretending

Let your toddler pretend to be a fish, bird and caterpillar. Show her pictures of the critters so she forms mental images of them.

Swim, little fish, in water clear.
Fly, little birds, up in the air;
Creep, little caterpillars, creep,
Sleep, little children, softly sleep.

Egg Beater. Turn a tire upright and, with you holding one side and your toddler holding the other, turn it in a circle. Move to the right, then to the left. Once she gets the idea, turn it faster and run around in a circle going to the right and to the left and adding different rhythms. Sing "Ring Around the Rosy," and when you sing, "All fall down," drop the tire while you both fall.

Locomotion

Your toddler loves to use his body to move in different directions and on various levels.

Jungle Story. Ask your toddler to be a snake and to squirm along the floor. Have your creepy crawler slither in and out of a tunnel fashioned from dining-room chairs and a blanket. Add this special rhyme to make it more interesting:

> *Walking through the jungle,*
> *What did I see?*
> *A slippery snake hissing*
> *At me, me, me!*

Seal Walk. Tell your actor to bark like a seal as he propels himself along the floor using his strong arms and dragging his feet. Get down on the floor and play with him; you will both develop upper-body strength.

Bubbles. The parachute is the grand finale in our classes, and children are always disappointed to end it. Let your toddler enjoy these two popular movements:

GHOSTS

Raise the parachute and let it float onto yourself and your toddler. Pretend to be ghosts, stretching your arms and lifting them up and down, making silly moaning sounds. Let your child be a friendly, funny ghost. After a few minutes lift the parachute into the air again and repeat.

JUMPS

Hold your toddler's hands and jump around in a circle as the parachute billows into the air. Once she gets going, let her attempt to jump alone. The bubbles may entice her to jump for a few minutes, or add this rhyme:

> *Jump-jump! Kangaroo Brown,*
> *Jump-jump, off to town;*
> *Jump-jump!*
> *Up hill and down,*
> *Jump-jump! Kangaroo Brown.*

MOVING OUT

According to optometrist Dr. G.N. Getman, the integration of all body movements is a prerequisite for the refined motions necessary to read and write and to become a functioning member of society. The following movements will challenge your child to explore the ways his body moves and the methods he can use to solve more difficult problems.

Partner Movements

TUMMY TIGHTENER

Value: Tummy muscles are sometimes neglected, but your go-getter will enjoy holding onto your feet while you strengthen those abdominal muscles. Then trade places!

Here's How: Why don't you start first: lie down and ask your helper to sit on your feet so you can do some bent-knee sit-ups. When you're through, tell your toddler it's his turn. If he needs a helping hand, offer it. At first he may use one elbow to boost himself. Once the abdominal muscles are strong enough, he won't need your help.

How Many: Begin with five and increase to ten sit-ups for your child, counting out loud as you go. You may do as many as you like, increasing by five each day.

Assistive Movements

GOING BANANAS

Value: Jumping is not an easy skill to learn. It requires much practice, especially when a toddler is trying to jump with both feet simultaneously. Two-footed jumping is a rhythmic movement necessary for superior control of leg movements.

Here's How: You have been assisting your toddler's jumping by holding both her hands. Now she may be ready to jump holding only one hand. Using an

inner tube trampoline, a bed or an old mattress, hold one hand and ask her to bend her knees and jump. Keep the rhythm going, saying, "Jumpety, jumpety, jump, jump, jump!"

As your child progresses in steadiness and confidence, gradually loosen your support to one finger, then nothing. Encourage her to jump in one place, rather than aiming for height.

How Many: Repeat the rhyme four times; may be repeated daily.

HIGH STEPPING

*Value:*As your adventurous moppet steps over the higher ladder rungs, she will develop eye-foot coordination, balance and spatial awareness.

Here's How: Place the big ladder between two tires, pillows, bricks or cardboard blocks. Ask your toddler to walk over the ladder rungs, raising her knees high, almost as if she were marching. Assist by holding one hand and offer her a reward at the end: a hug and kiss!

How Many: Two crosses; may be repeated daily.

ACROBAT WALK

Value: To walk backward on the beam, your balancer must bring one leg behind the other. Her goal is eventually to balance forward and backward with minimal stress, freeing her mind to concentrate on her surroundings.

Here's How: Place the beam 5 inches off the floor, and ask your mover to mount it. Offer one-handed assistance and lots of verbal support as you ask her to walk backward, her other arm outstretched for balance. When she reaches the end, ask her to turn around and walk backward again. Place a big ball or toy at the end of the beam, and encourage her to focus on it as she walks.

How Many: Two walks; may be repeated daily.

CLICKETY CLACK

Value: You now have a thoroughly experienced railroad engineer. During these two months teach him to walk backward on the sides of the track.

Here's How: Place the railroad track between two chairs. Have your engineer climb onto the chair, and tell him to pretend there is a river on the bottom and to remember his balance so he won't fall and get wet. Hold him gently under the arms, and let him walk backward on the sides of the track. Remind him to hold his arms out for better balance and gravity control. Say this rhyme, if you wish:

> One red engine puffing down the track,
> One red engine puffing, puffing back, back, back.

How Many: Two walks; may be repeated daily.

WIBBLE WOBBLE #2

Value: This movement helps your toddler balance as she tilts from side to side.

Here's How: Have your child sit on the tilt board with legs out straight. Holding only one hand, shift the board to the left, let her adjust her balance, then move her to the right. The idea is for her to maintain good sideways balance.

How Many: Four tilts to each side; may be repeated daily.

TUTTI FRUTTI

Value: This tumbling movement is difficult, but your toddler will learn more about space awareness, balance and body control as she attempts it.

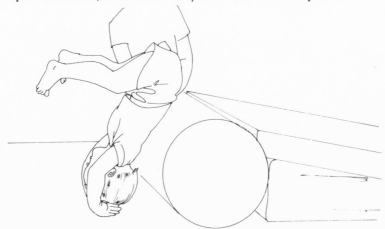

Here's How: We combine the wedge and bolster to perform this backward somersault. Have your tumbler walk backward up the wedge, sit on its edge and put his back onto the bolster to prepare for a backward somersault. Gently roll the bolster over until his hands touch the floor. Adjust his hands on the floor, place your hand on his tummy and ask him to flip his legs over his head. His movements will be so automatic that you'll be amazed!

How Many: Two backward somersaults; may be repeated daily.

Active Movements

BLAST OFF INTO SHAPES

Value: This sequence helps your toddler develop auditory memory while performing certain tasks. She will also increase leg endurance, body control and eye-foot coordination and learn to distinguish simple geometric shapes.

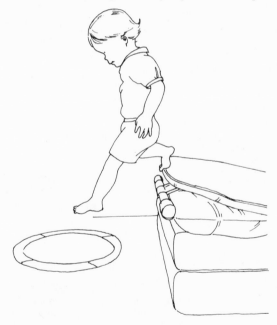

Here's How: Set up the ramp or wedge. Form geometric designs on the floor with masking tape, starting with a circle, then adding a square, triangle, diamond and so on. (Geometrically shaped pillows may also be used.) Ask your astronaut to run off the wedge and jump into each shape.

How Many: Two to four jumps; maybe repeated daily.

FUZZY WUZZY

Value: This movement allows your child to become an animal while developing body control, balance and spatial awareness.

Here's How: Lay the big ladder flat on the ground over a new texture, such as a foam pad or your fuzzy-wuzzy texture board. Ask your toddler to be a bear and step between the ladder rungs, using his hands and feet. A few growls make this difficult walk more exciting.

How Many: Two walks across the ladder; may be repeated daily.

BUG BOUNCE BACKWARD

Value: This favorite movement teaches your toddler to bounce an object backward. What a fun way to develop leg strength and control!

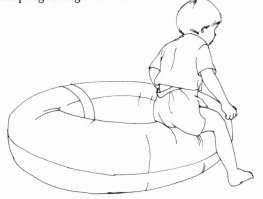

Here's How: Have your toddler straddle the tube and bounce it up and down going backward. Create a tale about a little bouncing bug.

How Many: Bounce until story is over; may be repeated daily.

FORWARD SOMERSAULT

Value: If you have not already taken home movies of your youngster's attempts to turn a somersault, get out the camera now!

Here's How: Tell him: "Put your hands down, touch your head to the mat, push with your toes and over you go!" He may need a little push on his bottom, but after a few goes don't be surprised if he turns to you with a look of disdain and says, "Do self!" What a thrill for him, and for you!

How Many: Two somersaults; may be repeated daily.

EXPLORING

Your child still needs plenty of room to explore and, because his attention span is short, he moves quickly from one activity to another. His playthings should be learning things and should fit his level of development. The playthings we offer here will fascinate him and focus his energies for longer periods of time. The suggested activities assure development in special movement areas.

Super Stuff

Ping-Pong balls are fun because they are so easy to control. Now, too, tots can do more than just throw and chase them. Ask your toddler to place his Ping-Pong ball on a smooth surface and blow on it so it will move. He will become aware of breath control, learning to take deep breaths or short, little ones to keep the ball rolling.

Next, have him roll the ball down an incline, where he can see a good demonstration of gravity. After he watches it a few times, give him a circular tube, such as a juice can with both sides taken off or an empty paper towel roll, and ask him to insert the ball through the tube. Ask him to bounce it on a table or smooth floor. A child enjoys tracking the Ping-Pong ball with his eyes and hearing its neat bouncing sound.

Plastic cushioning, used to wrap breakables, can be purchased in large sheets wherever packing materials are sold. Your explorer will love jumping on the sheets and popping the air bubbles. For a change ask him to walk softly or roll on the cushioning so he can feel the unusual texture with his entire body.

Show your toddler the differences and similarities between a Ping-Pong and *tennis ball*. Ask her to throw the tennis ball into a basket or box, using eye-hand coordination skills, then let her toss it between her legs, carry it under her chin or propel it on the floor with a rolled-up newspaper.

Plastic, tin or paper *dishes* are great playthings. Aside from their obvious use to serve a pretend meal, they can be balanced on different body parts while your child walks around a room. Tell her to stack the dishes or to line them in a row and count them. Outside, show her how to throw a plate like a Frisbee.

Plastic or cardboard numbers can be purchased wherever educational toys are sold. Place them on the floor and have your child step on them as you call out the numbers together. He can jump from number to number and walk in different patterns: tiny steps, giant steps, sideways steps, backward steps. He can crawl over them. Play wheelbarrow, holding his legs parallel to the floor and letting him place his hands on the numbers. And your learner's imagination will flourish the minute you let him do his own thing with them!

Silly Pool

It's that old favorite again! Put some flour in the wading pool and give your explorer a flour sifter, ice-cream scooper, spoons, cups and plastic dishes. This medium provides great eye-hand practice. If you haven't tried tortilla flour, use some alone or mixed with all-purpose flour for a fun variation.

Eye-hand coordination prevails as your tot tries to string a shoelace through large, round *macaroni*. Or give him a piece of construction paper and some glue and help him make a design with the pasta. Hang his creation on the refrigerator, where he can show it off to his little pals. Another time cook the macaroni and ask your toddler to pick some up with a toothpick. He will poke his fingers into the holes, tear it, squish it between his fingers and—of course—taste it.

Fideo is coiled pasta—a different texture and design to break, crumble, crush and uncoil. Show your tot how to stick a spoon through the coils, too.

ALL AROUND

Smelling and Tasting

Scientists claim that the average human is aware of two thousand odors, and that the sensitivity can actually be doubled with training. Imagine your toddler's joy with these!

Give your child some honey and other *sweet things* to taste. Let her feel the stickiness. Bears love honey; maybe you can relate the sensation to a cuddly bear story. When you fix ham and fish, let your toddler taste their *saltiness*. Children make remarkable faces when they taste *sour* foods. Give your toddler plain yogurt and watch her reaction. Let her drink a little quinine water, too. She will make a funny face at its *bitterness*.

When you offer a new food, talk about its *temperature and texture*: ice cream is cold and smooth; rolls are warm and chewy. Butter melts on a warm food because it is soft.

When you are cooking, offer your child samples of foods he may not taste for dinner but can *smell cooking*: cabbage or liver. Check out your *spice rack* and see what new aroma to offer your tot.

Seeing and Manipulating

Give your toddler a small box of raisins to *open and close*. He uses principles of eye-hand coordination to open the box and his pincer grasp to eat the raisins.

New balls are great fun. Teach him to make a foil ball. A foam football has a distinct feel when tossed. Give him a baseball-size whiffle ball with holes, too. Tie a string through one hole and hold it or attach it so he can hit it with a rolled-up newspaper or Ping-Pong paddle—a carryover skill for future sports prowess as well as reading and writing.

Stiff *cardboard books* are still favorites, as are pop beads. Your toddler can now not only pull apart the beads but push them back together.

When you are working outdoors, give your toddler a bucket of water and paintbrush so he can *paint the house with water*. The water will leave enough of a mark to satisfy him and dry quickly enough to make you happy. Let him help take down the *bird feeder* and fill it with seed.

Hearing and Language

It's important that you listen with obvious interest to what your child tells you. Encourage her chatter by making her feel that what she says is meaningful. Remember to speak slowly and clearly when you chat together, and use simple words and everyday phrases.

While walking outdoors or through stores, take turns *pointing*. Give your toddler a book and ask him to name objects he has seen in real life, like a cat, dog, truck, store and so on. If he can't name the objects, label them for him.

By now your toddler is able to describe a situation or object using *adjectives*. If he is wet, he can say, "diaper wet." He will often describe food: "ice cream, cold," or "soup, hot." Encourage these two-word sentences and continue to describe the properties of foods for him.

Use your feely bag now as a *language bag* by filling it with a sponge, brush,

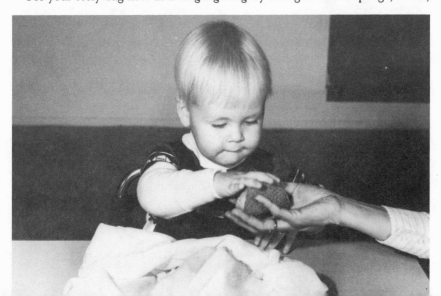

rock, rubber ball—all sorts of everyday objects. Request an item and have your child reach into the bag and find it without looking.

After you finish a *telephone conversation* with your spouse or a relative, give your tot a chance to hold a short conversation of his own. Continue to call his attention to *environmental sounds*: a cricket, frog, police siren or ice-cream truck (a favorite!). Ask him what makes the sounds.

Imitating, Imagining and Language

Your toddler learns wonderful secrets about himself if he has healthy role models and ample opportunities to observe people perform tasks. He asks simple questions and watches goings-on with hawklike concentration.

Give your toddler a large piece of paper taped to the floor or his table and show him new ways to *scribble*. Draw a circle or another geometric shape with a crayon, fountain pen or pencil, and watch again for a hand preference.

Shoe boxes fascinate youngsters. If you have several, ask your little one to insert one into another, from small to large. Show her new box shapes: a heart-shaped Valentine box, a round hat box and a rectangular shirt box.

Colorful plastic *geometric blocks* can be stacked high, built into tall buildings and, best of all, knocked down! Your child can make an obstacle and step, crawl or sit on it; he can push the blocks, carry them and pretend they are different objects. These blocks will have more uses over the next few years as your child's sense of fantasy develops.

In previous months your child pretended to drink from an empty cup. Now she pretends to drink a *special liquid*, like apple juice or coffee. Take her imagination a step further by asking if she would like sugar in her pretend coffee, then "spooning" some in and "stirring" it. Children love to *pretend-talk on the telephone*, too. Help your tot invent pleasant conversations by talking on her toy phone with someone she actually knows.

Give your toddler *simple household items* to substitute for imaginary objects, such as a scarf wrapped around his neck to pretend he is a superhero, pots and pans for pretend cooking, old shoes and jewelry to play house, and the like. When you look through a book or magazine, point to objects and ask your imitator to *pretend to use them*: if you see a toothbrush, let him "brush his teeth"; a comb, "comb his hair"; a chocolate chip cookie, "eat it" and so on.

Talk about what you just did and what you will be doing next so your child starts to understand and use the *concept of time*: past, present and future. "Yesterday we went to the store." "Today we are going to Toddler Play." "Tomorrow Grandma is coming to visit."

Teach your toddler to use *pronouns*: "I," "me," "you," "he," "it." The only way he learns these tricky parts of speech is to hear you use them: "I will help you," instead of "Mommy will help you." Don't criticize his mistakes at this age; that will discourage him.

Self-Awareness

As self-awareness matures, your child strives to further control her immediate surroundings. She constantly wants to try things on her own. Encourage these endeavors and guide her to success.

Your child is more and more aware of discomfort, such as a wet diaper. She will come to you, saying, "Diaper wet," and ask you to change it. Take care of her needs right away so she will continue her efforts to communicate.

Often we do too many tasks for our children, mainly in the interest of time. Get your child started with a simple task, *like washing his hands and face*. Give him a hand towel to wash with and one to dry with, and let him do the job himself. Let your child soap up in the tub, too, and *review body parts*—chest, shoulder, heel, shin.

Make a *handprint* of your toddler's hand. Cut a piece of 5-by-7-inch burlap to match your home's decor. Ask your artist to spread his hand on the burlap and, with a felt pen, outline it. Put his name at the bottom of the picture, along with his age. Unravel the ends of the burlap slightly, tie a pretty ribbon on the top and it's ready to hang!

Problem Solving

As your child plays, she learns to solve some problems by herself and decides to ask your help with others. Her selectiveness aids more crucial, future problem solving.

If she is ready, challenge your child to a more difficult puzzle—one with five or more pieces. Give her time to select and guide the correct piece into its slot. If she has trouble and begins to get frustrated, guide her hand to the right place.

Your toddler is ready for a famous *stacking toy*: placing the colored doughnuts on the spindle in their correct order. Tell him which end is large and which is small.

Make four circles, two small and two large, from cardboard, and glue pretty felt of the same primary color on all. Once your toddler can *match circles* of the same size, place one big and one little circle on the table and ask, "Please give me the big circle. Now please give me the little circle." Using the *plastic numbers*, ask your toddler to put the first three in order. Once he learns to do that, add two more.

Body Positioning

Allow your child time to *play outdoors*—running in every direction, jumping, climbing and rolling. Your child also enjoys the steady, sustained up-and-down movement of *swinging*. Climbing up and down hills develops this sensation, too, but your mover must exert more effort.

A simple, *short stroll* around the neighborhood allows your tot to pick up various objects for her nature basket. She can stop, bend and grasp items more easily now.

Socializing

In her book *Helping Children Grow Through Play,* Joan E. Cass states that children get immense value from playing with each other. Here is the real clash of wills among equals! Let your child try things out, make his own mistakes and work out his own fantasies.

Teach your helper cooperation by simply asking her to *pick up* her toys. If you get down on the floor with her and help, she will be more willing to cooperate. Let her put the toys where they belong and thank her for being such a good helper.

Your toddler still takes pride in *helping around the house* because he enjoys doing what adults do. Let him dust, scrub, help empty the dishwasher and put plastic bowls away. Be pleased with his efforts. If you have to redo the work, don't do it in front of him.

Short trips fascinate your child: a trip to the fabric store, car wash, drive-through bank, drugstore. Afterward talk about what you saw and ask your keen observer what he enjoyed most.

Your snuggler expresses feelings of affection through her attachment to certain possessions and may hold something close, saying, "All mine." One favorite object may be the stuffed animal that she seats next to her, wraps up and puts to sleep and feeds.

If your toddler is *afraid* of a certain person, animal or object, such as the doctor or a large neighborhood dog, ask her to play doctor or doggie. This helps overcome such fears by distinguishing between real and imagined danger.

Chapter 17

MINE, MINE, MINE!
Twenty-four Months

HOW DO YOU DO?

As your child approaches her second birthday, you begin to notice more substantial control in her activities. Her attention span is longer. She participates with more enthusiasm in circle games, loves to run up and down the ramp, balances on the beam, jumps off obstacles and propels herself up and down on the inner tube trampoline.

A child's little finger, hand and wrist actions are more coordinated now. Puzzles which were tricky are now easy to complete. Your toddler has fully developed right- or left-handedness, can manipulate more readily with one hand and can alternate from one to the other. She enjoys building a tower with six or eight cubes and is beginning to build upward with large plastic geometric blocks.

The whole job of childrearing becomes easier once your toddler begins to perfect language skills. Jargon is dropping out and sentences are dropping in. Not only is her communication improving, but she is asserting her wishes through phrases: "It's mine," "Go away," or "Don't want to."

In fact, her command of language is improving so fast that you can't keep count of her total vocabulary. For starters, she can now proudly tell you her first and last name. She is beginning to use the pronouns "me," "you" and, sometimes, "I" (though not always correctly). Distinctions between "one" and "many" are clear to her, and she understands the meanings of "another" and "more." She knows what "soon" means and is learning to wait, but don't expect her to wait a long time. A minute seems an eternity to your mite.

What a social bug she is becoming, too! In our classes, twenty-four-month-olds interact, in spurts, with peers. At this age children playing together harmoniously are lovely to watch.

Sometimes, as they complete their second year, children become complicated little persons who like to have their own way. New items in class can become catalysts for battles, since the students are all anxious to manipulate a new object at once. Sometimes aggressive tendencies emerge, with one child grabbing, pushing or hitting another. If this occurs redirect your child's attention to other activities and discourage the hitting. This helps her distinguish between acceptable and unacceptable behavior. Try to correct mistakes in a positive way, without scolding or criticizing, so as not to hurt your child's feelings. For the most part, she likes to please you and is struggling to accept and obey your rules.

Your tot is now capable of completing many tasks on her own. She can feed herself, drink from a cup and replace it properly on a table. She role-plays everyday domestic activities, paying more attention to finer details, like dialing the telephone and saying "hello" and "good-bye" to pretend callers. She is still a long way from being independent, however, and depends on you for all essential needs.

Note that the list of new exercises is a bit smaller, and the repeated movements are expanded. Each movement that has appeared in *Playful Parenting* has a progressive element to it; the more your child practices, the more she learns about certain aspects of body and space awareness: balance; forward, backward and sideways movement; changes in position due to gravity. Repeat movements from previous chapters which your child has particularly enjoyed, asking her to quicken her pace or strive for more accuracy. Where she started seated, ask her to stand for a movement; where she moved forward, add a backward element. Watching her progress from a hesitant, incomplete start to a clean, steady and complete finish is one of the greatest joys of the program.

Love and support your unique little person. You have nurtured her specialness these past two years; continue to pique her curiosity as you play and introduce new challenges. She will beam with self-esteem due to her accomplishments in each area of development. Congratulations for your hard work as we complete this wonderful second year of your child's life.

SUPPLIES

tire—one
big ladder
barrel of fun
chairs—two
big bolster
parachute
railroad track
beam
tilt board
tape
rope
tube
super stuff—golf tubes, Tootie Toss
silly pool—fresh and frozen peas, clothespins, rubber bands

GETTING READY

Your tot now imitates your movements with much better form. She is anxious to please you and will try anything that sounds and looks like fun.

Loosening Up

This pretty dance develops directionality as your toddler turns to the right and to the left. Create your own tune:

> *I can dance upon my toes,* [Move in a circle to the right and left.]
> *Tra-la-la-la-la.*
> *Softly, softly, on my toes.* [Repeat, to opposite direction.]
> *Tra-la-la-la-la.*
> *When the dancing tune shall stop,*
> *On the floor I'll gently drop.*

Body Awareness

At two your toddler begins to locate rather than name body parts. Make sure she is familiar with the body part and has had practice saying its name before you ask to find a specific part. Practice naming while changing clothes and bathing.

THIS IS THE WAY (USE THE TUNE OF "MULBERRY BUSH.")

> *This is the way we wash our hair, wash our hair, wash our hair,*
> *This is the way we wash our hair, so early in the morning.*
> Second verse: *This is the way we brush our teeth.*
> Third verse: *This is the way we turn our wrists.* [Move up and down
>   and turn around in a circle.]
> Fourth verse: *This is the way we move our ankles.* [Turn up and down
>   and in and out.]

Rocky Robot Says: Mom and Dad should get together to play this game.

> *Touch your knee to Daddy's knee.*
> *Oh! what fun he can be.*
> *Touch your toes to Mommy's toes.*
> *Tickle them and don't let them go.*
> *You're doing great;*
> *So let's all sit down and take a break.*

Finger Play

Your child can now move little fingers and hands in unusual ways. She will stare intently to imitate you during this rhyme. Let her repeat it until she gets it correct.

MY FAMILY

> *Here is my family, standing tall,* [Begin with thumb and touch each finger in turn.]
> *First there's me, and that's not all.*
> *Next comes my mother, pretty as can be,*
> *And my father, who's good to me.*
> *Then comes my brother, who's big and strong,*
> *And my baby sister, who goes "goo goo," all day long!*

Rhythms

For the young child, music and movement go together. He is uninhibited as he tunes in his little ears to the fun words in records or rhymes. In this rhyme do the actions indicated:

> *Wiggle your fingers, and clap your hands,*
> *And quickly turn around.*
> *Hop to the left,*
> *Hop to the right,*
> *Bend over and touch the ground.*
>
> *Wiggle your fingers and clap your hands,*
> *And quietly sit down.*
> *Lean to the left,*
> *Lean to the right,*
> *Sit without making a sound.*

Winnie Wedo Says: Body rhythms develop good timing and teach many words while describing actions:

ELEPHANT EARS

Bend your elbow out and in, away from your body. Say "out" and "in."

FLIPPERS

Lie on the floor on your tummy and raise your right and left hands, then slap them on the floor, saying, "Together, up and slap the floor."

Pretending

What a great pretender your little person is becoming! Sneak a peek when she plays; you'll be surprised at her vivid imagination.

BIRTHDAY CAKE

Today is [child's name]*'s birthday,*
Let's make her [him] *a cake;*
Mix and stir, [Do stirring action.]
Then into the oven to bake. [Pretend to hold cake in both hands.]

Here's our cake so nice and round, [Make a circle with arms.]
We frost it pink and white; [Action of spreading frosting.]
We put two candles on it,
To make a birthday light.

—LOUISE SCOTT AND J. J. THOMPSON

Race Car Driver. Hold the tire upright and ask your toddler to hold the other side. Gently roll the tire backward as your driver learns to roll it forward. When he gets the idea of handling it, make the game more complicated by moving the tire to the left and to the right, as if you were maneuvering around a curve, and ask your driver to turn the car to the left, then the right. Tell a story about a safe driver who watches out for other traffic.

Another time, have your safe driver roll the tire backward as you roll it forward. As he watches where he moves his "car," he is aligning posture and developing body control, coordination and space awareness. Play this game for two to three minutes each day.

Locomotion

Set up a simple obstacle course using the ladder, ramp, barrel, chairs and bolster. Create a fantastic story or let your mite invent something. To get her started on her trip, here is an example: "Once upon a time there was a little child who loved to run up and down the grassy hills in the country [use ramp, going up and down]. As she softly walked by a farm, she saw a horse galloping around [gallop around room]. She said, 'Hi, Mr. Horsey. How are you today?' He answered, 'Naaaaaaay.' She marched off into the woods, creeping and crawling [use the barrel, chairs] through the bushes. She came to a bridge [ladder] and crossed on tiptoe because she didn't want to wake the fish. She came to the top of a hill and decided to roll down [use bolster] and let the grass tickle her body. What a wonderful, adventurous day she had!"

Bubbles. Bring out the parachute to generate more spatial and body awareness excitement.

HOT DOG

Have your child lie on the end of the parachute and tell him you are going to wrap him like a pig in a blanket. Wrap him about five to eight turns. Then tell your tot you are going to unwrap him and pull the parachute toward you until he rolls completely off it. Do this two times, once a day.

SWINGING

Have your toddler sit in the parachute while you and Dad pick him up and swing from side to side, forward and backward and around in a circle to the right and the left. Bounce him up and down, too, by lifting the parachute slightly. He will develop good balance, spatial awareness and posture control as he rights himself to maintain balance.

MOVING OUT

According to N. C. Kephart, author of *Slow Learner in the Classroom,* "To explore and learn about his environment, the child must move about in his environment, and this movement must be *for the purpose* of contacting and interacting with the environment or parts of it." These developmental movements allow your tot to better understand himself and his surroundings. Keep your child's personality in mind as you explore, and remember to direct his attention to his *goal* instead of his *performance*. It is better for the child to possess lower skill levels in a number of activities than high skill levels in only a few.

Partner Movements

Now that everyone is warmed up, let's stretch!

TICKLE TOES

Value: Let's see if you two can touch your toes without bending your knees.

Here's How: Stand facing each other with your feet wide apart. Space your-selves, leaving enough room to bend over without bumping heads. Hold your tot's hands and guide them to touch her toes, right hand to right foot and left hand to left foot. Count toes, then come up to rest. Eventually he will do it alone.

How Many: Two toe-touches, increasing to four as flexibility increases; may be repeated daily.

Assistive Movements

DIVE ROLL

Value: We are now combining two movements: running and doing a somer-sault. As your "big kid" does this exhilarating stunt, he will increase his body and spatial awareness and further develop body control.

Here's How: Make sure there is plenty of moving space. Ask your child to run and roll over the bolster into a somersault. As he goes over the bolster, help him tuck his head and watch for hand placement. (You may modify the exercise by having him walk instead of run.)

How Many: Two rolls; may be repeated daily.

TARZAN CLIMB

Value: Your swinger needs to coordinate many muscles to reach the summit, then climb down the ladder.

Here's How: Lean the ladder against a chair and secure it snugly. Hold your climber's hand and ask him to climb the ladder, alternating feet, without holding onto it with his hands. When he arrives at the top, have him turn around and

climb down again, with your one-handed assistance. He will enjoy a big "Cheetah" hug as you sweep him off the floor.

How Many: Two climbs; may be repeated daily.

BACKUP

Value: Massaging your child's back for a few seconds before she takes off on this jaunt will make her even more conscious of her spatial and balancing progress.

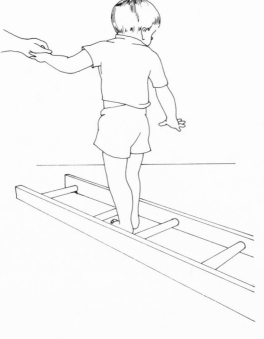

Here's How: Place the big ladder flat on the floor. Holding one hand, ask your toddler to walk backward over the rungs. Tell her how nicely she is walking.

How Many: One backward walk and back to starting position; may be repeated daily.

TILT 'N' LILTON

Value: This movement on the tilt board is more complicated than the last because your child must now stand. He must shift his weight to the center of the board to maintain balance while experimenting with gravity. Practice in shifting quickly to maintain balance helps avoid dangerous falls.

Here's How: Ask your child to step on the tilt board. Hold his hands while he tilts back and forth, exploring this new kind of balancing.

How Many: Balance for count of ten; may be repeated daily.

Active Movements

HAPPY FEET WALK

Value: Now that your child has developed enough confidence she will want to try walking alone on the beam.

Here's How: Place the beam 5 inches off the floor. Ask your child to mount it and walk forward. Tell her to watch the toy at the other end as you say this new jingle:

Cobbler, cobbler, mend my shoe
Get it done by half past two.
My toe is peeping through,
Cobbler, cobbler, mend my shoe.

How Many: Two walks across the beam; may be repeated daily.

MORE SHAPES

Value: Your toddler is learning to move in different ways along tape shapes!

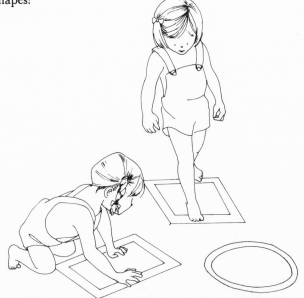

Here's How: Use any kind of tape (glass, masking, electric or colored adhesive tape) and create diamonds, ovals or pentagons on the garage, bedroom or kitchen floor. Ask your child to walk forward, backward and sideways on tiptoe on the shapes, naming each as she goes. Then have her crawl and jump on them. Ask her to invent her own movements!

How Many: Play for a few minutes, once a day. Remember to review old shapes, too.

BUMPY ROAD

Value: Your toddler develops total body coordination as he crawls over the rungs, relating his body in relationship to the ladder.

Here's How: Place the big ladder between two bean bags, books or bricks, four to six inches off the floor. Ask your toddler to pretend to be an animal and to crawl over the rungs on his hands and knees, then on his hands and feet. A poster of a make-believe animal—a dragon or unicorn—will encourage him to invent his own kind of animal.

How Many: Two trips across; may be repeated daily.

CHAIRS AND ROPE

Value: Add a few new twists to this fun whole-body exercise.

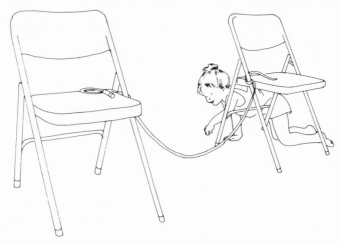

Here's How: String the rope across two chairs about two inches off the floor. Ask your toddler to jump over the rope, then step backward over it and repeat the process. Ask her to weave around the chairs in a figure-eight pattern, first creeping, then crawling under the rope. Playing Follow the Leader with an older sibling makes this game even more fun!

How Many: Two to four of each variety of movement; may be repeated daily.

DOUGHNUT BOUNCE

Value: This directional-learning movement usually brings giggles from your tot.

Here's How: Place the inner tube upright and ask your child to straddle and move with it, forward then backward. You will enjoy watching him handle this object in space.

How Many: Two to three minutes of play; may be repeated daily.

EXPLORING

Time to be free, to experiment with fun new media! Don't organize anything; just let your player use his imagination and fine-tune his tactile sense as he manipulates these objects.

Super Stuff

Golf tubes used to hold clubs in a golf bag, can be purchased in a sporting-goods store. Since they are very long, you may want to cut one in half and leave one long. Your toddler can step on them, roll her foot back and forth on them and insert small objects inside them. She will enjoy galloping like a pony on the long one, while the smaller one makes a great marching baton. Tape a streamer to it and let her run and watch the movement of her banner. Isn't she having a wonderful time?

A *Tootie Toss* is a circular object with a net stretched across it, which can be purchased in any toy store. Your child will make a game of hitting a big balloon with the launcher and watching it float into the air and return to him. He can hit a beach ball against a wall and bounce the ball on the floor. Watch him place one or more bean bags on the launcher, bounce them into the air and try to catch them. This is a terrific object to stimulate creativity and imagination.

Silly Pool

Watch your toddler's delighted expression when he feels partially thawed *frozen peas*. Help him count them and drop them into a jar. He will spend a lot of time picking them up, pressing each one between his thumb and forefinger, squishing them and, of course, eating them. When the jar is full, let him screw on a lid so he can shake them.

Next, give your tot *fresh peas* and show him how to shell them. If you are really daring, open a large can of peas and let him stomp on them!

Children love to play with old-fashioned *wooden clothespins* that slip over a line without being squeezed. Show your tot how to attach these around the edge of a coffee can. Paint three each in blue, red, yellow and green (there are 12 in a package) and ask her to put all the blue ones in the can, then the red and so on. When it's time to put them away, help her count them as she drops them in the can, then show her how to snap on the lid.

Rubber bands are unique, and your explorer will have a wonderful time making them big, bigger, biggest while he learns about elasticity. Let him use two hands, then two fingers, to stretch one. Show him how to put his hand through one so it wraps around his wrist, then ask him to wrap it around a rolled-up newspaper. Pound four nails, about 2 inches apart, into a 4-inch-square piece of wood and ask your toddler to loop a rubber band around two of the nails and, once he is successful with that, around all four. Supervise him while he creates more magic to see that he doesn't put the rubber band in his mouth.

ALL AROUND

Smelling and Tasting

Two-year-olds are reputed to be finicky eaters. They *do* have definite favorites. "Me want," is a common expression for a two-year-old; when you serve a favorite, your tot will show delightful affection toward the food—and you!

At this age your child prefers *whole foods*, like beans, chunks of potato, a whole banana and the like. He may not like the appearance of mixed foods, like potatoes and gravy. Research also shows that two-year-olds prefer *red and yellow foods*, so give him lots of corn, apples, watermelon, bananas and yellow squash. Talk about their color.

At the gas station tell your toddler about the smell of gas and oil. Let him watch Dad or the mechanic change the oil in your car and talk about its color. Take him to as many new *businesses* as you can find: orange-packing house, textile mill, furniture store, paint store.

Seeing and Manipulating

Once your child enters school, many demands will be placed on his fine motor coordination during coloring, drawing, copying and writing. These activities give your child a head start to develop superior eye-hand skills.

Until now, you have let your tot work free-form on the *pegboard*. Now give her a pattern to copy. Ask her to match the vertical line you form on the board, then show her how to create a horizontal line. Use only three pegs, increasing the number as she gets older. She'll still enjoy making free designs, too.

Two-year-olds like animal pictures, so give your tot a *jigsaw puzzle* of his favorite animal, with four or five large, separate, but more intricately shaped pieces. Also, when your tot has mastered stringing large beads, have him string shaped *beads*. Start with round ones. Another fascination is *screwing and unscrewing* large bolts or a variety of jars with lids. These exercises develop wrist agility.

Your child has been jumping, walking and touching geometric forms, so she will like putting the correct pieces in a *form toy* or puzzle. Give her new *colors* to learn, too. Glue felt onto two cardboard circles, using colors she doesn't know yet. Tell her the colors, then ask her to hand you the one you request.

Any type of *magnifying glass* is a new kind of visual stimulant. Ask if the objects are the same or different and if they are larger or smaller than life. Many types of *magnets* are on the market, too; choose some of these to interest your child, such as animals, numbers, letters, geometric forms. Let him touch them and hang them on the refrigerator door.

Children are always fascinated by a *flashlight*; to them it's a magical object that creates light when they switch it on. In a semi-dark room, let your explorer point one all around. Ask him to point up and down, to the right and left and in circles. Show him how to make the light big, then small. Visual tracking, necessary for following words across a page, is the main purpose of this game.

Hearing and Language

At two children can name almost everything familiar and, if they are encouraged, they love to relate their daily experiences. Your child may say "boom" if something falls or "out" to go outside. She is also beginning to apply the rules of grammar; in learning to use the word "feet," she may progress through "feet," "foots," "feets," and finally, return to the correct "feet."

Add something soft, hard, squishy and cold to your *language bag*. Ask your tot to reach in and tell you what she touches.

Bring *water sounds* to your child's attention, whether you are near an ocean, a harbor, a lake, a stream or a pond. Rocking boats, swishing waves, water slamming against rocks, fishing reels being cast and cooing sea gulls are all unique to water. See how many water sounds you can find at home.

Our two-year-old class loves to hear their little voices *echo* when they yell inside the auditorium in our school. This becomes a chain reaction: as they enter the building, one child starts to shout, and the rest follow suit. They have arrived!

One day, by accident, we *let the air out of a balloon*, creating that familiar high-pitched squeal. Several children ran over immediately to locate the source of that noise, so we showed them how to pull a blown-up balloon to make the noise. We talked about air escaping and let them feel the breeze when the balloon was collapsed. The activity was a big hit!

Every child loves a *parade*. Our toddlers use different noisemakers: bells around wrists and ankles, bells with handles, tambourines, sticks and so on. This can be great fun for a play group or at a family party.

When you and your child are looking at objects, *ask questions like* "Where is the toaster? What does it say?" Let him point and give its sound. Buy him a *string toy* that make noise when pulled or pushed. Toddlers also like *books about sound.*

For some real novelty play this *listening game* with your two-year-old: choose three distinct objects, like a whistle, a shaker and an alarm clock. Ask your toddler to close her eyes and listen carefully to each sound, then to identify them. Repeat one if she cannot guess and praise her when she is correct. Then let *her* make the sounds while *you* guess.

While she watches, drop a ball, a spoon and a wallet on the bare floor. Have her turn around, and drop one of the objects again. *Ask her to tell you which one it was.* Add more sounds to both parts of the game as her abilities progress.

Let your child record his voice on a tape recorder while you play games or sing nursery rhymes. He will be fascinated and amused to hear the results. If you are fortunate enough to own a movie camera with sound, he will think he is quite a star.

Imitating, Imagining and Language

Maria Montessori asks: "Is the child's mental horizon limited to what he sees? No. He has a type of mind that goes beyond the concrete. He has the great power of imagination."

Bedtime has always been a traditional *storytelling time*, because you have a captive audience. Make up a story or read one to your child.

Your toddler is ready to scribble on her own *chalkboard.* Using colored chalk, show her how to make large circles, having her move from the shoulders to develop good writing muscles. Draw vertical lines, instructing her, "Up and down," and horizontal lines, saying, "Left to right." Draw a simple animal or smiling face and ask her to add the nose and ears.

Give your artist one *finger-paint* color and ask her to paint a picture for you. She'll go wild creating a masterpiece. Next time use two colors and let her mix them to form a third.

Ask your child to *mold some clay* into a ball. Her fingers will become quite dexterous while you help her make a simple person or animal figure. *Puppets* are popular with two-year-olds, too. Children kiss and wave bye-bye to them, and even follow their directions when they would not normally listen to a parent or teacher. Winnie Wedo and Rocky Robot make successful puppets whom children are happy to please. Ask your tot questions, and the puppet is likely to answer!

Your child now *pretends to feed and bathe* her stuffed animals and treats them very nicely. On occasion, though, you may hear her scold an animal, saying, "No, no!" Does this remind you of anyone?

Let your child *dig and plant* his own garden. Give him a pack of seeds and show him how to plant them. *Doctor kits* also provide hours of tender caring for sick animals, friends and parents. Nothing is funnier than getting a dental check-up from your child.

When talking with your child, be sure to stress the use of *proper names* instead of nonsense words. Even if your tot says "bow-wow" or "wee-wee" and you know what he means, repeat the correct words and he will eventually imitate your vocabulary. School reading and comprehension will be more easily acquired if he hears good grammar and adult vocabulary at home.

Self-Awareness

Selma H. Fraiberg states in her book *The Magic Years*:

> Now, the more conscious the child becomes of himself as a person, an
> "I," the more he values this body which encloses his psychic integrity,
> seems to be closely bound up with the completeness and integrity of the
> body.

This is the *age of the bandage*. Whenever your toddler cuts, scratches or
bruises himself, he wants to put a piece of gauze adhesive on his injury to feel
"whole" again—one step beyond the ice cube. He is greatly concerned with
being safe and intact and feels immediately restored once that cure is pasted
on!

Your child should know and be able to locate certain *body parts*: eyes, ears,
nose, mouth, head, hair, teeth, chin, neck, shoulders, arms, elbows, wrists, hands,
fingers, thumbs, back, chest, stomach, navel, legs, knees, ankles, feet and toes.
We have tried to include these in Body Awareness activities. If your child knows
all of them, give her new parts to learn.

Problem Solving

Give your child simple *counting and number toys* and check her ability to nest
bowls and barrels in their proper order. Introduce *snap-together toys* and see if
she can take them apart and put them back together. Gear these toys to your
toddler's abilities; you don't want her to become frustrated.

Your child will enjoy playing with a *sand machine*. He can discover that the
weight of the sand turns the wheels. In fact, try to give your twenty-four-month-
old opportunities to solve problems presented in *everyday situations*: climbing in
and out of spaces, dropping and picking up, dressing and undressing. Don't rush
to do something for your tot unless he seems overwhelmed. Instead, see if he
comes to you for help.

Body Positioning

Your child will exercise different muscles and joints while maneuvering these
objects. He is furthering space awareness and body control.

Your tot loves the sensation of bouncing up and down and back and forth on
his *rocking horse*. Add a *gym set* for a real bounty of movements: swinging,
climbing, hanging, gliding and sliding. When small friends visit, be sure to
supervise their play, especially near moving parts. Try incorporating the ladder
and slide into your developmental movements.

Take your child on *walks*. Don't hurry him; give him time to explore and remember that his legs are shorter than yours! Tote your *nature basket* and collect treasures he can show Dad.

Build a clothes rod and pegs for your helper to *hang up clothes*. Give him a place to hang his towel, washcloth and toothbrush, too.

Socializing

Arrange for your twenty-four-month-old socializer to play with peers two or three times a week. The children will rarely interact but will enjoy being together. Your tot still has problems *sharing*, because he has to understand ownership before he can learn to let go. For now, "it's mine" is what you frequently hear. Reinforce your child's right to hold onto his own things, especially when other children are present, and redirect them to different toys. Once your child

feels confident that his things will be returned to him after play, he will share graciously.

Even though your child seems much more mature now, she is still capable of creating mischief. Provide her with a *play center* where she can keep occupied. A small table and chair in the kitchen, her bedroom or a corner of the basement might allow her to be near the action while exploring her own activities. And having a fenced-in backyard for a play center allows her tremendous freedom.

More *conscious of people*, your tot may now be shy around strangers, especially adults. Once he becomes acquainted with a newcomer, though, he will bring out his favorite toys to share.

Part IV

MINI PLAY

Twenty-five Months to Three Years

INTRODUCTION

Happy birthday! The second birthday is exciting, because children are so much more aware of their celebration. Make your child's special day meaningful. Child psychologist Dr. Kevin O'Shea suggests letting your child help plan a party. Bake a cake or cupcakes and let him add a personal touch by decorating with a tube of colored icing. Invite three to four little guests to visit for a few hours, listen to records and play with toys. Have fun—and take lots of pictures!

Babyhood is over. Your child now looks more grown up and has matured dramatically during his first two years: socially, emotionally, physically and intellectually. During this third year he will consolidate these gains, making sense out of the countless fragments of life that he has experienced.

Your little person continues to show genuine excitement about physical activities. And his eagerness is paying off in obvious ways. By the end of this year, he will be jumping from various heights; walking precisely in all directions; climbing the stairs; throwing, kicking, striking and catching more objects; and developing strength, flexibility, endurance, healthy body image and total body coordination.

To keep pace with your child's dramatic growth, new twists have been added to the program as he begins the third year. Although he still needs familiarity and consistency, there is now greater emphasis on new concepts. The program will offer more opportunities for imaginative play, allow him to think through and solve problems and let him plan and carry out complicated activities. Mini Play includes movements and activities to help your child master the basics, refine his skills, move with better coordination and proficiency and add hundreds of new words to his vocabulary.

You will notice a theme for every two months of activities. These were chosen to be meaningful for your child's age: My Family, Visiting the Farm, What People Do, Going to See the Circus, Seasons, and ME! Use each theme as a guideline to new involvement with the program. Much of the excitement this year can be generated by peripheral information from daily life: conversations, field trips and family outings that relate to the bimonthly themes.

Many categories in Mini Play stay the same; however, your child will expand his abilities by repeating movements until he is thoroughly successful. We will continue to do Loosening Up activities in GETTING READY, but your child is now more capable of understanding tension and release. Gradually he will relax and contract the proper muscles at will to develop good body management and coordination.

Body Awareness will teach your child the basics of bending, stretching, twisting and turning and will unveil whole new variations in forward, backward and sideways movement. Finger Play will place emphasis on fine motor skills, adding rhythm to increase his attention span and listening ability.

Rhythm is now entwined with locomotion, so your child learns to keep a steady pace during everyday movements. Pretending and Locomotion encourages him to move about his environment more efficiently, constantly exploring every available space. By age three your child will have better running balance, endurance, strength and coordination and will start, stop and turn more easily. Climbing, a fundamental retained from his creeping days, is used to conquer obstacles while furthering balance, body and space awareness and eye-hand and eye-foot coordination. A new challenge is combining jumping with tumbling stunts, and hopping, galloping and rolling are added this year.

We have taken the fun a step further by incorporating a child's first love: pretending. You'll find several stories and many more story ideas to tell your child while he performs on an obstacle course. These will offer him the opportunity to hear and visualize an idea, expand his vocabulary and stretch his imagination. What could be a better developmental asset?

Exciting new categories have been added to MOVING OUT: Balancing Movements, Up and Away Movements and Playing with Objects in Space. We chose these categories because each addresses an important aspect of learning and because our little students love them!

Balancing Movements involve floor play (floor exercise) and use of the beam, big ladder, railroad track and tilt board. The difference between your child's left

and right side is again stressed, because laterality is necessary to successful reading and writing (for sustained left-to-right progression across a line of print).

Since your child will jump off nearly anything he can climb onto, we have
included fun airborne activities in Up and Away Movements. The box, inner
tube trampoline, ramp, big bolster and wedge are used to channel your child's
endless energy into exploratory movement. A variety of other large-muscle activities challenge his motor skills, creativity and imagination. The benefits are
better muscular control and coordination, healthy posture and more mature
balance.

Playing with Objects in Space brings four terrific areas of play into focus—
activities involving throwing, catching, striking and kicking. Here your youngster is requested to use many objects, such as balls and bean bags, in structured
activity, in contrast to EXPLORING, where random movement is the name of
the game.

Because your child's tempo is so greatly expanded, movements are now listed
as oral directions to your child. Going through the lists at your own pace is
refreshing and more supportive of your child's progress and needs. Attempt at
least one suggestion from every category daily and add more and more of your
own ideas as you progress through the year. And if your youngster doesn't
understand a new concept from your explanation, don't hesitate to demonstrate
it. He will model your behavior and comprehend the movement even faster. He
may even pat you on the back for your effort!

Super Stuff is now the single ingredient of EXPLORING, since two-year-
olds are simply not content to be confined to a wading pool anymore. ALL
AROUND activities for the entire year are listed together at the end of Chapter
18 to facilitate your time and energy and your busy doer's talents. Refer back to
this single list throughout the third year.

As your child enters this intense period of learning independence and self-
control, patiently concentrate on his good qualities. Since he is still curious and
persists in touching everything, when problems arise, redirect his attention to
something he is allowed to touch.

One of the reasons a two-year-old's life is so complex is his realization of so
many possibilities: yes or no, come or go, give or take and on and on. Your child
is struggling to maintain his self-control as he balances these alternatives.

In the meantime playing with little friends in familiar surroundings is an
important "distraction," making him more independent and preparing him for
an upcoming adjustment to school. Children must be allowed to imitate each
other, communicate in their own language and learn social skills. In our classes
we see more children take turns, share toys, peacefully agree and disagree and
cooperate at this age, but a great deal of time must still pass before they truly
understand and empathize with each other. Keep an eye on their play, from a
distance, to prevent hitting or arguments.

While your child plays, you'll be acutely aware that his language is becoming
clearer and more refined. Remember that you and Dad are still his best role

models. As he listens to your broad vocabulary, his own language skills become more adult and he begins to express his views about everyday situations. In fact, by the time your child is three, he will have a vocabulary of a thousand words!

And language skill is just one indication of his growing independence. He has unique ideas and creates activities without much guidance from you. In our Mini Play classes we hear, "Don't help me," "I can do it myself," and the ever-popular, "No, no, no! Go away!" He knows what he is doing and will try very hard to succeed at it. As much as he protests, though, he likes to have you nearby to watch and praise his efforts.

Toward your child's third birthday, he will be able to handle complicated manipulative tasks like drawing pictures and lopsided circles to represent a favorite pet or toy. Make-believe becomes more vivid, with your child using a block to represent something that is not even present: a car, a flower, a building. Our young daughters often used a banana as a phone to "talk" to Daddy at the office.

Your child is reflecting upon events and situations so much more than when he was one! His two-year-old concept of life is that everything that moves—like a leaf blown by the wind or the clouds drifting in the sky—is alive and conscious. And, despite a few false notions to overcome, his outlook is charged with the same electric liveliness. Welcome your birthday child into Mini Play. Take a deep breath together, and let's take off!

Chapter 18

DELIGHTFUL COMPANY
Twenty-five and Twenty-six Months

We dedicate this section to "My Family" because, during your child's third year he becomes a true contributor to the family circle. He is beginning to reach out to all those around him, instead of receiving pleasure just from his primary caretaker. He now knows more about himself; therefore, he can accept others into his life more easily. The family takes on new meaning as he better comprehends everyone's position, including other brothers and sisters, nearby grandparents, very close aunts, uncles and cousins and, sometimes, your adult friends.

The next two months' activities emphasize his relationship with the family and help him understand his base of operation. Talk with him about these people in his daily life: what they do, how they help each other and what they mean to each other and to him. By the end of the year, he will eagerly reach out even further to include little friends in his social family.

SUPPLIES

felt board
butcher paper
Hula-Hoop
tires—three or four
expandable tunnel—collapsible cloth tunnel
ramp
wedge
parachute
beam
big ladder
railroad track
tilt board

box
inner tube trampoline
big bolster
objects in play—tennis ball, sponge ball, basketball, beach ball, cloth diapers, balloon, punching man, tissue paper
super stuff—doughnut-shaped, inflatable beach toys; cotton balls; four-square ball; 18-inch dowels

GETTING READY

Loosening Up

I've just come in from playing; [Jog in place.]
I'm as tired as I can be; [Bend over at waist and dangle arms.]
I'll be just like Raggedy Ann;
I'll flop onto the ground.
And lay as still as I can;
My head won't move;
My arms won't move;
I'll just be still;
Because I can.

Body Awareness

1. Show your child some baby pictures and some recent photos. Talk about the changes in his eye and hair coloring.

2. Have him lie on a long piece of butcher paper and trace his outline. Let him name body parts as you both color them.

3. Draw simple pictures of different family members and have your youngster color their body parts. Talk about similarities and differences, such as Daddy having hair on his head but Grandpa having no hair.

Rocky Robot Says:
"Show me how you touch your ear to your shoulder."
"Touch toes to toes."
"Can you put your ear on the chair?"
"Touch the part of your body you smell with."
"Touch Mommy's back with your head."
"Touch your chin, neck, elbows, ankles, chest, hip, heel."

Finger Play

Continue to work on individual finger strength and finger coordination and begin symmetrical training, so your child learns to use both hands together to work on a project.

MY LITTLE HOUSE

This is my little house, [Put fingertips together.]
This is the door. [Put index fingers together.]
The windows are shining, [Pretend to polish windows.]
And so is the floor. [Pretend to polish the floor.]
Outside there is a chimney, [Hold hands up high for chimney.]
As tall as can be,
With smoke that goes curling up. [Wave hands slowly above head.]
Come and see.

—ELIZABETH MATTERSON

GRANDMOTHER'S GLASSES

These are Grandmother's glasses, [May substitute other name. Join
  forefinger and thumb.]
This is Grandmother's hat; [Place hands on head.]
Grandmother claps her hands like this,
And folds them in her lap.

These are Grandfather's glasses,
This is Grandfather's hat;
This is the way he folds his arms,
And has a little nap.

Rhythms

By now your youngster may tug at your hand and say, "Mama, music!" She may enjoy making music, listening to it or endlessly moving to it. The following games let your beautiful child move rhythmically to the music he hears.

Winnie Wedo Says: "Let's play . . ."

MOMMY'S DAY

Mommy's cleaning, Mommy's cleaning,
Dust, dust, dust.
Picked up [tot's name] *little toys,*
And threw them in the chest.

Mommy's cooking, Mommy's cooking,
Stir, stir, stir.
Picked up [child's name] *favorite cake,*
And put it in the oven to bake.

Mommy's done, Mommy's done,
Hip, Hip hooray!
Now it's time to have some fun,
For the rest of the day.

Pretending and Locomotion

Acting out simple make-believe stories allows your youngster to express his ideas. Locomotor activities—traveling from here to there—provide a pleasant variety of sensations to improve balance, posture control, coordination and agility.

Let your child inject his ideas into the following story. Between the two of you, the most exciting adventures will occur using the Hula-Hoop, tires, expandable tunnel, ramp, wedge, parachute, bolster, rope, chairs and rhythm instruments.

MY FAMILY

Once upon a time there was a handsome child named (tot's name) who lived with his Mother and Father and (name other family members, including pets). They all lived in a funny house. It had a round door. (Step through a Hula-Hoop.) And all the rooms were round. (Put tires in a row and have child jump

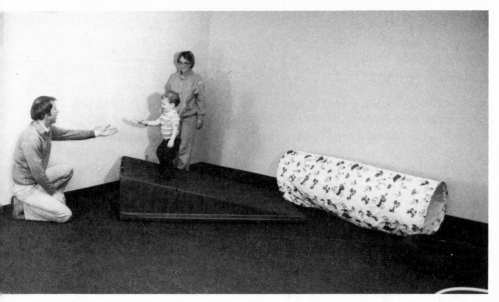

from one to another.) Here is (child's name) room. Here is the kitchen, bathroom, etc. (Have youngster supply names of rooms, or count them.) To get out the back door, he had to crawl through a long, round tunnel into the bright sunshine of his backyard. (Crawl through expandable tunnel.) He liked to climb to the top of the nearby mountain (go up ramp anyway he wants to), go merrily down through the soft clover on the other side (turn somersaults, roll, slide on tummy down wedge), and swim in the cool pond (move on tummy and back across parachute). Then he would run all the way home (run around room) and his mommy would give him a big hug and kiss!

MOVING OUT

Balancing Movements

Now that your cutie pie is warmed up and happily involved in play, her mind, senses and muscles are receptive to the developmental movements. Let's begin with balancing activities, for if your child has good balance, her movements are integrated, freeing her mind to concentrate on abstract matters.

Always direct her focus to a specific spot, follow her tempo and give her plenty of smiles and praise. Do one or two suggestions from each category daily.

Floor Play. (Always followed by tickles and hugs!) Ask your child to:

1. Sit on the floor with hands and feet touching the floor and push up her tummy to make a table. (Pretend to eat off your child's "table.")

2. Pretend to be a bunny rabbit, hopping forward on both feet with your hands by the sides of your head for big ears.

3. Do a three-point balance with: hands and one knee; bottom and two hands.

Beam. Place the beam 5 inches off the floor and ask your child to:

1. Crawl forward and backward like a kitty prowling along a high fence.

2. Walk and carry a baby doll or umbrella.

Big Ladder.

1. Lean a ladder against a chair. Have your child climb to the top, sitting on each rung as she goes.

2. Place the ladder on its edge. Hold it while he straddles it and walks forward and backward.

Railroad Track. Tell your tot:

Place the track on the floor and let's play Follow the Leader across it. I'll do whatever you do. (You may need to give suggestions at first.)

Tilt Board. Ask your child to:

1. Sit cross-legged on the flat board. (Give one-handed assistance.)

2. Kneel down on the flat board. (Give two-handed assistance.)

Up and Away Movements

Box. Ask your child to:

1. Place the box right side up. Push it forward and backward, to the right and left. (Let her get in while you push, too!)

2. Place the box upside down. Push the box fast when it is empty, slowly when it is full.

Inner Tube Trampoline. Ask your child to:

1. Jump and clap hands at the same time.

2. Can you jump with your eyes closed? I will hold your hand.

Ramp. Ask your child to:

1. Run up and down the ramp backward like a frisky puppy.

2. Walk small when you go up the ramp and walk tall when you come down.

Big Bolster. Ask your child to:

1. Do a somersault over the bolster, wearing Grandmother's old hat.

2. Show Daddy how Uncle Bill the logger walks on logs. (Assist your child under his arms, and he will move the bolster with small walking steps.)

Wedge. Tell your tot:

1. Let's play roller-coaster. Chase me down the wedge, rolling over and over. I will chase you up the wedge, rolling.

2. How many people are in our family? Let's take big steps up the wedge for Dad, medium steps down the wedge for Mom and small steps back up for you. (Make up other steps for different family members.)

Playing with Objects in Space

Your child's success at play and, eventually, in sports depends on his throwing, catching, striking and kicking proficiency. Expose him to objects that vary in size, shape and weight. You should each have the same object during demonstrations so your child will keep her eyes open and move with both sides of her body while manipulating hers. Try to do at least one activity from each category daily.

Throwing. Ask your child to:

1. Toss a sponge ball into the air and watch it come down. Next, toss a basketball into the air and watch it land and bounce.

2. Stand on a chair and throw cloth diapers into the laundry basket.

Catching. Tell your tot:

1. Let's sit in a circle and play catch in our laps with a large sponge ball.

2. How does a turtle catch a sock? On its back!

Striking. Ask your child to:

1. Show me how you hit a balloon into the air with your hand.

2. Will the punching man fall over if you hit him with this rolled-up newspaper? Try and see.

3. Tap this dangling piece of tissue paper softly with your hand. Strike it hard with your fist.

Kicking. Ask your child to:

1. Kick the sponge ball with your right foot, then your left. (Pat the proper foot while naming it.)

2. Can you kick the beach ball backward with your heel?

EXPLORING

Super Stuff

We call the first objects *doughnuts* because that is what one little girl named them when we introduced them in class. These are the familiar inflated beach or swimming-pool toys that go around a child's waist. Children learn to identify body parts as they wear the toys around their necks, arms, legs or waists. Your child can do a silly shuffle walk with both feet in one, a single shuffle walk with one foot in and one foot out or a crazy dance with a foot in each toy. What a super imagination your child is developing!

The next time you are in a drugstore, purchase a large bag of *cotton balls*. Their size and softness please your half-pint, and a wonderfully silly time may be had by everyone during a cotton-ball fight. Cotton balls can be gathered up, squashed into a bigger ball, lined up, counted, stuffed under arms, carried on an open palm to a container and piled high on a paper plate. Help your little creator make cotton-ball people and see what other delights she makes happen.

A *12-inch four-square red heavy rubber ball* quickly becomes a treasured toy. Your child can sit, roll and lie on it, drop it from the top of the kitchen stool, push it with her head and carry it between her knees. Just watch your wondrous inventor!

We suggest that you add several more *dowels* to your supply box. They can be laid side by side or end to end, rolled down the ramp, used to make shapes, taped down like ladder steps and walked on or over, tucked under a chin or arm, rolled down legs—the possibilities are endless! Your bright one will talk up a storm describing his tricks with the sticks.

ALL AROUND

Don't rush your child during play; just provide him with many learning situations and let him digest whatever information he can. Arrange toys, books, costumes and the like where he can manage them himself, so he will initiate some experiences. Keep in mind his ability and special interests. Break down a new task into smaller steps, if necessary, but don't help him when he can finish by himself. And remember to praise his good efforts.

Try to match his energy with the following sensorimotor experiences—and don't neglect the ALL AROUND ideas from previous chapters. All of these will satisfy his curiosity, develop his creativity, expand his imagination and develop his self-confidence and independence. Pick one adventure in each category and work on it until your child is ready for something new. Carry out chapter themes when possible, and stress concepts: alike-different, inner-outer, curved-straight, nothing-something, fat-thin, light-dark.

Seeing and Manipulating

Your child can benefit from *interlocking toys* by using his hands to create exciting structures and objects. Kiddie Links are easy to manipulate, feel good and come in bright colors. Once he learns to put them together, he will begin to make lovely designs with them. Trucks connected by magnets are great toys for two-year-olds, since they come apart more easily than those that snap together. These are easy to maneuver and rearrange for hours of imaginative play. Bristle Blocks have prickly textures children like and can be interlocked and built in many directions to create a story. Large Legos will give your child hours of play, too. Begin with a starter set that interests your child—airplane or police car—then more complicated ones, such as hotel and grocery store.

Your child can learn to screw and unscrew *Reels and Wheels* into a spindle. Your *little carpenter* will also want to participate in any nailing and hammering done around the home. Give him scraps of soft lumber, short nails and a light-weight hammer. A Pound-a-Peg Box with a small mallet is a safe toy to start with. And with a *cogwheel board*, your child will learn to insert the correct wheel to make another turn.

Toward the end of the third year, give your child *scissors*. Preschool or kindergarten scissors designed for right or left hands are highly recommended, because they have rounded ends and large finger holes. Draw lines across the corners of a piece of paper and show your child how to snip the small pieces. Then draw a straight thick line, a thinner line, curves and angles and, finally, pictures for him to cut out. Teach your child how to pass the scissors to another person and how to walk with them pointing down, too.

Tracing books help you monitor your child's progress. Tracing around simple cookie cutters is fun, too, and you can purchase templates to trace figures. Make simple *dot-to-dot* designs for your child to follow, or purchase very simple books with large number or letter dot-to-dots.

Teach your child to sort the *pegs in a pegboard set* according to color. Then, on an index card, make a design using the same color as the pegs and have your child transfer that design to the pegboard with the same color. As he gets older, make more complicated designs and combine colors.

Show your eager learner how to use *common household items*: small stapler, hole puncher, large paper clip, clipboard, egg timer, stopwatch, music box, alarm clock, radio, can opener, air pump. Also demonstrate how to *pour* from one container to another. He will learn with your encouragement, even if he makes a spill here and there. Let him help cook; show him how to *squeeze oranges* on a squeezer plate to make orange juice.

Teach your child to *focus on different objects*. Sit in front of her and place four small objects in her line of vision. Place one to her left side and, as she names the object, place one to the right, then repeat. Change the objects quickly enough to make your child move her eyes from left to right. Stress *eye* movement rather than *head* movement. Ask her to do the same for you.

Give your child a large *magnet on a string* to lift small metal objects off the floor. Find a scrap of loosely woven *burlap* about one foot square and a large-eyed plastic *needle*, and show your little seamstress how to push the needle through the material and back to the other side, using yarn for thread.

Continue *chalkboard* activities. Encourage large arm movements as your little

person makes circles, lines, pictures, curves and stick people. Invest in a large chalkboard, if possible, for your child will benefit from it for years. And keep an ample supply of colored chalk.

Place a lipped cookie sheet on a small table and fill it with generous amounts of *messy media*: pudding, gelatin, rice or petroleum jelly. All-purpose flour and little cars provide soothing activity on a rainy day, too. Bringing out these silly old media will make your child laugh now that he is "all grown up!"

Seeing, Hearing and Language

Communication is an essential activity. Help your child learn to talk by naming and describing what she sees. The more she sees, the more she will want to talk and will learn to listen to your explanations.

Storybook dolls are great playthings for both boys and girls. They wear little aprons and, as you read their stories, the cloth page is flipped and the next page has a new face. These are perfect to carry on a trip or to the doctor's office. Your child will also enjoy *participation books*. His attention span and interest in reading will increase as he is introduced to pop-up books, where he lifts up certain objects; finger-puppet books, where he moves a puppet as a story is told; and string books which have certain objects connected to strings.

Talk-about books give your child information about colors, matching, differences and likenesses, seeking and finding, counting, numbers and so on. Try to relate these to each chapter theme. You can also read *books on subjects* in which your child shows interest or about situations within the family, like books on family relationships; science books (a favorite is *The Very Hungry Caterpillar* by Eric Carle, published by Collins-World); and animal books, which are popular and perfect for the farm theme. Many *hardboard books* familiarize a child with the toys, clothing, other children and food in his life. The Golden Books and Random House series provide wonderful, inexpensive books for you to read to your child; and don't forget fairy tales and poetry. If the story isn't too long, your child will also enjoy books with records. During a relaxing time you can help him turn the pages along with the music. After you read a book ask questions like, "Tell me more about the animal."

Your child will enjoy a *tape, coloring book and crayons* around his third birthday. He listens to a tape, then draws his version of the story in a blank coloring book. Your child will also enjoy a *record player* that comes with several different records he can play himself. He will learn the songs happily.

Your child will have endless creative moments with a *marching band*. A drum, in which the top can be lifted, contains a set of castanets, cymbals, a harmonica, maracas, a tambourine and sticks to hit the drum. He will get years of use from this set.

Play adjective and adverb games to supplement your child's predominantly noun vocabulary: the "big" truck, the "round" ball, the "new" dress; run "quickly," walk "slowly" and so on. Ask him to describe what he and other family members are wearing, using colors, fabrics and the like.

Acquaint your child with the *outside world* when you go on small trips, such as the meaning of the three colors in a stop light. Pretty soon he'll shout, "Go!" every time the light turns green and will check to the right and left to see if the road is clear. Ask him to name everything he sees in order on the way to the store, church and playground.

Add even more objects (or different ones) to your *language bag*. Tell her to find a certain object for you, or pick one and have her describe it.

Play *word games* on trips. Every time you see a little car, say, "love bug," or a flag, say, "red, white and blue." Ask your child to name and *classify objects* and activities into categories: vegetables, fruits, furniture, animals, cars, toys, colors. Talk about his activities—Mom's and Dad's, his friends', relatives' and so on. He must visualize as he talks, expanding his vocabulary. Say a word and have your child give you the *opposite*: "big"–"little," "soft"–"hard."

Between the ages of three and six, your child's ability to absorb a second language reaches a peak. She will learn it like English. She needs to hear it spoken frequently, naturally and fluently by someone who speaks it like a native.

Imitating, Imagining and Language

Your child's imagination will develop if you give him a chance to think for himself, develop his own concepts, find solutions to his problems and seek answers to new questions. Allow these experiences to stimulate the diversity and richness of his imagination.

Children like to assume the roles of their parents or siblings as they *play house*. Set up an area in your child's bedroom, the family room or outdoors where she and her friends can act out scenes and experiences from the adult world. A kitchen set lets your child sort utensils, set the table and pretend to wash pots and pans after she is through cooking. Dolls to feed, bathe, change and put to bed teach your child about giving love and growing up.

Give your actor a trunk or boxful of clothes to use for *dramatic play*. To make the pretending more exciting, offer him props: doctor kit, telephone, old hats or novelty hats, jewelry, high heels or man's shoes, scarves, purses, makeup. If you're really industrious, create sets with a card-table house. Sew four pieces of material together for sides and a square piece to connect them on top and slide over a card table. Use different fabrics: make one side a circus, one a farm, one a space station or one a skyscraper.

Water can become anything. For *water play*, give your child containers to fill, pour, empty, squeeze and so on, and household items to explore with, like sponges and paintbrushes. He will be fascinated by learning to manipulate a small plastic water pump, funnels, a baster and measuring spoons and cups. He likes to squirt bottles to spray the plants and help you wash the windows, and give him plastic cups with a sprinkling of holes so he can watch water spray out the bottom and sides.

Remember the *wading pool*? Give your child boats and other bathtub toys and set him outside on a sunny day for joyful play. Let him play with the hose, under your supervision, and show him how to operate the faucet to water the yard. Let your child play in mud puddles, touch rain and inspect a creek or slow-moving stream with shallow water.

Your child is an individual, and her *art* is very special to her. Elaborate on how colorful her work is, rather than asking, "What is it?" Working with art materials develops her dexterity, expresses her memory and makes her aware of shapes, colors and textures, which will carry over to language, science and mathematics.

Continue to give your tot big, *fat crayons*, because they don't break as fast as the thin ones. Later, add felt pens, pencils and fountain pens. Let her experiment with paper plates, brown wrapping paper and newspaper. Give her different sizes of *pads of paper*. Aside from letting her pretend to be a waitress taking your food order, a conductor taking your train ticket or a stewardess taking your boarding pass, these pads come in handy for drawing while traveling.

Spread newspaper over the floor, set up the easel and small tin cans or milk cartons with water, and give your artist an assortment of paintbrushes and three *poster paints* to create whatever her little heart desires. Don't forget to hang the masterpiece.

With a sponge, wet the surface of white shelf paper or glossy finger-paint paper. Have her dip her hands in *fingerpaint* (two or three primary colors) and spread it over the entire area, moving fingers, hands and elbows. (You can add food coloring, to toothpaste or hand lotion to make your own paints.) For a different texture have your child use a small sponge, a mascara brush, a comb, a block or whatever he can think of!

Blot painting—applying paint to the crease of a folded piece of paper, pressing the sides together and rubbing—and *string painting*—dropping one end of a string or yarn into the paint and dragging it across a paper—are also fun painting pastimes.

Your child will continue to enjoy tearing, pulling, bending, squeezing and rolling *clay*. Give him flat-ended toothpicks, pipe cleaners, popsicle sticks, shells, corks and washers to poke and design whatever suits his fancy.

Anything that can be pasted—papers of all sorts, feathers, cotton balls, sequins, ribbon, buttons, yarn, eggshells, dry cereal, toothpicks—is good material for a *collage*. Let your genius's imagination run wild!

Expand your child's love of puppets; build a *puppet theater*. Use a cardboard box and drape a piece of satiny material over the cut-away side. (You can also purchase a curtain that fits into most doorways.) Your child will love watching a puppet show presented by members of his own family! By the end of the third year, he may even be able to start handling large puppets and making up stories, though he'll probably prefer to just watch.

Purchase a *firehouse* or *play house* to teach your tot about the community and help spark pretend play. Keep an ample supply of *blocks* on hand and try to coincide this play with stories from the GETTING READY sections.

Show your child *different means to achieve a goal*. For example, she can pound with a rock instead of a hammer. *Explain things* in very simple terms. Describe what it takes to accomplish a project: what ingredients go into baking a cake or what parts are needed to fix a toy.

Play the *prepositions game*: give your learner a small box and a block and ask him to put the block in, out, below, under, above, beside and behind the box. Help him only if he needs it. Then arrange two to four blocks in different *patterns* and ask your child to copy the patterns with identical blocks.

Self-Awareness

When you are helping your child *dress*, mention the corresponding body part: "Put your right arm into this sleeve." "Put your left shoe on your left foot." Children like to know about *animal parts*, too. Purchase a dinosaur puzzle with four well-defined body parts that are simple for your child to understand.

Give your child books that *picture a situation* and ask if a corresponding statement is true or false, like, "A child is hanging upside down on the bars, true or false?" These are great fun! You can also draw a person whose body parts are misplaced, like an arm coming from the head or one eye missing. Ask your child, *"What's wrong with this picture?"*

Problem Solving

Let your child try to complete these problem-solving games himself. Whenever possible, relate the situations to the real world, like the geometric forms that can be seen in traffic signs, pictures that are in the house and colors that are in his clothes. Give him ample time to be successful, even through trial and error, and praise him for his efforts.

According to research, there is a high correlation between doing *jigsaw puzzles* and learning to read. Once a child has learned the shape and form of letters, he uses the shape and form of words as one cue to their identity. Choose puzzles carefully, looking at them as a child would.

Several puzzle types are interesting for children:

A *stop sign with shapes* comes in four basic, bright colors and has as puzzle parts "stop," "slow" and "go." *Crepe puzzles* are popular in our classes, mainly because of their nice rubbery texture. *Color puzzles* reinforce color, as the child must pick up pieces from an inlay of the same color. A more complicated version has three different bugs, each with two colors written on it. In a *number puzzle* the pieces of each puzzle coincide with the number: the number "1" has one piece, "2" has two pieces, and so on. Lots of reinforcement! *Family puzzles* are hard to find, so grab one if you see one. These have parents, two children and a dog, usually with a small number of pieces. Finally, *sequence puzzles* come in a wooden play board where the pieces can be stood up. Animals, cards, people, snowmen and the like must be placed into their slots according to size.

Purchase this game, or make one yourself! In *Pass the Bag*, your child puts her hand into a bag and feels for a shape (no peeking allowed) that she needs to fill a card. Each shape comes in several colors, adding more challenge. Two years of age is the right time to start *matching colors*. Begin with red, blue and yellow—the primary colors. Cut colored construction paper into circles or squares. Make two sets so you can put one set on the table and give the other to your child. Ask him to match each color. Once he is matching well, ask him to identify each colored piece. Play the game of naming colors throughout the house, in clothing, looking at pictures, going for walks in the neighborhood or when you are shopping.

Teach your child to *count to ten*. Show him how to count his fingers and toes, and ask how many ears, eyes, hands and feet he has. Branch out to include other objects of interest. Ask him how old he is or how many cookies he has. Give him numbers cut out of sandpaper and let him trace them with his finger. (This is great for letters, too!)

Place three Ping-Pong balls and a square block on a table and ask your child to give you the one that is *different*. Then ask for those that are the *same*. Try other household items, too, like three spoons and a fork or three plates and a cup.

Body Positioning

Your child is using many muscles together to perform tasks. Allow her to run, climb, play games and experiment with toys so she adjusts posture, balance and rhythm throughout everyday life.

A *train* with a handle in the back is great to push. Weigh it down with blocks, little friends or favorite stuffed animals. A *wagon* is sturdy enough to fill with favorite treasures and fun to pull. Let your child have a great time learning to maneuver a *stroller* around the house and neighborhood for more pretend play.

Toward her third birthday, give your child a *tricycle*. You'll know she is growing up when you first see her trying to ride her new trike. Have the camera ready for this exciting moment! Also around the third birthday, many parents begin to look at swing sets for their child. We suggest that, instead, you continue to use the equipment suggested thus far in this book, which will give your little learner years of use. As she gets older, alter the equipment enough to create more challenges.

Your child can now have lots of fun learning to balance on *roller skates*. Start on grass with the lightweight plastic type. As your child gets the feel of skating, test his abilities on the sidewalk. He will take a few tumbles, but that's the only way he'll learn.

Remember the ol' *tire swing*? Placed in an old tree, this is a favorite pastime, for your child is now big enough to sit there *alone!* A *circle swing* (or a rope swing with a circular platform) is another fun swing for your two-year-old, requiring that he squeeze his legs and hold on with both hands. He can lean back, close his eyes, swing off a low bench and twirl in a big circle. What terrific sensations!

"Guess what I am?" A simple game of *Charades* will have the whole family in stitches. Let your child guess and act out brushing teeth, playing ball, eating spaghetti and the like.

A pipe *chinning bar* may be set up outside or in an interior doorway to give your youngster a good arm-muscle workout. Place an old mattress under the bar, and be sure he can reach the bar by standing on tiptoe.

All kinds of *grass play* makes your love bug laugh, especially if neighborhood children chime in. Play Statue, Duck Duck Goose and London Bridge, and enjoy spinning games, wheelbarrow and upright handwalk races and a short game of croquet.

Have your child stand stiffly, hands at his sides and feet together, and let him fall back into your arms. Show him how you and Daddy play *Tower Fall* first, to give him the idea. What wonderful trust you are developing!

Socializing

Your growing child has received so much love, attention and acceptance that he will expect the whole world to be friendly and kind. Let him play near others, participate in family circles, express his opinions and make independent decisions. He is truly "all grown up."

You're probably getting much more help from your two-year-old *around the house*: setting the table, emptying ashtrays, cleaning spills, putting toys away, sweeping floors, clearing his place at the table, loading the dishwasher and helping carry small grocery bags. Encourage your good little helper in these *household duties* and tell him you appreciate his work.

Since your child is curious about how things grow, how they look and how they feel, take *science and nature trips* to the pumpkin patch, woods, parks, lakes and mountains, and talk about events and discoveries that pertain to your trip. If you take a walk through a forest, talk about the shapes and colors of leaves, trees and flowers. Tell him everything is related: "The leaves turn red in autumn, then fall off the trees because the sun doesn't shine as much."

Let your two-year-old *plant seeds* in a milk carton, pot or egg carton. Talk about the importance of water and sunlight or shade to keep the plant alive. Tomatoes are easy to grow, and your child will beam with pleasure when he sees the first bud.

Hamsters, gerbils, mice, rabbits, turtles and goldfish are easy *pets* to care for and give your child a feeling of responsibility. Show him how to hold them correctly, show tenderness and learn about their diets and homes.

Weather affects your child directly, for it determines what type of clothing she wears and whether she can play outdoors. Talk about how wind affects her: "It's too windy to play outside today because the dust is blowing." Point out machines that "make" wind," like the hair dryer, fan, air conditioner and heater—hot and cold air! Talk about snow, which is very cold water. "You can pack snow to make snowmen and snow forts." *Reinforce the elements* mentioned in Chapter 22 throughout the third year.

Your social butterfly will like *outings* of almost any kind—as long as other children his age are going, too! Find all the social spots in your town to take your child and some playmates: parks, beaches, ball parks (to watch Dads), amusement parks, shopping centers and, especially, other people's homes. As long as you are near and other children and toys abound, he will have a grand time.

Your child will like to be consulted sometimes in deciding "*Where would you like to go?*" Ask about going for a drive, out to eat, to a friend's house, for a walk and the like. You'll find out what good ideas she has.

Many libraries have simple *story hours* for children two years of age and older. These usually involve several short stories, perhaps a short cartoon and a game or two. If it is done nicely, this can greatly spark your child's interest in books, and the librarian will generally be helpful in selecting appropriate books for your child. Naturally, he will love the presence of peers, and this is just about the right time to introduce sitting *quietly* in a group!

Chapter 19

TALK, TALK, TALK
Twenty-seven and Twenty-eight Months

Two-year-olds' fascination with farm animals is reflected in the great number of stories about animals, many of which are given human characteristics. Farm-animal rhymes have taught generations of children about moral values, fears, temptations, feelings, wisdom and natural phenomena. Through observing, touching, feeding and listening to farm animals, your child learns to distinguish between human and animal bodies, food, shelter and companionship.

It seems a natural progression, then, to dedicate these two months to "A Visit to the Farm." Your two-year-old will love learning about the other creatures that share his world and how they help each other in the chain of natural events. Embellish the next two months with simple stories about farm life. Visit places that relate to farming, such as a dairy, a horse farm or a chicken ranch. Your curious one will enjoy himself immensely, talk, talk, talking about his visit to the farm.

SUPPLIES

> felt board
> clay
> wedge
> tires—three or four
> chairs (two) and rope
> box
> parachute
> beam
> bean bags
> big ladder
> railroad track
> tilt board

inner tube trampoline

ramp

bolsters—big and small

objects in space—yarn balls, cardboard shapes, net ball, large sponge ball, four-square ball, athletic socks, badminton racket, Ping-Pong paddle, balloon, lightweight bat, beach ball, empty milk cartons, pieces of foam, Hula-Hoop

super stuff—bicycle tires, foot launcher, section jump ropes, long streamers

GETTING READY

Loosening Up

TEN LITTLE CHICKS

Ten little chicks on the chicken pen floor, [Bend over.]
Scratching for worms or something more. [Run fingers around on floor.]
Ten little chicks on the roost up high, [Reach up on tiptoes.]
One little chick lets out a big sigh.
The big brown eyes of the cunning fox, [Bend side to side at waist.]
See the ten little chicks up on the box. [Look up.]
Quickly he jumps! But the chicks fly away, [Jump up, run around.]
And hide in their snug little nests all day. [Tuck up on floor.]

Body Awareness

1. Share farm pictures and talk about the people, animals, machinery and food you find on a farm. Make your own scrapbook of favorite farm photos.

2. Create clay figures of farm personalities: farmer, chicken, cow, pig and so on. Talk about what sounds they make and what their body parts do.

3. Dress your youngster in a farmer's hat, a bandana, jeans, old boots or whatever you have on hand, in front of a mirror.

Rocky Robot Says: "Be a Stalking Cat":

When all the house is quiet, [Pretend to be sleeping.]
And the moon begins to shine, [Raise arms up.]

Out stalks the cat, [Get on hands and knees.]
And this is what he finds:
He walks around on silent paws,
Looking for mice out in the barn.
He twitches his tail and arches his back; [Wiggle bottom, arch back.]
Scares a mouse, and says, "I like that!" [Jump forward.]

Finger Play

FOUR PUPPIES

Four little puppies scratched at my door, [Hold up four fingers of
right hand and move up and down.]
One, two, three, four. [Touch fingers.]
I gave them some milk.
And they trotted out the door. [Walk fingers away.]

FIVE LITTLE PIGS

This little pig ate corn. [Begin by touching thumb on child's out-
stretched hand.]
This little pig didn't get up till morn.
This little pig ate wheat,
This little pig danced on tiny feet,
This wee little pig ran as fast as he could
Into the wood.

Rhythms

Music and young children go hand-in-hand. Play a variety of music and let your
two-year-old explorer realize her physical capabilities.

POKEY SNAIL

Pokey snail, pokey snail,
You crawl so s . . . l . . . o . . . w;
Hop toad, hop toad,
This is how you go;
Noisy cricket, noisy cricket,
Why do you jump so high?
Only little birdies fly up in the sky.

LITTLE ROOSTER

> *I'm a little rooster, singing cock-a-doodle-doo,*
> *See me strut all around asking, "How do you do?"*
> *I flap my wings and stretch my crown,*
> *Turning right and left and way down to the ground.*

Winnie Wedo likes to:

1. Feed the chickens. Throw one arm out toward the floor, then throw the other arm out. Alternate for a series of three on each hand.

2. Chase the sheep. Run around the room, waving arms and saying "Shoo, shoo, shoo!"

Pretending and Locomotion

Correlating his movement choices with an idea fulfills a young child's need to show independence. Let him begin with familiar subjects and use simple ideas to give him many opportunities for free movement. How about . . . A visit to a farm? Incorporate the wedge, tires, chairs and rope, box and parachute into your obstacle course and invent a tale about your child's visit to see the corn patch, galloping horses, chicks, ducks and cows that belong on a farm.

MOVING OUT

Balancing Movements

Now that your child's skills are smoothing out, put more emphasis on concepts. Give simple instructions and repeat key words, such as: "scoot sideways," "walk backward," "take giant steps," "walk high," "crawl low." See if he will repeat your key words and, perhaps, make up his own short sentences in response to your questions. You will proudly notice how amiable he is—more satisfied with himself, more adaptive to situations and always talking, talking, talking! Do one to two suggestions from each category daily.

Floor Play. Ask your child to:

1. Do a horse kick. Kneel on hands and knees and kick one leg out straight.

Do two with each leg. (A good whinny and perhaps a little pawing add to the merriment.)

2. Sit on your bottom, lean back on your hands and hold legs straight out for a few seconds, then pound your feet up and down on the floor, together or alternating. Pretend to squash "no-good bugs" that eat the harvest.

3. Walk straight and tall with a bean bag on top of your head: forward, backward, in a circle.

Beam. Place the beam five inches off the floor. Ask your child to:

1. Pretend to be a chicken, grasping her hands behind her back and walking forward, stepping over her eggs (bean bags).

2. Lean hands on the beam and take giant farmer steps sideways.

Big Ladder. While the ladder is placed flat on the floor, ask your child to:

1. Pretend to be a beautiful stallion and prance forward and backward over the rungs, one foot in and one foot alongside the ladder.

2. Crawl and find your way to the end of this ladder with your eyes closed, like a newborn kitty. While I hold the ladder on its edge, show me how you crawl through backward in the spaces.

Railroad Track. With the track placed on the floor, ask your child to:

1. Be a silly goat and walk forward with one foot on top of the track and one foot on the side of the rail.

With the track placed twelve to eighteen inches off the floor, tell your child:

2. A farmer's helper must have strong arms for feeding the animals and tending the garden. Let's see your arms move you sideways to the right and to the left in an upright handwalk. (Offer your assistance.)

Tilt Board. Ask your child to:

1. Show me how a rooster would balance with one foot in front of the other one on the raised board. (Let your child stand with right foot in front, then switch to the left. Give assistance.)

2. How would a tired baby duck fall asleep on the flat tilt board? Perhaps he would sit, bend his knees and rest his head on them. (If your child invents another position, praise his good idea and offer any assistance he needs.)

Up and Away Movements

Box. Ask your child to:

1. Sit on the box and push it backward with your legs.

2. Hold two scarves and jump off the box like a baby bird learning how to fly. Now show me how far you can jump!

Inner Tube Trampoline. Ask your child to:
1. Jump on hands and knees like an angry dog, barking.

2. Jump in a circle to the right and to the left.
(Touch your child's right side, then her left, as you tell her which to use.)

Ramp. Ask your child to:

1. Run and jump into a Hula-Hoop. (Move the hoop further away with each jump and praise him for being such a good jumper.)

2. Slide down the ramp like a wet piglet.

Bolsters. Ask your child to:

1. Be a playful skunk, rolling continuously on the big and little bolsters (as you move them forward).

2. Push the bolster slowly up the wedge, then down and across the room as fast as you can move.

Wedge. Ask your child to:

1. Do a frog jump down the wedge. What does a frog say?

3. How would a turkey walk up the ramp and jump off?

Playing with Objects in Space

Throwing. Tell your tot:

1. Let's pretend the family is picking apples. Stand on a chair and throw yarn balls a short distance into one tire and a longer distance into another.

2. Make a large cardboard circle, square, rectangle, diamond, triangle and oval, and cut out the centers. Lean them against a wall and ask your youngster to throw a net ball through whatever shape you call out.

Catching. Tell your tot:

1. Let's set up the chairs and rope about six inches off the floor and sit opposite each other. We'll toss the large sponge ball back and forth over the rope. (Make sure child is successful by "pouring" ball into her arms.)

2. I'll roll a ball fast down a hallway. Catch it by lunging on it!

Striking. Tell your tot:

1. Use your badminton racket to swing at the balloons. See how far you can hit them—or how high!

2. Let's play baseball! (Give your two-year-old slugger a lightweight plastic bat and position him sideways. Stand fairly close and gently pitch a lightweight softball while someone helps him swing the bat a few times. Soon he will be hitting the ball past the pitcher!)

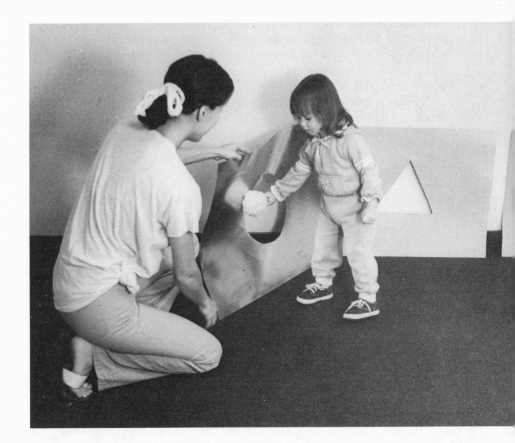

Kicking. Ask your child to:

1. Use both feet and kick over a row of empty milk cartons. Count, one, two, three and so forth.

2. Take a Hula-Hoop and two smaller circles (made from hose in graduated sizes). Kick a ball through the large circle; now the medium-size and small ones. Lay the circles down inside one another and identify them for me.

EXPLORING

Super Stuff

Most two-year-olds like wheels—tractor, tricycle, wagon, stroller, motorcycle, car or train—because of the motion. If this sounds like your child, he will certainly enjoy playing with *bicycle tires.*

You can get two or three used tires (without tubes) at your local bicycle repair store. Spread some newspaper on the garage floor and let your helper assist you in painting the tires bright or fluorescent colors. Once they are dry, see how many games your child invents: hopping in and out of them, playing Tug-of-War, forming patterns on the floor, stacking them, throwing objects through them and walking on them. Compliment your thinker on all his good ideas, and don't forget to chat about the concepts he is refining: around, in and out, bending, twisting, stretching, pulling and so on.

A *Tootie Launcher* demands that your child pay special attention to eye-foot

movement. Her eyes must tell her feet where she wants to go, where she wants to stop and how she wants to move. This sounds simple enough, but some children have difficulty mastering the sequence. When your child steps on the *Tootie Launcher* in the precise spot, balls of all sizes, bean bags, sticks, quarters or shoes fly into the air! Soon she will be able to launch the items with either foot and catch them, too!

Your live wire will discover that, because of the stiff plastic sections but manageable quality of a *section jump rope*, he can form shapes, wiggle it, wind it around his wrist, swing it around, walk on it, jump over it or into shapes, curl up in a shape around it and on and on. Partner activities are also great fun: Tug-of-War, turning in a circle while each holds an opposite end and running together while holding onto it.

We hope that you have been enjoying many types of music during activities. *Long streamers* (five or six feet) lend themselves nicely to light, happy music, fast, furious music or slow, lumbering music. These are the most colorful, bouncy objects to twirl, shake and weave around the room with. Direct your supermover to shake one in front of and one behind you, between his legs and to his right and left. Long streamers of thin plastic or crepe paper are also terrific outdoor companions on a windy day. Running up and down hills builds your child's heart muscles and gives him a feeling of flying. Enjoy!

Chapter 20

THE PLAYMATE
Twenty-nine and Thirty Months

"What would you like to be when you grow up?" Your child will be asked this question over and over from the time she begins to talk. This question of recognition is someone's way of saying, "Look how nicely you are growing! You are becoming an important member of our society. How would you like to help when you are bigger?" It responds to your youngster's deepening curiosity about her world and her reaching out to the people around her.

We are going to expose your two-and-a-half-year-old to many different occupations—to "What People Do." Not only is it fun to learn about singing, painting, fishing, selling, building or acting, but these experiences will help her decide what activities appeal to her. Though many years will pass before she must decide, there are so many opportunities that the search is stimulating and challenging.

Let's help your playmate explore some possibilities through rhymes, games and movement. Expose her to a variety of occupations: watch the person tossing dough at the local pizza house, the mechanic at the gas station changing an air filter or the woman down the street painting her shutters. Adults will delight in your child's looks of "Can I play, too?" and most will be happy to answer her questions.

Since her attention span is still short, a brief look and a quick explanation will usually suffice. You are just whetting her appetite about life so that, later, she will ask more searching questions. Even now her clever comments let you know that parenting is a thrilling experience.

SUPPLIES

ramp
parachute
bolsters—big and small

Hula-Hoop—two
chairs and tires
box
wedge
beam
big ladder
railroad track
tilt board
inner tube trampoline
objects in play—balls: net, whiffle, tennis, Ping-Pong; yarn; balloon; wastebasket; small broom; plastic bat
super stuff—Chinese jump ropes, bubbles and things, cardboard blocks, round foam discs

GETTING READY

Loosening Up

DANCER

> *High upon my toes I go,*
> *Up down, up down,*
> *Rising quickly and then down slow*
> *Up down, up down.*
> *When the dancing music stops*
> *I will gently flop, flop, flop.*

Gracefulness is not limited to dancing. Most things in slow motion appear quite graceful. Move to this rhyme as though in slow motion.

DRIVING A STEAMROLLER

> *Here is a steamroller, rolling and rolling,* [Roll arms up.]
> *Ever so slowly, because of its load.*
> *Then it rolls up to the top of the hill,* [Stretch on tiptoe.]
> *Puffing and panting, it has to stand still.*
> *Then it rolls . . . all the way down!* [Roll arms down to floor.]

Body Awareness

Talk to your child now about some of the working people he may know, so he will learn about their relationship to his world. Stress the roles of people he sees frequently.

1. What part of your body does the dentist look at?

2. The cook in the restaurant fixes your food for you to put . . . where?

3. How does a carpenter hammer? Show me how he saws.

Rocky Robot Says: "Show me . . ."
"What a nurse does." (Feel forehead, wrist.)
"What a truck driver does." (Move arms, like steering.)
"What a mother does." (An activity related to her occupation or hobby.)
"What a father does." (An activity related to his occupation.)

Finger Play

FIVE LITTLE FIREMEN

Five little firemen sit very still, [Hold up five fingers.]
Until they see a fire on top of a hill;
Number one rings the bell, ding-dong; [Bend down thumb.]
Number two pulls his big boots on; [Bend down pointer finger.]
Number three jumps on the fire engine red; [Bend down middle
    finger.]
Number four puts a red fire hat on his head; [Bend down ring
    finger.]
Number five drives the red fire truck to the fire, [Bend down little
    finger.]
As the big yellow flames go higher and higher. [Spread arms.]
Whoooooo-oooooo! Whoooooo-oooooo! hear the fire truck say,
As all of the cars get out of the way.
Shhh! goes the water from the fire hose spout, [Rub palms.]
And quicker than a wind the fire is out! [Clap hands.]

—LOUISE SCOTT AND J. J. THOMPSON

Rhythms

Once your child enters school, classroom tasks won't seem hard if he knows that he is in control of himself. Moving smoothly and rhythmically will aid his reading readiness and other academic challenges, and his alert responses make these games even more pleasurable now.

THE CAPTAIN AND HIS JET

> *The captain and his jet fly by,* [Stretch arms out.]
> *All around the sky.* [Make arms go around.]
> *He zooms up high,* [Lift arms.]
> *He zooms down low.* [Lower arms.]
> *And you can bet,*
> *He flies fast as he can go.* [Arms outstretched, turn body around.]

Winnie Wedo Says: "Follow me . . ."
"Walk like a silly clown, just like me."
"Run like a cowboy is after you."
"Hop like a zoo keeper, just like me." (Hop on one foot.)
"Slide-step like a dancer." (Lead with one foot.)

Pretending and Locomotion

Vocabulary growth takes place whenever you talk and play with the junior member of your family, especially when you integrate movements with an imaginative story. Let your helper set up the obstacle course, using the ramp, the parachute, the bolster, two Hula-Hoops, the box and wedge, and create an adventure based on her favorite occupations. Here is a start:

WHEN I GROW BIGGER

When I grow bigger, I'm going to do something special, just you wait and see. Maybe I'll be an astronaut and fly up to the moon (run up ramp and jump off), or maybe I'll be a sailor and sail a ship far across the rolling sea (roll over and over on billowing parachute). It would be exciting to be in the circus (dive roll over bolster), or drive a race car around the track (make figure eight around two Hula-Hoops). I might work in an office and type and type all day (sit on box and pretend to type), or teach little children how to read and play games (circle, holding hands).

MOVING OUT

Balancing Movements

Ann and Townsend Hoopes, in their book *Eye Power,* write that "vision is the principal sensorimotor link between the brain and the outside world." The following movements let your child harmoniously coordinate his eyes, brain, hands and feet—while having a glorious time! Continue to give visual reference points in the room as your child responds to one or two suggestions daily.

Floor Play. Tell your tot:

1. Football players do many push-ups. Let's try to keep our balance while doing squat push-ups (bend knees, touch floor, stand up). Concentrate on the bright disc on the floor.

2. How would you sidestep something sticky (bean bags)?

Beam. Place the beam twelve to eighteen inches off the floor. Tell your child:

1. March forward carrying a flag like a soldier. Hold it first in one hand, then in the other. Focus on a noisemaking toy at the other end.

2. Let's be tugboats chugging out of the harbor. Straddle-scoot across the beam and I'll follow you.

Big Ladder. Tell your tot:

1. A sign painter walks very carefully across planks when he works. Pretend to be a sign painter and follow me, walking forward and backward on the floor on the sides of the ladder. (Place the ladder flat on the floor and offer assistance, if needed. Place a bright ball at the other end for a focal point.)

2. Show me how a farmer would take giant steps over two rungs at a time, like stepping over furrows in a plowed field.

Railroad Track. Tell your tot:

1. Sailors must have good balance when they are at sea. Show me how a sailor walks backward along the deck with one foot on top and one on the side of the rail.

2. Lifeguards need strong arms to save people. Let's do an upright handwalk backward, from the top down the slanted track (against chair) and then back up. (Give your lifesaver a scrumptious hug and kiss for this mighty effort; it is a difficult exercise.)

Tilt Board. Tell your tot:

1. Let's balance on the right foot, then the left, on the raised board. (She may need assistance in the beginning. Have her focus on your belt buckle.)

2. Pretend the floor is the ocean and we are drilling for oil on this platform (flat side up). Let's balance together; now you balance alone.

Up and Away Movements

Box. Tell your two-year-old:

1. Here are three Hula-Hoops on the floor with colored discs (painted paper plates) in them. Jump into the Hula-Hoop with the colored disk I call out. What a smartie you are!

2. Push the box around and in between the chairs and tires, like a strong dock worker.

Inner Tube Trampoline. Ask your child to:

1. Jump and land on his bottom. (This is important for future seat drops on a trampoline.)

2. Be a singer! Sing while jumping:

Jumping, jumping, jumping so high,
Jumping, jumping, till you touch the sky.

Turn in a circle, round and round,
Turn in a circle, all about the town.

Ramp. Tell your tot:

1. Do a slide-together sidestep up and down the ramp.

2. How would a clown drive a jerky old Jeep on this steep road?

Big Bolster. Tell your youngster:

1. Let's set the big and little bolsters up on end. I'll steady them while you climb on top and jump off!

2. Here's our old favorite: the dive roll! Approach it quickly, like a runner; slowly, like an old woman; gracefully, like a model; businesslike, like a banker.

Wedge. Ask your child to:

1. Be a candy maker and tuck yourself into a little ball. Roll down the wedge like through soft, gooey chocolate.

3. Show me how a "happy you" dances all over the wedge.

Playing with Objects in Space

By now your walkie-talkie may be trying to run the whole show, so we want you to begin designing even more of your own activities. Encourage him to do as many variations as he can think of. See if he will explain what he is doing, with what object he is playing and how he is doing it. Use background music to accompany some of these eye-hand and eye-foot movements, but allow quiet sometimes, too. Do at least one variation (ours or yours) from each category daily.

Throwing. Ask your child to:

1. Roll a ball to me from between your legs. Can you make up a song to go with the motion?

2. Toss a small ball into the tube lying on the floor. Throw the ball overhand through the upright tube. Remember to practice using both arms!

Catching. Tell your child:

1. Sit on the box while I sit on the floor. Let's play catch with the yarn balls, throwing them up and down to each other.

2. Let's wedge the tube between chairs and play catch with the balloon. Can you catch it with your feet?

Striking. Ask your child to:

1. Use the small broom to knock down milk cartons. Try big swings and little taps.

2. Use the plastic bat to hit the whiffle ball, sitting on top of the T-ball stand, which is a little league baseball stand made out of heavy rubber. It is adjustable and comes with a plastic ball. The ball sits on top of the stand and the child tries to hit the ball with a plastic bat. Swing hard . . . soft . . . like a spaceman.

Kicking. Ask your child to:

1. Play kick the ball with you on different surfaces: carpeting, wooden floor, grass, cement, dirt.

2. Kick a series of objects of different sizes, weights and textures: big ball, small ball, yarn ball, net ball; foam piece, small box, balloon, paper roll, and other things.

EXPLORING

Super Stuff

Chinese jump ropes are stretchy, looped ropes that can be purchased in a dime store. Their unique elasticity makes them conform to whatever shape your child wraps them around: toes and hands, feet and neck, knees and head. He can stand up, lie down, roll or jump with one, or hook it around his body and an object like a chair or a doorknob.

Partner activities are fun, too. Bend and twist with it, play tangle or horsey. Supervise your enthusiastic roper to be sure he doesn't get carried away and stretch the rope so taut that it snaps.

The iridescent and weightless qualities of *liquid bubbles* never cease to relax and captivate children. Allow your child now to shake, twirl and blow his own bubbles. He'll probably find a way to use the wand that you never even imagined!

Let him experiment catching bubbles, too, using the wand, a plastic dish and his hand. When popping see how fast he can pop them with his hands, feet, elbows, bottom and head. Let him hit, poke or swat them with a dowel, paper plate, scarf, Ping-Pong paddle or rolled-up newspaper. And don't forget to include little friends: playing Pop the Bubbles with companions is especially joyful.

Cardboard blocks have been suggested before and will continue to get years of use. They can become so many imaginary objects: walls, trucks, cars, houses, freeways, animals or furniture. When your child acts out an imaginary setting with them, go along with the game. Ask if you can wash your car at his gas station or buy groceries at his supermarket. Your youngster will love you for taking part in his imaginary world.

Chapter 21

DRESSING UP IS GREAT
Thirty-one and Thirty-two Months

What two-and-a-half-year old—not to mention fifteen, forty-five- or eighty-five-year-old—is not drawn to the music, lights, colors, animals, popcorn smells and dust that are the circus? The atmosphere vibrates with excitement for a young child, and your learner will look in every direction, watch the people and animals, laugh and applaud. She may be a little frightened, too, and need some reassurance, but she'll be enchanted by the high-wire performers, fascinated by the animals' antics, delighted by the clowns and, undoubtedly, exhausted by the whole wonderful experience.

A trip to the circus will have an impact that will show up in the coming months in her vivid chatter and imaginary play. She will love to dress the part (just wait till Halloween!) and try to juggle balls or put her dog on a leash to do tricks.

Together, watch television programs about the circus, and read books about acrobats and play story records with circus sounds. Get into the circus spirit during the next two months and you'll share many lively adventures with your lion tamer!

SUPPLIES

felt board
wedge
tires—three or four
parachute
tube
box
ramp
bolsters—big and small
chairs (two) and rope

rhythm instruments
beam
big ladder
railroad track
tilt board
inner tube trampoline
objects in play—sponge ball, small basketball hoop, tennis balls, Hula-Hoop, yarn balls, plastic bat, small broom, balloons, four-square ball, bean bags, beach ball
super stuff—long, soft, thick rope; pillowcase or similar bag of stretchy material or large brown grocery bag; empty one-gallon ice-cream containers; toe puppets

GETTING READY

Loosening Up

THIS LITTLE CLOWN

This little clown is fat and gay;
This little clown does tricks all day;
This little clown is tall and strong;
This little clown sings a funny song;
This little clown is wee and small,
But he can do anything at all!

—LOUISE SCOTT AND J. J. THOMPSON

PEANUTS

See the little peanuts lying in the pan, [Lie in tuck position.]
Feel the little peanuts wiggle in your hand, [Wiggle on floor.]
Crack the peanuts open, [Stand up and stretch.]
Pop them in your tummy, [Big hop forward.]
Run along home now—yum, yum yummy! [Run in circle, rubbing tummy.]

Body Awareness

1. Describe people in the circus. See if your child can guess who each one is.

2. Identify body parts by function: What does a seal walk on? (Flippers.) What do you walk on? What does a trapeze artist swing by? (Arms, legs.)

RIDING THE MERRY-GO-ROUND

Ride with me on the merry-go-round, [Gallop in big circle.]
Around and around and around;
Up go the horses, up! [Gallop on tiptoe.]
Down go the horses, down! [Gallop bent over.]
You ride a horse that is white; [Gallop fast.]
I ride a horse that is brown; [Gallop slowly.]
Up and down on the merry-go-round, [Gallop, smiling around in a circle.]
Our horses go round and round.

—LOUISE SCOTT AND J. J. THOMPSON

Finger Play

COUNTING AT THE CIRCUS

One, one; the circus is lots of fun! [Hold up hands with fingers extended; bend down one finger for each line.]
Two, two; see a kangaroo!
Three, three; see a chimpanzee!
Four, four; hear the lions roar!
Five, five; watch the seals dive!
Six, six; there's a monkey doing tricks!
Seven, seven; elephants eleven!
Eight, eight; a tiger and his mate!
Nine, nine; penguins in a line!
Ten, ten; I want to come again! [Bend down last finger, then clap hands.]

—LOUISE SCOTT AND J. J. THOMPSON

Rhythms

Winnie Wedo Says: "Let's play . . . "

THE ELEPHANT

The elephant walks with great big feet, [Bend over and walk.]
Clump, clump, clump.
He swings his trunk from side to side, [Clasp hands, swing as from side to side.]
Thump, thump, thump.
And when you greet him, shake his trunk up and down, [Clasp hands and arms up and down.]
He will think you are a clever clown! [Smile!]

MONKEY SEE, MONKEY DO

> *A little monkey likes to do,*
> *Just the same as you;*
> *When you sit up very tall,*
> *Monkey sits up very tall;*
> *When you pretend to throw a ball,*
> *Monkey pretends to throw a ball;*
> *When you try to touch your toes,*
> *Monkey tries to touch his toes;*
> *When you move your little nose,*
> *Monkey moves his little nose;*
> *When you jump up in the air,*
> *Monkey jumps up in the air;*
> *When you sit down in a chair,*
> *Monkey sits down in a chair.*

—LOUISE SCOTT AND J. J. THOMPSON

Pretending and Locomotion

A circus is filled with magic for a two-and-a-half-year-old. Take a pretend trip to the circus, using the Hula-Hoop, three or four tires, expandable tunnel, ramp, wedge, parachute, bolster, rope and rhythm instruments. Your performer will love being the ringmaster and directing the circus activities as he navigates the obstacle course. He may even want you and Dad to be the performing animals in your tale!

MOVING OUT

Balancing Movements

Floor Play. Ask your child to:

1. Walk like a lumbering elephant across the room. Clasp hands, bend over at the waist, and swing your arms from side to side. Take slow, lazy steps. Finish with a loud elephant roar, lifting your arms up and leaning back.

2. Hop like a kangaroo with feet together, hands up, elbows bent and taking small jumps across the room.

Beam. Place the beam 5 inches off the floor and tell your tot:

1. Bears are special circus performers because they balance well. Let's do a V-sit on the beam, holding onto it with our hands and lifting our legs to form a V

like the big polar bears. (The goal is for him eventually to let go with his hands, too.)

2. Do a silly clown walk backward, then sideways, along the beam. (Your child must work at changing directions. He may need one-handed assistance at first.)

3. What circus performer would you like to be? Could you balance on the beam on your tummy? On your back?

Big Ladder. Place the ladder flat on the floor and ask your child to:

1. Walk face down along the ladder, hands on ladder sides, like an impish chimpanzee. Let's get the toy at the other end of the ladder. (Assist with your child's legs.)

2. Let's raise the ladder off the floor on bean bags. Begin to walk forward on the rungs, do a half-turn and finish walking backward. What a good ladder walker you are!

Railroad Track. Ask your child to do these activities:

1. Be a balloon man! Walk sideways on top of the rail to the right and left, as though moving through the aisles. Carry a balloon under each arm. (Track should be flat on the floor. She may need one-fingered assistance.)

2. While I hold your legs, walk on your hands like a trick dog: forward halfway, then sideways to the end and turn, then backward halfway and sideways to the end. (Give directions one phase at a time.)

Tilt Board. Ask your child:

> How would a circus elephant stand on the raised board holding a Hula-Hoop?

Up and Away Movements

Box. Ask your child to:

1. Climb on top of the box and jump over the rope like a circus tiger. (Move the rope and chairs further apart after each jump and vigorously applaud your talented tiger.)

2. Trained otters jump off the box and roll over three times, then stand up. Can you act like a circus otter?

Inner Tube Trampoline. Tell your tot:

1. Trapeze artists warm up before they perform, just like we do! Run in place fast, then grab this dowel and let me swing you down onto the floor.

2. Circus horses turn circles on their hind legs. Can you turn circles with your legs spread apart and your arms held up like the front legs of a circus horse?

Ramp. Ask your child to:

1. Put the bolster at the top of the ramp. Push it and let it roll down and out onto the floor, then run after it and do a dive roll over it, like one of the tumblers!

2. Begin at the bottom and scoot up the ramp backward, pushing the bolster like the strong man.

Big Bolster. Ask your child to:

1. Straddle the bolster and pretend to be popping circus popcorn.

2. Combine the big and small bolsters, and you can ride them like an elephant as I move them along.

Wedge. Tell your tot:

1. The circus crew works hard to set up the equipment. Show me how a worker would sidestep up and down the wedge, first with your left foot, then with your right, while carrying this big pillow.

2. Run up the wedge, stop and jump through the Hula-Hoop as though it were a ring of fire and you were a circus tiger!

Playing with Objects in Space

Throwing. Tell your tot:

1. Let's attach a toy basketball hoop to the refrigerator and throw sponge balls through it.

2. At the park or in the yard, throw a ball as far as you can, using both arms. Wow! You could be a circus strong man!

3. Throw two tennis balls up at the same time, like the juggler.

Catching. Ask your child to:

1. Stand in the center ring (Hula-Hoop) and catch yarn balls in a hat.

2. Let go of a ball at the top of the ramp, race it to the bottom and catch it. Run fast!

Striking. Ask your child to:

1. Hit the sponge ball on the floor with a plastic bat between two chairs, first wide apart, then close together.

2. Lie on the floor and hit a ball suspended over your head with a rolled-up newspaper, using both hands.

3. Using a small broom, sweep several balloons into this large box, turned on its side, like the circus crew cleaning up.

Kicking. Ask your child to:

1. Drop the ball, then kick it hard along the ground, first with one foot then the other. You are kicking with your right/left foot.

2. Kick bean bags across the floor, using shuffle kicks, like a sad clown.

3. Kick and run simultaneously, using the beach ball. You'll make a good circus performer someday!

EXPLORING

Super Stuff

Purchase a 15- to 20-foot piece of soft cotton or nylon *rope*, ½ inch in diameter. Your little shadow will probably need little instruction to use it. He'll wiggle, coil, curve and zigzag it and make squiggly designs with it. Play Follow the Leader around his squiggly curves or Mary Matchmaker (he must do whatever you do and vice versa).

Laying the rope out straight and walking in different patterns is also fun. Siblings and friends may come up with some complicated designs involving direction, speed, levels and qualities. See how your mimic does and praise his own ideas.

Of course, playing jump rope is the greatest challenge: snakes, hurdles (jumping over) and limbo (sliding under). Wait till Dad tries these! Supervise this activity when your child is playing with the rope alone.

Trying to walk, hop, run and roll in a *sack* is a challenge without compare.

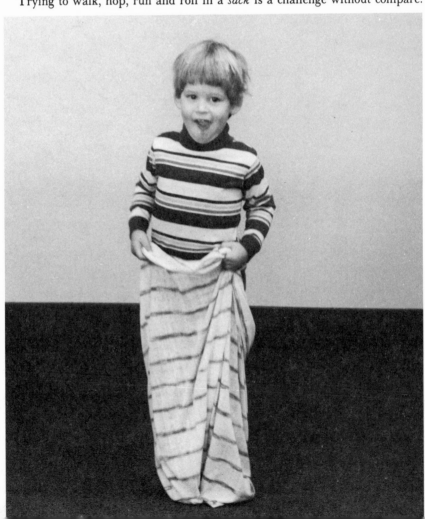

Several children playing with sacks make the fun even sillier! Keep the events lighthearted and, if you hold races, make your child feel like a winner even if he can't keep up. Paper sacks make neat noises, pillowcases are soft, and stretchy ones give you more freedom of movement, though burlap is still the traditional sack material. Your child can also use these to play a ghost, stretch monster or crayon-colored character. What fun to be two!

Though most people associate puppets with hands only, *toe puppets* can be equally pleasurable and charming. They can be crocheted or cut out of paper. (Use thick construction paper, fasten into a ring and slip around the toe.) Wait till you see how often you find your child lying on the floor, feet in the air, telling himself a story! How about making some circus-animal toe puppets?

Chapter 22

NATURE LOVER
Thirty-three and
Thirty-four Months

With their dramatic changes, the four seasons affect all of us. Even your youngster must learn that a change in seasons promotes certain activities and curtails others. Depending on where you live, the weather will have a greater or lesser impact on play activities, but most places do have seasonal shifts in food and drink, clothing, recreation, travel and socializing.

The seasons are so integrated within our everyday lives that we forget to talk much about them except to grumble about the weather being too hot or cold, rainy or dry. A child, however, finds nature fascinating: animals born, new plant growth, thunderstorms, chipmunks gathering food for winter, spring flowers and fall winds.

We hope to convey some basic concepts about the seasons to your lively little one through play and to answer questions like, "Why does it snow?" Expand on the listed suggestions by sharing your seasonal preparations: canning food in the summertime, chopping wood in the fall, lighting a fire in the winter, seeding and planting in the spring.

The seasons are really a timeless subject. This chapter will unlock only the beginning of a bounty of wonders for your child to experience through his communion with nature.

SUPPLIES

    box
    wedge
    ramp
    parachute
    rug squares

ladders—big and little
tires—two
expandable tunnel
tube
Hula-Hoop—two
beam
railroad track
tilt board
inner tube trampoline
chairs (two) and rope
big bolster
objects in play—tall box, yarn balls, 12-inch four-square ball, beach
    ball, feather, badminton racket, fly swatter, tape balls, soccer ball
super stuff—cardboard or heavy plastic foot- and handprints, twin-size
    bed blanket, feathery things, small sandbags

GETTING READY

Loosening Up

RAIN

I hear thunder, I hear thunder; [Drum feet on floor.]
Hark, don't you, hark, don't you?
Pitter-patter raindrops, [Indicate rain with fingers all the way to the
    floor from tiptoes.]
Pitter-patter raindrops, I'm wet through, [Shake all over vigorously.]
So are you! [Laugh and point to each other.]

LITTLE FLOWER

Oh, little flower in the ground, [Tuck position on floor, on feet.]
Now it is spring, and I have found; [Look all around, side to side.]
That the earth is warm, [Look down.]
And the sky is blue, [Look up.]
Come out and stretch your arms so new, [Stand up and stretch arms
    out.]
Please, pretty flower, I love you. [Hug self.]

Body Awareness

I AM A SNOWMAN

I am a snowman, cold and white;
I stand so still through all the night; [Stand up tall.]
With a carrot nose, [Point to nose.]
And head held high,
And a lump of coal to make each eye. [Point to eyes.]
I have a muffler made of red,
And a stovepipe hat upon my head. [Place hands on top of head.]
The sun is coming out! Oh my! [Make circle for sun.]
I think that I am going to cry; [Start sinking to the ground.]
Yesterday, I was so plump and round;
Now I'm just a river on the ground. [Sink to floor.]

—LOUISE SCOTT AND J. J. THOMPSON

IN WINTERTIME

When wintertime is cold and gray. [Stand up and shake.]
We bundle up and go out to play.
We put warm hats upon our heads, [Hands on head.]
And mittens on our hands. [Rub hands.]
Boots go on our feet just so, [Bend over, pretend to pull on boots.]
And earmuffs on our ears. [Cover ears with hands.]
We run and hide and play outside, [Run in place.]
Until it's time to go inside
And take off all our wraps. [Sit down and pretend to take off hat, etc.]

Rocky Robot Says: "Jack Frost likes to nip at little boys' and girls' . . . what?" (Noses, ears, fingers, toes; parent touches body parts.)
"How do the wipers on your car go when they wipe away the raindrops?"
"What does an umbrella keep dry when you use it in the storm? Sit under the umbrella."

Finger Play

Holidays are very much a part of seasonal changes, and two-year-olds love to be included in making tree trimmings or preparing ethnic foods. Here is a finger play to introduce your child to a unique American tradition.

THANKSGIVING

Every day when we eat our dinner,
Our table is very small. [Show size with two hands.]
There's room for Daddy, [Hold up tall finger.]
And Mother, [Hold up pointer finger.]
And me, that is all. [Hold up little finger.]
But when Thanksgiving comes,
You can't believe your eyes.
For that same table stretches, [Stretch arms.]
Until it is this size!

Rhythms

FALL LEAVES

Fall leaves are floating,
Floating to the ground,
Bright reds, oranges and browns,
Twirling, twirling all around
Floating, floating till they touch the ground.

THE WIND

The wind came out to play one day. He swept the clouds out of his way; [Make sweeping motions with arms.]
He blew the leaves and away they flew. [Make fluttering motions with fingers and move sideways.]
The trees bent low and their branches did, too. [Lift arms up and down.]
The wind blew the great big ships at sea; [Move arms back and forth overhead.]
The wind blew my kite away from me. [Raise arms and run around room.]

—LOUISE SCOTT AND J. J. THOMPSON

Winnie Wedo Says: "Let's . . . "

"Throw snowballs with the right and left hand, up in the air and down. Pretend to pack snow into a snowball."

"Stomp through mud puddles, lifting knees high."

"Go swimming, swinging arms back and forth in big and little strokes."

"Make thunder: pound your hands on the floor softly, loudly."

Pretending and Locomotion

IT'S SNOW!

You need: wedge, ramp, parachute, rug squares, little ladder, tires (two), expandable tunnel, tube and Hula-Hoop.

Once upon a time there was a little boy named (child's name). He lived with his mommy and daddy and (other family members) on (name street). One morning he awoke (stretch) and there was snow all over the ground. He jumped out of bed (jump up high) and ran down the stairs (run in place, knees high). Crunch, crunch, crunch went the snow under his feet as he tiptoed out to the garage to get his sled. He had to climb up on a box and reach up high to unhook his sled from the wall. He jumped down and carried his sled up the nearest hill (walk up wedge with arms above head) and zoomed down on his tummy (pull down ramp on tummy). Wheeee! Then we made angels in the snow by sweeping his arms from his sides up over his head and down (lie on back on wedge, covered with parachute). Afterward, he skated on the pond (skate on parachute) but it was getting late so he followed a snowman's footprints (step on rug squares) all the way home . . . over the bridge (cross little ladder, raised between two tires) and through a curved ice tunnel (bend expandable tunnel), crawled carefully around an ice hole (crawl around tube) and walked in the door (walk through Hula-Hoop). "I'm home," he said, and his mom swung him around, shaking off the snow and tickling him until he was warm all over.

MOVING OUT

Balancing Movements

Floor Play. Ask your child to:

1. Show me how a jackrabbit hops across the snow in wintertime.

2. Animals like to "kick up their heels" in the springtime. How would a donkey do this? Make braying sounds.

Beam. Place the beam 5 inches off the floor and tell your child:

1. Balance on your hands and knees on the beam. Lift up one leg and stretch it out straight to the side. Set it down and lift up the other leg.

2. Pretend to be crossing hot sand in summer. Walk to the middle of the beam, balance first on your right foot, then on your left, and then continue to the end of the beam. (May need one-fingered assistance.)

3. I'll hold two Hula-Hoops on end on the beam. Walk along the beam, stoop down to step through the hoops, then finish walking across the beam.

Big Ladder. Place the ladder between two chairs and ask your child:

1. How would a raccoon cross a babbling brook in springtime? (Have her crawl across on hands and knees or feet.)

2. Let's move the ladder flat on the floor. Be a bear coming out of hibernation and stretch. Grumpy papa bear walks slowly and stooped; mama bear walks at medium speed and medium height; baby bear walks on tiptoes and looks all around.

Railroad Track. Ask your child to:

1. Be a gray squirrel gathering nuts to store for winter. Let's place the track between two chairs so you can handwalk forward and backward, picking up bean bags and dropping them into your nest.

2. Slant the track against a chair so you can scamper up its sides, using your feet and hands, like a chipmunk playing in the crisp, spring morning. When you are halfway up, stop, turn around and go down backward.

Tilt Board. Ask your child to:

1. Pretend to be a newborn foal just learning how to stand and balance. Turn

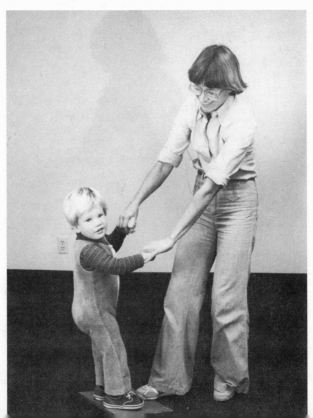

the flat side up and stand on one half, facing me. While I step on the other side to balance and then step on the board, you must keep your balance.

2. Balance on the raised board while you look at the spots that I tap with a stick, like a robin looking for the worms.

Up and Away Movements

Box. Ask your child:

1. What would happen if you were an autumn leaf on a high limb (box), and a big wind blew you right off into this stack of leaves (soft pillows)?

2. Jump from the box onto the top of the wedge and roll down the hill. What season is it? What animal are you?

Inner Tube Trampoline. Ask your child to:

1. Jump in the center like a rabbit hopping through snow.

2. *Jump, one, two, three. Jump on knees.*
   Jump, one, two, three. Jump with legs out straight.
   Jump, one, two, three. Just like me!

Ramp. Tell your tot:

1. When fall comes and the leaves fall, they must all be raked up and hauled off in the wheelbarrow to be burned. Pretend to be a wheelbarrow going up and down the ramp.

2. How would you climb this hill if it were cold and rainy? . . . bright and sunshiny?

Big Bolster. Tell your child:

1. Vault over the end while I hold the bolster.

2. Lie on your back while I put the bolster on your feet and hands. Now toss it off like a butterfly emerging from its cocoon.

3. Push the bolster forward with your lower legs, like a snow plow.

Wedge. Tell your tot:

1. It's very foggy and you cannot see well. How would you go up and off the edge of the wedge?

2. Be a frisky baby goat: run up the wedge, jump off and do a forward somersault. (Do three or four times.)

Playing with Objects in Space

Throwing. Remember to use one hand and then the other. Ask your child to:

1. Sit inside a tall box and throw yarn balls up and outside it, like a squirrel discarding nutshells.

2. Throw a ball up a flight of stairs: high, higher, *highest!* See if you can fetch it when it bounces down.

Catching. Tell your tot:

1. Catch the beach ball with your whole body, wrap around it and roll over onto it. (Roll ball to your child.)

2. Pretend you have melted from the hot sun and have to lie on your side to play catch.

Striking. Encourage your child to use one hand at a time. Ask him to:

1. Swing at the feather with your badminton racket. (Drop feather from above.)

2. Use the flyswatter to swat the tape balls I throw to you. When you catch one, pick it off and put it in a pile.

Kicking. Ask your child to:

1. Kick the ball through the human tunnel that Dad and I form with our hands and feet. Now you be part of the tunnel!

2. Push the soccer ball down the hallway with your head or elbows.

3. Stand behind the tape line. Kick the ball across this other tape line (6 feet away). What a mighty kicker!

EXPLORING

Super Stuff

Footprints and handprints can be cut out of oilcloth, which seems to adhere to most surfaces, or cardboard. Make six to ten pairs of feet and hands (right and left) in bright, matched colors. Use these to set up paths for your private eye. Design a challenging course, making the prints small, giant, zigzagged, turning in circles, turning back, stepping heel-to-toe, crossing over slightly (that's a toughie!), going up ramps, stopping in front of the bolster and picking up on the other side and on and on. Let your child help lay them out, and have *everyone* play. Include handprints and you can use a wheelbarrow style, too.

Your child can also use the prints to count, match colors, stack and make designs. How perfect to be developing eye-hand and eye-foot coordination, laterality and space awareness while playing a great game!

If you have not played *horsey under a blanket* with your half-pint, now is the time. Let him be the front or back and go through all the motions of pawing the ground, rearing up, galloping, trotting and neighing while the movie camera rolls. It does get hot under the blanket, so after a short period of horsey play, use the blanket to play caterpillar (adding other family members or friends), blanket swing, tent, ghosts, cocoon and butterfly and whatever else you can think of.

Feathery things do charming floats, glides, drapes, wraps, twirls, dances and curls. A feather sash or boa feels so smooth, too—let your cherub wear one while standing nude in front of a fan.

Small sandbags are 2-by-4-inch sacks made of pinwale corduroy filled with fine-grain sand. Have about twenty to thirty of them on hand; perhaps you and a friend can set aside an afternoon to cut, sew and fill a set for your children (or share a set to cut down on cost). Your youngster will watch the production with great anticipation of the building, stacking, hopping on, jumping over, putting end-to-end, counting and arranging into shapes he can do with them. Small sandbags can also be used in developmental exercises in any number of ways. Remember to discuss their concepts in simple and pleasant terms.

Chapter 23

ALL GROWN UP
Thirty-five and
Thirty-six Months

These last two months of the program are aimed at the "all grown up" child in your house, who now jubilantly calls himself *Me*! This final chapter showcases his astonishing talents and long list of successes. Your child takes pride in his accomplishments, because you have nurtured them with love and praise. You have done your job well. He loves himself, as he should.

It seems only fitting, then, to focus on your child as you approach his third birthday: who he is, where he has come from and what kinds of activities he has perfected. Let him *hear* that you like him; let him *see* your undisguised joy in him. Let him *know* that he is wonderful!

SUPPLIES

    felt board
    wedge
    tires—three or four
    parachute
    tube
    box
    ramp
    bolsters—big and little
    chairs (two) and rope
    rhythm instruments
    beam
    broom handle
    big ladder
    railroad track
    balloon
    tilt board

inner tube trampoline

Hula-Hoop

objects in play—sponge ball, 18-inch playground ball (made out of scuff-resistant, waterproof heavy red rubber); paper plates, Ping-Pong balls, yarn balls, cloth diapers, 12-inch four-square ball, bean bags, beach ball, punching bag, 18-inch dowel

super stuff—silky material, Tune Tubes, plastic paddle, whiffle ball, old media

GETTING READY

Loosening Up

READINESS

> *Close your eyes, head drops down,*
> *Face is smooth, not a frown;*
> *Roll to left; head is a ball;*
> *Roll to right; now sit tall!*
> *Lift your chin; look at me.*
> *Take deep breaths, one, two, three;*
> *Make big smiles, hands in lap;*
> *Make believe you've had a nap.*
> *Now you're rested, from your play.*
> *Time to work again today.*
>
> —LOUISE SCOTT AND J. J. THOMPSON

TO THE SKY

> *To the sky my arms they go.*
> *Bend my knees and touch my toes.*
> *Flop to the left,*
> *Flop to the right,*
> *Now lay down and say night, night.*

Body Awareness

1. Weigh and measure your child. Draw the outline of her foot and hand and show her the difference from when she was younger.

2. See if she can learn the name of your street and city. Talk about the neighborhood and its people.

Rocky Robot Says: "Let's do 'Can You Pound . . .' "

Can you pound with your two hands?
Pound, pound, pound!
Can you roll with your two hands?
Round, round, round!
Can you slap with your two hands? [Slap sides of legs.]
Slap, slap, slap!
Can you clap with your two hands?
Clap, clap, clap.

I CAN

I can hop on two feet, two feet, two feet.
I can hop on two feet. Let's see you.
You can hop on two feet, two feet, two feet.
You can hop on two feet. You can too!

I can blink with two eyes, etc.

I can wiggle one hand, etc.

I can wiggle two hands, etc.

DRAW A CIRCLE

Draw a circle, draw a circle,
Round as can be; [Draw a circle in air with pointer finger.]
Draw a circle, draw a circle,
Just for me.
Draw a square, draw a square, [Draw a square in air.]
Shaped like a door;
Draw a square, draw a square,
With corners four.
Draw a triangle, draw a triangle, [Draw a triangle in air.]
With corners three;
Draw a triangle, draw a triangle,
Just for me.

—LOUISE SCOTT AND J. J. THOMPSON

Rhythms

I WENT TO SCHOOL (Move around room doing appropriate actions.)

I went to school one morning and I walked like this,
Walked like this, walked like this.
I went to school one morning and I walked like this,
All on my way to school.

I saw a little robin and he hopped like this, etc.

I saw a little pony and he galloped like this, etc.

I saw a tall policeman and he stood like this, etc.

I heard the school bell ringing and I ran like this, etc.

SLIP ONE AND TWO

Slip one and two [Join hands and take two sliding steps to the left.]
Jump three and four, [Make two little jumps and drop hands.]
Turn around swiftly,
And sit upon the floor. [Sit on floor with legs crossed.]
Clap one and two,
Nod three and four,
Jump up again,
And be ready for more. [Join hands and repeat, if desired.]

Winnie Wedo Says:
"Follow the Leader" (Play music and have your child follow you. Change commands as quickly as your youngster can respond.)
"Place hands on head."
"Place thumbs in ears."
"Hands on knees."
"Tap with finger on back of hands."
"Camel walk: bend over, hands on back."

Pretending and Locomotion

Here's your opportunity to create a masterpiece of imagination for your child. Talk about his favorite time of day (morning?), his favorite meal (breakfast?), game, toy, space movie and so on. Help him invent a story using these elements, such as "One typical day . . ." Be sure to use a good sprinkling of the equipment—especially his favorites. You may even start with a basic story and elaborate over the next two months. Your child will think he is really special when you pull out a pad and pencil and write down what he tells you!

MOVING OUT

Balancing Movements

Floor Play. Ask your child:

1. Would you like to learn how to skip? Let's sing this rhyme as we skip along: (This may take a few months for your child to perfect.)

> *Skippety skip to the candy store*
> *To buy some candy bars.*
> *One for my brother Lars,*
> *One for the man on Mars.*

2. Be a top. Jump and turn a half-turn. Can you make a full turn?

Beam. Place the beam 5 inches above the floor. Tell your child:

1. Hop across the beam. Let's count your hops.

2. Walk forward, dipping one foot and sweeping along the side of the beam while the other foot is on top. Point your toes and alternate your feet. Extend your arms for balance and hum a little tune!

3. Here's a tricky one, so listen carefully. Walk forward, squat, turn, stand up and walk forward again. How clever you are!

4. Vault over the beam. Place your hands on it, jump and swing your feet over to the other side. (She may step on the beam at first. This is the beginning of a cartwheel.)

Big Ladder. Tell your tot:

1. Today is a brand new day. Show me how you would like to walk the ladder. Are you happy, sad, excited, worried, mad? You have such good ideas!

2. Turn the ladder on its side. Let's play Follow the Leader, with your friends weaving in and out of the spaces.

3. Let's combine two things at once; I'll lead, you follow. Clap your hands each time you step over a rung. See? What fun!

Railroad Track. Ask your child to:

1. Slant the track against a chair. Tell your feet and eyes to walk you forward along the sides of the rails up the track while you carry a large beach ball. Throw it backward over your head and come down backward. You can do it! That's terrific!

2. Show me what kind of animal you are, walking slowly on the track. What kind of noise do you make?

Tilt Board. Ask your child to:

1. See if you can balance all by yourself on both sides of the tilt board.

2. Balance like a statue, penguin, dancer, umbrella.

Up and Away Movements

Box. Ask your child to:

1. Jump backward off the box. (She may need assistance at first.) Now turn a backward somersault or shoulder roll.

2. Be a superduper space jumper. Jump off the box, forward onto a surface a few inches higher: couch, chair, bed.

Inner Tube Trampoline. Ask your child to:

1. Do jumping jacks. Count: say, "Open, close," "Out, together," "Open, shut."

2. Try a seat drop (depending on the spring of the surface). Jump, jump, jump, sit down, landing with legs out straight in front and hands at sides to help push yourself back into a standing position.

Ramp. Tell your tot:

1. Be a color and walk up and down the ramp: red (mad), yellow (warm), blue (cold), purple (funky), pink (happy) and so on.

2. Run, jump and turn in mid-air. Whee! What fun!

Big Bolster. Ask your child to:

1. Run and do a fast somersault over the bolster. Drag your feet and do a s-l-o-w somersault.

2. Set the bolster up on end. Run, tackle it, and jump over it.

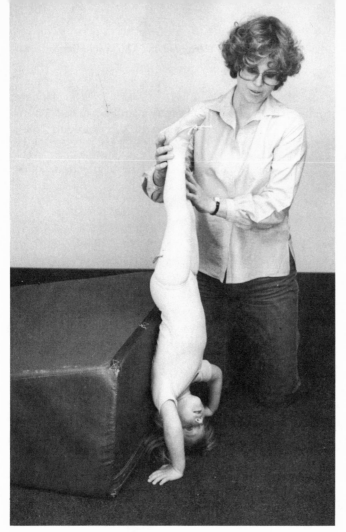

Wedge. Ask your child to:

1. Be an alligator and crawl slowly up and off the end.

2. Control the ball while backing down the wedge, using your feet.

3. Do a headstand against the wedge, and spring your legs up onto the top. Sit up. (This can also be done on a couch.)

Playing with Objects in Space

Throwing. Ask your child to:

1. Bounce an 18-inch playground ball with both hands, then with right hand alone, then with left.

2. Place a bean bag on a paper plate and toss it up. Can you catch it?

3. Let's play Hot Potato! Sit on the floor, and we'll toss a ball back and forth, getting rid of it as fast as we can.

Catching. Ask your child to:

1. Let's play Anny Anny Over in the backyard (over a low wall) or house (over a tall chair). I'll throw the sponge ball over, saying, "Anny, anny over!" See if you can catch it or yell "*Boom!*" when it lands. Now you throw and I'll catch.

2. Throw the ball up, clap and catch it. (This may take some time, so make it fun. He will be *so* earnest in his attempts. Can also be done bouncing and clapping.)

Striking. Ask your child to:

1. Give the ol' punching bag a workout! Swing with arms straight: right, left, right. Clasp your hands and double punch it!

2. Play indoor croquet. Use the dowel to hit Ping-Pong balls across the floor. Swing your stick level with the floor.

Kicking. Ask your child to:

1. Play kickball with the neighborhood children. (Let your youngster pitch, kick and run bases. Explain to the other children that this is the way a little child learns. Make exceptions for him, but let *all* the children feel good about their efforts.)

2. Play soccer! (Let your child have many kicks, always coming out a winner. Kick the ball between chairs, too.)

EXPLORING

Super Stuff

By now your child knows all about superheros and their exciting escapades. Nothing suits his imagination more than a large piece of silky material to use as a *supercape*. The material should feel so soft and tingly that he cannot help but feel capable of great feats: moving wildly, softly, sneaking about rooms behind furniture and flying off low couches onto pillows. With music the cape becomes a beautiful dancing companion to zip through the air or float gently to the floor. It can immediately become a practical partner to wrap around dolls or to camouflage a card-table hideaway. Don't be surprised if the cape truly does develop "super" qualities while your wonder bug senses feelings of power and glory or expresses joy, puzzlement, agility or relaxation.

Three-foot pieces of clear, corrugated-plastic tubes amuse your sound buff when he whips these *Tune Tubes* through the air. Your experimenter *par excellence* will discover how to make the tubes moan, groan and whistle happily as he manipulates them at different speeds.

We have exposed the junior member of the family to a variety of objects that he can swing at and strike other objects with. Here is one final suggestion: a giant *paddle and whiffle balls*. An oversize paddle requires him to coordinate eyes and hands with the rest of his body while enjoying the play. You can bat whiffle balls back and forth to each other over a low net, or hit them as far and high as you can, against the garage door or at a pitchback. Your child will also learn to balance and carry objects on the paddle.

Your child is at a fantastic age for learning to play simple games, as long as they are fun rather than being demanding. Suggest, for instance, that he keep his eye on the ball until it hits the paddle, but don't load him down with heavy instructions or criticisms. Show him to laugh at mistakes and move on, praising and encouraging his participation.

Now let's clean out our storage closet and rediscover the media that have been untouched for months in a real *superpotpourri*. Perhaps several can be combined for extra fun: the parachute and ribbons, pinwheels and golf tubes or doughnuts. Turn on a fan and some music and let your happy user amaze you with new ideas. Because of his refining of abilities, he will get even more mileage out of the old media.

Bring out the camera for this *grand finale* of ideas and fun. You can look back in the years to come at the expressions of confidence, exuberance and zest that belong to your three-year-old, to that feeling of being *me*!

Part V

WHAT'S IN THE FUTURE?

Whew! Where have the three years flown? There is a diploma in the back of this book that says you have completed the program. Accept it with pride and joy. You may wish to put it in your child's scrapbook as a memento of the close personal moments you have spent meeting your child's basic needs for love, attention and acceptance.

You may feel a mixture of excitement and sadness as you finish the program. You have provided the best possible beginning for your child, but have reached the end of the intimacy of infancy. Now that you have a healthy, expressive, capable, aware and happy three-year-old, you wonder, "Where do we go from here?"

Wonderful adventures lie ahead for your child. Exciting dimensions of movement and sensory education—games, exploration, rhythms, dance, sports, stunts—will bring him hours of enjoyment. These activities will provide continued emotional, intellectual and physical growth. He will learn to function in group situations—to share, lead, laugh, think critically, work with others toward goals and react reasonably in stressful situations. He will continue to realize his own capabilities and will be able to compete more effectively in life.

It has been our experience that three-, four- and five-year-olds continue to need sensorimotor stimulation. You can provide worthwhile, fun activities at home or in facilities such as parks, beaches and farms. Search out preschools with movement and sensory programs, check your local Y's schedule and inquire at gymnastic schools, community services and other available facilities. Read through our Bibliography to see if any titles stimulate your curiosity about a particular aspect of parenting.

We believe that parents must also take an active role to ensure that motor and sensory education continue to be integral parts of their child's formal education, from kindergarten on. Support local school sensorimotor programs. Campaign for local school bonds. Participate in parent organizations to aid educators in curriculum decisions, making sure that sensorimotor activities are included in classroom lessons from grade school through high school.

Most important of all, participate with your child in a variety of activities that include the whole family: camping, touring museums, visiting zoos, attending concerts, swimming, hiking, bicycling. Teach your child the importance of being fit, so that he or she will pass along the joys to the next generation.

Congratulations—and good luck!

APPENDIX

PLAY DOUGH

1 cup water
1 cup flour
½ cup salt
2 tablespoons vegetable oil
2 teaspoons cream of tartar

Cook over medium heat. The mixture will quickly form into a ball. Knead three or four times and add food coloring, if desired.

SUPPLIES

Precise descriptions of each medium and piece of equipment are found as they are introduced in the SUPPLIES, EXPLORING and ALL AROUND sections.

Much of the equipment is easy to make in a garage, spare bedroom or basement. Use the diagrams that follow and the written instructions in each chapter to construct your child's playland.

If you wish to purchase mats, wedges and bolsters, write for a catalog to: Skill Development Co., 1340 N. Jefferson, Anaheim, Calif. 82806. For gymnastic equipment like the balance beam and inner tube trampoline write: Constructive Playthings, 1040 East 85th Street, Kansas City, Missouri 64131. For records and instructional media, write: Educational Activities, Inc., Freeport, N.Y. 11520. For wooden puzzles: The Puzzle People, Inc., P.O. Box 144, Line Lake, Ga. 30072 and for toys keep in mind the Semper baby toys made in Sweden. For Tootie equipment write: John Hanson, Creative Ideas Co., 5328 W. 142nd Place, Hawthorne, CA 90250.

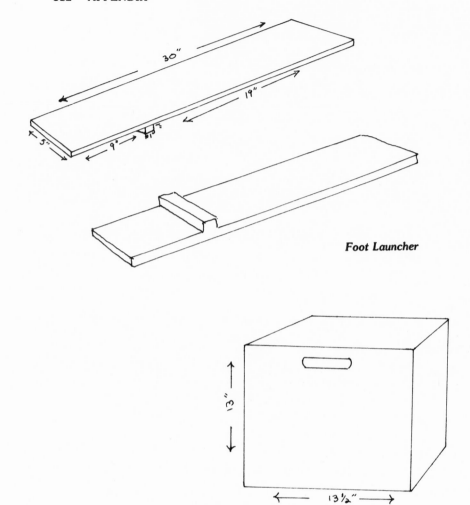

Foot Launcher

Box

Tilt Board

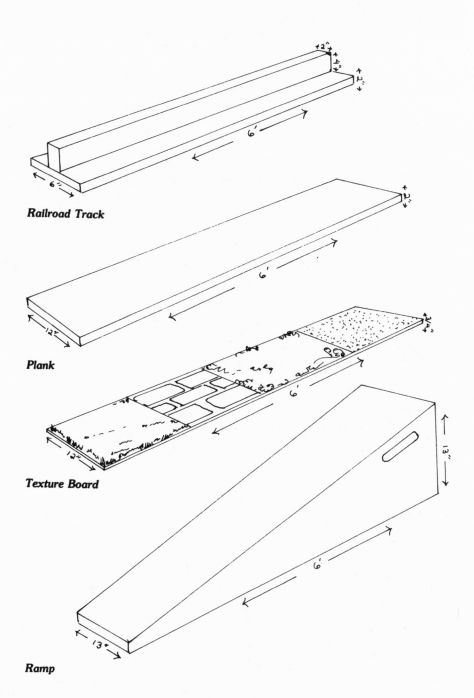

Railroad Track

Plank

Texture Board

Ramp

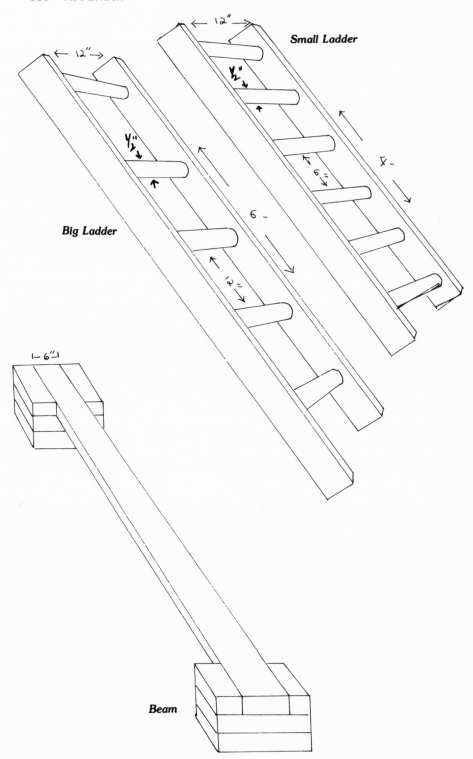

Small Ladder

Big Ladder

Beam

BIBLIOGRAPHY

Arnheim, Daniel D., and Robert A. Pestolesi. *Developing Motor Behavior in Children*. St. Louis: The C. V. Mosby Co., 1973.

———. 1978. *Elementary Education*. St. Louis: The C. V. Mosby Co., 1973.

Arnheim, Daniel D., and William A. Sinclair. *The Clumsy Child*. St. Louis: The C. V. Mosby Co., 1975.

Ball, Thomas S. *Itard, Sequin and Kephardt: Sensory Education—A Learning Interpretation*. Columbus, Ohio: Charles E. Merrill Publishing Co., 1971.

Banas, Norma, and I. H. Wills. *Prescriptive Teaching*. New York: Charles C. Thomas, 1977.

Bayley, Nancy. *The Development of Motor Activities During the First Three Years*. Society of Research and Child Development, 1935.

Beck, Joan. *How to Raise a Brighter Child*. New York: Trident Press, 1967.

Bowers, Tom. *The Perceptual World of the Child*. London: Fontana/Open Books and Open Books Publishing, 1977.

———. *A Primer of Infant Development*. San Francisco: W. H. Freeman and Co, 1977.

Bayley, William. *Daily Sensorimotor Training Activities*. Freeport, N.Y.: Educational Activities, 1968.

Brazelton, T. B. *Infants and Mothers*. New York: Delacorte Press/Seymour Lawrence, 1974.

———. *Toddlers and Parents, a Declaration of Independence*. New York: Delacorte Press/Seymour Lawrence, 1974.

Caplan, Frank, general ed. *The First Twelve Months of Life*. New York: Grosset and Dunlap, 1973.

Caplan, Frank, and Teresa Caplan. *The Second Twelve Months of Life*. New York: Grosset and Dunlap, 1977.

Cass, J. E. *Helping Children Grow Through Play*. New York: Schocken Books, 1973.

Crandell, J. M. *Early to Learn*. New York: Dodd, Mead and Co., 1974.

Cratty, Bryant J. *Physical Expressions of Intelligence*. Englewood Cliffs, N.J.: Prentice-Hall, 1972.

Cratty, Bryant J. and M. M. Martin. *Perceptual-Motor Efficiency in Children*. Philadelphia: Lea and Febiger, 1969.

————. *Some Educational Implications of Movement*. Seattle: Special Child Publications, 1970.

————. *Intelligence in Action*. Englewood Cliffs, N.J.: Prentice-Hall, 1973.

Dodson, Fitzhugh. *How To Parent*. Los Angeles: Nash Publishing, 1970.

Emery, D. G. *Teach Your Pre-Schooler To Read*. New York: Simon and Schuster, 1975.

Engelmann, S., and T. Engelmann. *Give Your Child a Superior Mind*. New York: Simon and Schuster, 1966.

Fraiberg, Selma. *The Magic Years*. New York: Charles Scribner's Sons, 1959.

Furth, H. G., and H. Wachs. *Thinking Goes To School*. New York: Oxford University Press, 1974.

Gesell, Arnold L. *The First Five Years Of Life*. New York: Harper and Row, 1940.

Gesell, Arnold L. and Frances L. Ilg. *Infant and Child in the Culture of Today*. New York: Harper and Row, 1943.

Getman, G. N. *How to Develop Your Child's Intelligence:* Irvine, Calif. Research Publication, 1962.

Glazer, Tom. *Eye Winker, Tom Tinker, Chin Chopper, Fifty Musical Fingerplays*. Garden City, N.Y.: Doubleday and Co., 1978.

Godfrey, B. B., and N. C. Kephart. *Movement Patterns and Motor Education*. New York: Appleton-Century-Crofts, 1969.

Greenstein, T. N., ed. *Vision and Learning Disability*. St. Louis: American Optometric Association, 1976.

Grover, Eulalie Rosgood, ed. *Mother Goose: The Classical Volland Edition*. Northbrook, Ill.: Hubbard Press, 1971.

Hoopes, Ann, and Townsend Hoopes. *Eye Power*. New York: Alfred A. Knopf, 1979.

Jacobs, Frances E. *Finger Plays and Action Rhymes*. New York: Lothrop, Lee and Shepard Co., 1970.

Jordan, Diana. *Childhood and Movement*. Oxford, England: Basel, Blackwell and Mott, 1967.

Kephart, N.C. *The Slow Learner in the Classroom*. Columbus, Ohio: Charles E. Merrill Publishing, 1971.

Koch, Jaroslav. *Total Baby Development*. New York: Wyden Books, 1976.

Larrick, Nancy. *The Wheels of the Bus Go Round and Round*. San Carlos, Calif.: Golden Gate Junior Books, 1972.

Lawrence, C. C., and L. C. Hackett. *Water Learning*. Palo Alto, Calif.: Peek Publications, 1975.

Lehane, Stephen. *Help Your Baby Learn*. Englewood Cliffs, N.J.: Prentice-Hall, 1976.

Lerner, J. W. *Children with Learning Disabilities*. Boston: Houghton Mifflin Co., 1976.

Levy, Janine. *The Baby Exercise Book*. New York: Pantheon Books, 1975.

Matterson, Elizabeth. *Games for the Very Young*. London: Penguin Books, 1969.

May, Betty. *T.S.K.H. (Tickle, Snug, Kiss, Hug)*. New York: Paulist Press, 1977.

Mayhard, Fredelle. *Guiding Your Child To a More Creative Life*. New York: Doubleday, 1973.

McDiarmid, N. J., M. A. Peterson and J. R. Sutherland. *Loving and Learning*. New York: Harcourt Brace Jovanovich, 1975.

Montessori, Maria. *The Absorbent Mind*. New York: Holt, Rinehart and Winston, 1967.

Painter, Genevieve, *Teach Your Baby.* New York: Simon and Schuster, 1971.

Piaget, J. *The Origins of Intelligence in Children.* New York: New York University Press, 1936.

Plese, Elliott, and Kay Plese. *Key to Basics.* Walnut Creek, Calif.: Charles Holbrook, 1979.

Prudden, Bonnie. *How to Keep your Child Fit from Birth to Six.* New York: Harper and Row, 1964.

Prudden, Suzy, and J. Sussman. *Creative Fitness for Baby and Child.* New York: William Morrow and Company, 1972.

Pulaski, Mary Ann Spencer. *Your Baby's Mind and How It Works.* New York: Harper and Row, 1978.

Sava, S. G. *Learning through Discovery for Young Children.* New York: McGraw-Hill, 1975.

Skinner, Louise. *Motor Development in the Preschool Years.* Springfield, Ill.: Charles C. Thomas, 1979.

Spock, Benjamin. *Baby and Child Care.* New York: Pocket Books, 1976.

―――. "How Creativity and Imagination Enrich Your Child's Development." *Redbook,* June, 1980.

Tinker, M. A. *Preparing Your Children for Reading.* New York: Holt, Rinehart and Winston, 1971.

Wickstrom, R. J. *Fundamental Motor Patterns.* Philadelphia: Lea and Febiger, 1970.

White, Burton, *The First Three Years of Life.* Englewood Cliffs, N.J.: Prentice-Hall, 1975.

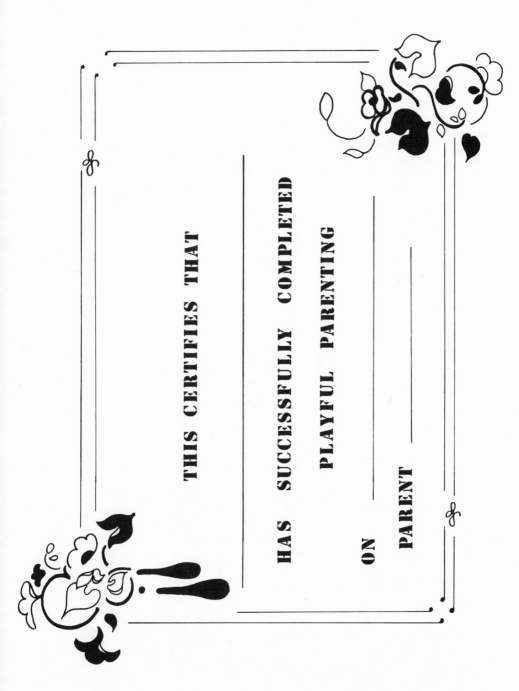

THIS CERTIFIES THAT

HAS SUCCESSFULLY COMPLETED

PLAYFUL PARENTING

ON _____

_____
PARENT